CORSICAN COMMAND

CORSICAN COMMAND

A dramatic first-hand account
of clandestine operations in the
Western Mediterranean,
1943-1944

Patrick Whinney

A William Kimber book
published by

PATRICK STEPHENS LIMITED

First published 1989

© Patrick Whinney 1989

British Library Cataloguing in Publication Data

Whinney, Patrick
Corsican command
1. Mediterranean region. Anti-German
espionage, 1939-1945 - Biographies
I. Title
940.54'86'410924

ISBN 1-85260-090-X

Patrick Stephens Limited is part of the
Thorsons Publishing Group,
Wellingborough, Northamptonshire, NN8 2RW, England

Printed in Great Britain by Biddles Limited, Guildford, Surrey

1 3 5 7 9 10 8 6 4 2

CONTENTS

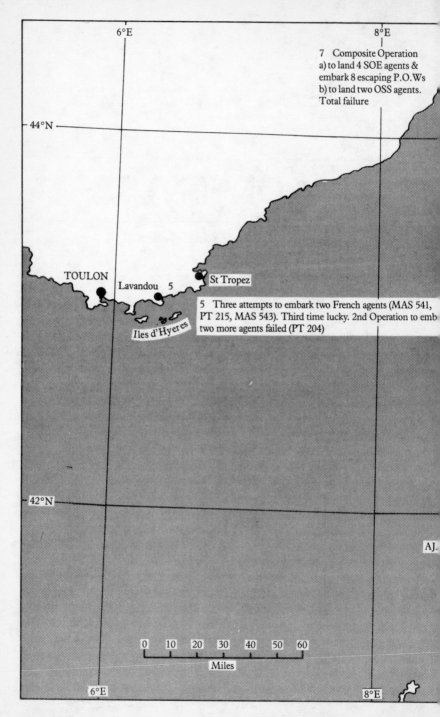

7 Composite Operation
a) to land 4 SOE agents &
embark 8 escaping P.O.Ws
b) to land two OSS agents.
Total failure

44°N

TOULON   Lavandou   5   St Tropez

5   Three attempts to embark two French agents (MAS 541,
PT 215, MAS 543). Third time lucky. 2nd Operation to emb
two more agents failed (PT 204)

Iles d'Hyeres

42°N

AJ.

0   10   20   30   40   50   60
Miles

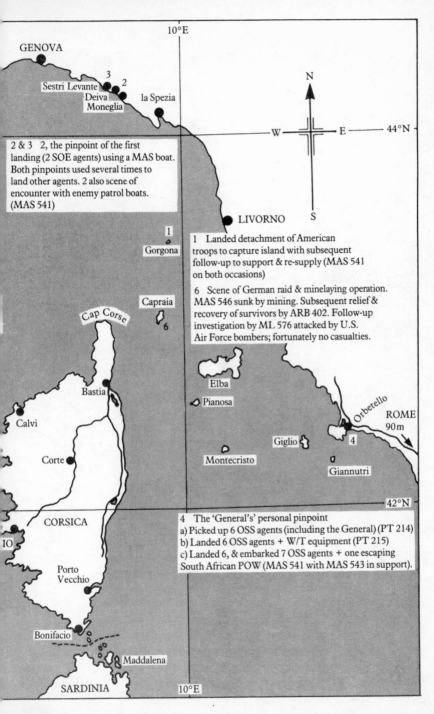

GENOVA

Sestri Levante
Deiva
Moneglia
la Spezia

3 2

2 & 3 2, the pinpoint of the first
landing (2 SOE agents) using a MAS boat.
Both pinpoints used several times to
land other agents. 2 also scene of
encounter with enemy patrol boats.
(MAS 541)

N

W — E — 44°N

S

LIVORNO

1
Gorgona

1 Landed detachment of American
troops to capture island with subsequent
follow-up to support & re-supply (MAS 541
on both occasions)

6 Scene of German raid & minelaying operation.
MAS 546 sunk by mining. Subsequent relief &
recovery of survivors by ARB 402. Follow-up
investigation by ML 576 attacked by U.S.
Air Force bombers; fortunately no casualties.

Capraia

6

Cap Corse

Bastia

Calvi

Elba

Pianosa

Orbetello

ROME
90 m

Corte

Giglio

4

Montecristo

Giannutri

42°N

CORSICA

4 The 'General's' personal pinpoint
a) Picked up 6 OSS agents (including the General) (PT 214)
b) Landed 6 OSS agents + W/T equipment (PT 215)
c) Landed 6, & embarked 7 OSS agents + one escaping
South African POW (MAS 541 with MAS 543 in support).

IO

Porto
Vecchio

Bonifacio

Maddalena

SARDINIA

10°E

7

PREFACE

On the principle of 'one day, perhaps, but not just yet' the manuscript of this book, written not long after the war, lay mouldering in a drawer until the 'one day' arrived out of the blue last year. Having delayed so long, why now? I can only answer that with the old cliché, 'because it was there'.

Shortly after the book was accepted for publication I went to see a friend of mine of nearly fifty years. During the war, with typical generosity, he agreed to let me write his biography at some future date, should I wish to do so. He is by way of being the most courageous man it has been my good fortune to meet, with a truly astonishing career behind him. On our recent meeting I reminded him casually of his earlier agreement, and asked him if he was still of the same mind. He smiled, shrugged, and replied apologetically that he had come to the conclusion that he no longer wished anyone to write his story. When I asked him what had made him change his mind he replied, 'My dear friend, when a few people are asked to describe in detail the simplest event which all have just witnessed their accounts tend to vary so much as to make one believe that each of them is talking about a totally different event. Where lies the truth, then, in a life story?'

It made me feel pretty small — to the extent, almost, of wishing to cancel this book. But not quite; it was already written.

I make no claims of verbatim accuracy for the many conversations recounted, but they certainly occurred, and in spirit if not in actual words they are true to the occasion. Portable tape-recorders were but a dream in those far-off days, and memories were thereby a good deal sharper.

As to the photographs I owe an embarrassing debt of gratitude to many people: Without their generous help, given often at some trouble to themselves, this book would have lost much of what interest it contains. I am especially indebted to the big contribution from the old members of RON 15, the American flotilla of PT boats with whom we worked so well, and to the Italian donors, official and unofficial. The manner in which these photographs were collected together is explained in the book itself, but before leaving the reader to get on with his reading I would like to mention those who gave so kindly of their time, trouble, and quite a lot of postage and correspondence.

Stanley Barnes, ex-CO of RON 15, Dave Morrison, ex-PT boat Captain, Simon Dickinson, 'Uncle Richard's' son, Tom Maxted, of the African Coastal Flotilla (ACF) Jim Bates, of ACF, Joan Sylvester-Bradley, widow of Peter ('Prof') First Lieutenant of ACF the Marchese Giulio Centurione, Lisabetta Salviati, Ann Nicoletti, Andrew Croft, CO of the SOE contingent, Paddy Davies, the Intelligence Officer on SOIS's staff, the Ufficio Storia in Rome, the Imperial War Museum, and the Naval Attaches of both American and Italian Embassies in London.

Patrick Whinney
Guernsey
January 1989

Chapter 1

MOVE FROM SARDINIA TO CORSICA

'And where, d'you reckon, we're going to sleep tonight, sir?'

Looking back over the years that question still seems to have been the real starting point of a fascinating interlude.

The time — September 1943: the place — Bastia, the island's second largest port two-thirds of the way up the east coast of Corsica. I was standing outside the office of the Commandant du Port, feeling rather more than irritable after a noticeably unsatisfactory interview with the Commandant, himself. Not that he had been uncooperative, far from it, but because of the state of almost total chaos in both port and town following the uproar of the recent German withdrawal from the island. In their flight they had still had time (and the will) for a show of malice by pouring more than a million litres of good red wine down the gutters in the streets. How good it actually was is impossible to guess — the local claim for 'excellence' was hardly borne out over succeeding months: the act itself, apart from infuriating the Corsicans, had no more than a fleeting effect on wine supplies to the Allied Forces (via the cafes and bars, of course). The only positive result was the capture of two German soldiers so intoxicated by the freely flowing booze that they failed to join their retreating unit before it left.

Earlier in the afternoon I had arrived in a 110 ft 'B' class ML (Motor Launch) from the recently established British Naval Base at Maddalena, Sardinia's most northerly port, a charmless place, its only boasts being lowering skies, a scrubby, rock-strewn landscape, olive-green carabinieri uniforms, and the unsmiling sallow complexions of its inhabitants. I was very glad to be away from it. By comparison the confusion of the badly-damaged French port, with its fiendish passion for red tape thrown in, was something to look forward to.

My orders were to carry out a general reconnaissance of Bastia, to try to assess the damage to the port installations, the jetties, cranes, warehouses, offices, and so on, and to obtain all information possible on enemy minefields in and around the harbour. All these details were needed with a view to making a quick transfer of the base from Italian to French territory.

The Naval-Officer-in-Charge, Maddalena, as he then was, one of the principal characters in this narrative, had a very proper sense of belligerency, and was keen for the forces under his command to maintain close, harassing contact with the enemy now in retreat up the spine of the Italian mainland. Geographically, it is worth noting, perhaps, that Maddalena and Anzio are on the same latitude, 200 miles apart, while Bastia lies as much as 100 miles to the north; at the same time it is less than 25 miles from the island of Elba. In peacetime such distances seem trivial: in war a hundred yards may be vital.

No one knew much about Bastia when I arrived, although, in theory at least, plans were already afoot to move up there as soon as practicable. Such a step would represent an important saving in high-octane fuel used in huge quantities by the flotillas of British, Canadian and American fast craft assembled at Maddalena, not to mention the Italian boats taken over by the Allies after the Italian surrender on 7 September 1943. From Bastia a much longer stretch of coast could be patrolled for a longer time at sea per boat. As the battle on the Italian mainland moved north, so Bastia would be nearer the scene of action.

In my efforts to acquire as much information as possible I had, earlier in the afternoon, tried to 'make my number' with the Commandant de la Ville, a mildly interesting experience but wholly unproductive of useful intelligence. The Commandant had taken over what must have been some part of the former German GHQ. The building itself was a rabbit-warren of interconnecting offices, few with any furniture to speak of, and now crammed with men, women and a fearful lot of children, all vociferous in their demands for help and attention.

As a matter of self-preservation the Commandant had worked out a simple but effective technique. Aided occasionally by members of his staff he kept constantly on the move, threading his way adroitly through the milling throng, talking to almost everybody while saying nothing to anyone. He would have made a fine diplomat. Once he had said his few words here and there to the individual or family he was gone, escaping like Houdini into an adjoining office from where he would repeat the process. Once, while I watched, I thought he had been outwitted by a group of four determined ladies who drove him into a corner from where escape seemed hopeless. I hadn't noticed, nor had the ladies, the existence of some french windows close by: in a flash a young member of the Commandant's staff, anxious for

12

promotion no doubt, glided in to separate his boss from the group, and the next second the Commandant de la Ville was out on the terrace moving swiftly away, to re-appear half a minute later at the head of the main staircase, a comfortable protective wall of humanity now established between himself and the angry matrons. He would have been good in music-hall, too.

Against such a polished performer there could be no competing. Instead I decided to return to the offices of the Commandant du Port. Once again my luck was out: so was the Commandant, and nobody knew where he was or when he would be back. To do him justice, however, I found out next day that he was virtually tireless in touring the port, always on foot, probing, searching, inspecting, directing labour, in a ruthless drive to restore order, assess damage, and locate the not inconsiderable number of German-laid mines. On his infrequent visits to his own office he preserved a calm, polite welcome for all visitors with genuine business; others were treated more curtly, but never with rudeness. Surprising in one under such pressure, nothing short of astounding in a French civil servant at any time.

Daylight was just beginning to fade as I emerged on to the pavement to stand a moment, pondering the next move.

'And where, d'you reckon, we're going to sleep tonight, sir?'

The question echoed my own thoughts at that moment so closely that I hesitated before replying. Moreover, it was spoken in English. Without having to think I replied,

'I haven't the faintest notion.' Then I added, 'Got any bright ideas?'

Only then did I turn round. There, close beside me, were two British sailors, both Leading Seamen, one fair, one dark, both well-built. They were correctly, even smartly dressed in the circumstances, and they were now regarding me with some interest. To the best of my knowledge I had never set eyes on either of them before, but then, there had been so many surprises during the day that their sudden appearance seemed unremarkable.

'Well, sir, we bin havin' a bit of a dekko round the place while you bin talkin' to the froggies, an' there seems quite a lot of empty 'ouses about. Some looks as though they might be quite comfortable, too, wouldn't you say, sir?'

The expression of earnest concern on the fair one's face seemed incongruous even in that moment when he was voicing exactly what had been going through my mind, what I had been hoping to hear from the Commandant de la Ville for the greater part of the afternoon. It was the innocence of his expression which was the incongruous bit. It wasn't until later that evening that, all at once, I found the refrain, 'Oh, 'tis my delight on a shining night in the season of the year ...' that

13

I realized who he was. He was the Lincolnshire poacher in person. Now I asked, 'And where did you find these empty houses?'

The dark one, an unmistakable cockney, made a vague gesture in the direction of the rising terrain leading out of the town. 'Up the back, sir, on the 'ill, like. Can't be much more'n a coupla 'undred yards from 'ere.'

A flicker of hope was, surely, excusable after such an afternoon of frustration; but caution was essential.

'I see. And tell me, where do you come from? To whom do you belong?'

Both looked stunned. 'Belong, sir? Us, sir?'

'Yes, you. You two, to whom do you belong?'

'Why, to you, sir. We come up in the ML — with you, sir.'

I had no recollection of seeing either of them on board, but that was hardly surprising as I had been talking to the captain and officer-of-the-watch most of the time.

'On whose orders did you embark?'

'Petty Officer Bates, sir.'

Ah. Now I knew who Bates was. He really did belong to me, having only the week before been sent up from Algiers as the first Coxswain-designate of the odd collection of fishing craft which I was supposed, ultimately, to command — when I had found and requisitioned them.

* * *

It's time I filled in some of the background.

The reason for my being in that area of the Mediterranean was to organize and run a clandestine 'water-taxi' (sometimes 'water-bus') service for the benefit of that courageous band of brothers *and* sisters, referred to in this narrative quite simply as 'resisters'. This omnibus title included straightforward intelligence agents sent in to gather all manner of information, saboteurs, propaganda specialists, important politicians, escape organizers for fugitive prisoners-of-war (shot-down pilots and the like), anyone, in fact, who worked 'underground' against the Axis. All had a common need, to be transported to and from enemy-occupied territory. Some went by air, were parachuted in, and brought out by a Lysander pick-up operation; others couldn't or wouldn't go by air, especially if their destination was anywhere near the coast; the sea was easier and more convenient.

The ideal 'vehicle' for these sea operations was a vessel with good sea-keeping qualities, a good turn of speed, and the ability to approach a coast silently. Such craft existed in substantial numbers but repeated pleas for the allocation of even a few had nearly always been turned down flat by the very people — the high-ups in Planning and Operations in all the services — who pressed hardest for secret information, on the grounds that all craft with those qualities were required for more warlike tasks. It was, of course, an unarguable policy in the sense that every gun- or torpedo-boat capable of fighting was needed to prosecute a vigorous campaign against the enemy at sea — but it didn't help us much. We were advised, instead, to make use of stealth where and whenever we could. We should seek out along the indigenous coasts some stout local fishing craft; we should requisition them, and man them with special volunteer crews who would, during operations, disguise themselves as fishermen. A tall order you may say, and so it was, but we had been doing it for some years prior to the time we are talking about.

In home waters, it is true, one or two fast craft (new ones) had been allocated for cross-Channel operations to the coasts of Normandy and Brittany, and, indeed, one highly unorthodox 'fishing vessel' had been specially constructed, capable of a rare turn of speed — when no one was looking ie, during the dark hours. A second such vessel was later built for the Mediterranean only to arrive a bit too late: we could have made good use of it twelve months earlier. All these craft were obtained by the Churchillian 'blood, sweat, and tears' in the teeth of strong opposition. It was a situation which would, today, most likely be labelled as 'catch twenty-two', but the book hadn't been written at the time. (Truth to tell even after reading the book I'm not sure what the title means, except that you can't win.)

Overseeing all such operations was an officer in London, who was nothing if not tenacious. He certainly needed to be. It is unlikely that without him this book and more serious ones on the same subject, would have been possible. Let me say something about him.

In 1914 Frank Alexander Slocum got off to a rather abrupt start to his naval career when he was appointed to serve in the Grand Fleet. He was only seventeen at the time, a tender age to be thrust into action against such a formidable foe as the German navy then was. His circumstances were not unique, there were many like him, in spite of some public protests against sending such youngsters off to fight.

One of his forebears was Joshua Slocum, the illustrious solo navigator, who, seeking to combat loneliness and hunger at a single stroke in his lengthy voyaging, conceived the idea of taking a goat to sea with him, thereby ensuring a constant supply of fresh milk, an occasional bleating noise to stave off loneliness, and, in emergency, several weeks of delicious meat. During the voyage the goat may have sensed the unfairness of the last part of this design, and decided to get her blow in first by eating the great man's precious charts: to have

15

eaten, say, the sails or his clothes would not have been half so telling. She was a shrewd goat.

Although Frank Slocum followed the ancestral example by qualifying as a navigator, there is, as far as I am aware, no record of him ever owning a goat. His career in the Navy was subject to the usual number of changes, but nothing spectacular enough to gain the coveted promotion to Commander at a period in the early 1930s when competition was at its fiercest. Unlike the less fortunate amongst his contemporaries he was offered, and accepted employment outside the Navy while still in his thirties. This was not to last for long. The second round of the contest against the Germans saw him once more in uniform, this time as a Commander. Not many months were to elapse before he was promoted to Captain and appointed as Deputy Director of Operations (Irregular) — DDOD (I) for short — in the Admiralty, a post hitherto non-existent but one which was to become essential to the many Allied clandestine services operating in Europe, and later, further afield.

When I reported to him in 1940 the first impression he gave was of lean liveliness. He was still a Commander. Jokingly, he used to claim to be 'above average height'. If he was, it was by an emaciated whisker. He moved quickly, wide-open eyes on the constant alert, the somewhat prominent jaw-line more than hinting at what was probably his outstanding characteristic, doggedness, which some senior officers came to interpret on occasion as 'bloody obstinacy', but without which he could never have achieved all that he did. His uniform was, at all times, immaculate, and he wore it well. By no means the least of his qualities was a large heart, for he was ever thoughtful of others, especially his immediate staff.

For five years, from 1940 to 1945, Frank Slocum held the post of DDOD (I) in the Admiralty, with the responsibility of transporting all types of resister by sea between Allied territory in Europe and the Western Mediterranean, and enemy-occupied territory. During those years he earned the respect and liking of hundreds of officers and ratings engaged in this odd service. Many of the 'resisters', too, came to rely heavily on him, their numbers reaching into the four figures, travelling on the various DDOD(I) 'lines'. To the best of my belief those, so to speak, 'lost in transit' totalled substantially less than one per cent. None was ever captured in transit.

This record must, in large measure be attributed to the Slocum passion for accuracy of detail in all that he took on. At times his fussiness, for that is how we often thought of it, was positively tooth-grinding, but he was right far more frequently than we were, and many of us learned from it lessons which stood us in good stead in our later

16

peacetime occupations. Overall, however, it was his unremitting persistence which made his organization what it was. He never gave up — even when it seemed certain he had done so.

He ended the war, and his career in the Navy, as Captain F. A. Slocum, CMG, OBE, plus an impressive number of foreign decorations from the Americans, the French, and other grateful Allies. Even he must have recognized that to be unusual.

Before he sent me out to Corsica he appreciated fully that the job really required fast craft, but — as always — where to get them? None being available, we would have to go at least through the motions of procuring local fishing boats, until something better turned up. I had already done much the same thing twice before, the first time in Gibraltar in 1941, and the second time, a year later, in Algiers. Both of us hoped that, on this occasion, fortune might be kinder. As we shall see, with the aid of a hefty shove from the redoubtable Naval Officer-In-Charge (NOIC) Maddalena, we were not to be disappointed.

Back, then, to where we started.

* * *

'What are your names?'

A momentary shuffle, a quick swallow as if the question contained an element of embarrassment. The 'poacher' replied for both of them.

'Me, I'm Downes, sir. An' this,' with a sideways nod of his head, 'is Johnstone.'

'I see. And what, exactly, were Petty Officer Bates' orders to you both?'

'Well, sir, 'e said as you was off up 'ere on a recce for a new base,' his eyebrows rose a fraction while he angled his head slightly to one side, 'could that be right, sir? — an' we thought that there wasn't much doin' down in Maddalena, so perhaps we could give you a 'and. Petty Officer Bates, sir, 'e thought it was a good idea — yea, 'e thought so, too ...' His voice trailed off into an uncertain silence.

'He may have thought it a good idea — maybe — but did he order you?'

Johnstone was already ahead of me. 'We bin followin' you round town, all afternoon, sir, wonderin' when we could 'elp. Never seen anythin' like them froggies for natterin'.'

Sometime in the near future a chat with Petty Officer Bates seemed important; in the meantime, however, there was no alternative — I would have to have another go with the local authorities before it got too dark. Perhaps a little sharply I cut short some interesting revelations. 'Never mind about the French. I'm going back to the offices of

17

the Town Commandant. You know where that is?'

They nodded. 'We seen it, sir. You was there.'

'Well, meet me there at six o'clock. Meanwhile you can look around and see what you can find for accommodation — just for tonight. But be sure it's empty before you look too far.'

'Aye, aye, sir.'

There was a quick exchange of looks between the two, like a couple of dogs promised an unexpected walk. Downes made a move to take my suitcase but reluctantly I had to refuse his offer; in it was a large sum of money and some secret documents. As I moved off they both gave me a smart salute; I left with a feeling that before long I might be glad of their presence and offers of help.

The second attack on the Commandant de la Ville was planned with care. Biding my time in the dense throng milling through the building I spotted a corner which had neither doors nor windows within ten feet, and there I waited. Sure enough, within five minutes the Commandant appeared on the scene to glide swiftly down the main stairs, skirt round the hall, and then he was in my corner and I was blocking his path with my suitcase. To jump over it might have been to risk an undignified fall. He halted, and I told him my needs. Frantically he was searching for an escape route as he answered. '... *mais, oui, parfaitement ... une question de logement, Commandant ... bien sûr, c'est difficile ... pour combien de personnes? ... Ça, alors ...* (he shrugged enormously) *... Je vous en prie...* '

He could provide nothing, at least not off the cuff, just like that, but he would lend me his driver and an open military truck in which to tour the town despite the fact that night was upon us and, officially, the black-out was in operation. There was nothing to be lost by trying, one could never tell, something might turn up: like Johnstone and Downes.

We set off, the driver and I, at breakneck speed and, of course, no lights. Quite soon we went headlong into a crater 3 ft deep in the road. The vehicle capsized on to its side and we both fell out into the rubble at the bottom. For a second or so there was silence while we were both making up our minds that neither of us was hurt, then, out of the darkness came the sound of many running feet; all at once invisible hands spurred on by much shouting righted both us and the vehicle, and once more we were on our way, but rather more cautiously. However, by now my enthusiasm had waned to the point that I asked the driver to return to the office of the Commandant de la Ville.

There, Johnstone and Downes were waiting. Even by the dim light from the office doorway I could see that they were beaming with confidence. It was then that I discovered that my suitcase had gone; it must have fallen out when we nosedived into the crater. Leaving an astonished pair of sailors the driver and I shot back to the bomb crater. Both of us scrambled and scrabbled inside and outside the crater, over-turning boulders, and bumping into one another — but no suitcase. The driver's language was original, lots I'd never heard before. When once more we stumbled into the road he could only gasp, '*La police. Il faut aller tout de suite à la police. Montez, Commandant, montez vite dans la voiture, la gendarmerie est tout près d'ici, à quatre cents metres.*' He made it seem like twenty metres.

An almost deathly calm prevailed at the gendarmerie; either the force was well organized, or more probable, not organized at all. It was difficult to find anyone to take any interest in us. Eventually we ran the chief himself to earth in his office where he was sitting gossiping with three or four of his officers. He listened politely in silence to my story, occasionally nodding, the ash of a Gaulloise stuck in the corner of his mouth. All the others breathed heavily, exuding such pessimism that when I had finished it seemed almost pointless to ask what chance there was of recovering my case. (I remembered, as a crumb of com-fort, that I had locked it.) The Chief regarded the blotter on his desk with a critical squint before raising his shoulders, arms, and finally his eyes in a huge slow-motion shrug.

'The Commandant will know how many thieves there are about in these difficult times,' he said slowly. 'Moreover, it is now dark. We cannot use torches to search ...' The cigarette in his mouth had now burnt so short that no matter how much he put his head on one side the smoke still went up his nose and in his eyes. He sneezed, and with a rapid gesture of his hand disposed of the result before finishing his sentence, '... and I have so few men.' He turned away for a second sneeze, this time into the waste paper basket at his side. 'Comman-dant,' he lied, 'I am desolate for you.'

I then mentioned the possibility of a reward. The atmosphere underwent a dramatic change: the Chief's hand paused in the act of stubbing out the offending cigarette, just long enough to subject me to a quick searching look. Then he leaned back in his chair with studied nonchalance as if the matter was no concern of his: how big a reward, he asked, was the Commandant thinking of offering? I offered the equivalant of £20 — which was a lot of money and all I had on me. I had to have that case back immediately.

The policeman's eyebrows rose fractionally as he reached forward for a pad on which he scribbled a few words; the result he tore off and handed in silence to one of his subordinates. The subordinate read the note, bobbed his head briefly first to his chief, then to me, and left the room. We could all hear his footsteps receding down the flagstone passage as he started to call out instructions to invisible inferiors.

For a time the silence continued while the Chief regarded his nails as if he had never seen them before. He tried biting one, spitting the fragment on to the floor. This was not a success and he stuffed both hands in his trouser pockets, not without difficulty as he was built on the plump side. When he had managed it he was still uncomfortable. Removing both hands again he shoved them into the leather belt carrying his official revolver. That gave him the confidence to resume his earlier diatribe about the number of thieves and pillagers in the town. Would the Commandant really like to wait? Or would he, perhaps, prefer to come back tomorrow morning? Oh, *pardon* — would the Commandant have a French cigarette? One of the remaining subordinates obliged, and I thanked him. The Chief also took one, lit it, and thanked no one. A further heavy silence was broken by a return to his commentary on the difficulties of his task; this he said with more than a touch of pride would be impossible without his '*tuyaux*', his lines of information. He encouraged all his staff to build up their '*tuyaux*', rather as if it were some body-building exercise.

I listened in vain for any sounds of activity on the other side of the door; no boots were tramping purposefully in our direction, no cars were starting up. I knew there were no carpets out there any more than where we were sitting. Could it be just a very quiet police station? I thought not.

The minutes went by and the Chief had reached the end of his small talk when there really was the sound of approaching footsteps. The door opened, with no preliminary knock, and there was our subordinate, my suitcase in his hand, doing his best to give the impression that he had been running from afar in retrieving the lost property. The relief was so great that instinctively my hand reached into my inside pocket. Everyone, including the runner from afar, stopped breathing until the money was seen to be on the table. Before paying I examined the locks. They were intact, and untampered with. I dared not open the case in front of them so I handed over the equivalent of £20 and shook the Chief by the hand to thank him. He responded with a small inclination of the head. But no smile. Perhaps the matter was too grave.

As I went down the steps I heard subdued laughter coming from the office I had just left. Well, I had had a bad fright, they had got some money out of it, and I didn't begrudge them their amusement.

Johnstone and Downes were waiting patiently for me where I had so hurriedly abandoned them. This time I let Johnstone take the case from me.

'Glad to see you got it back, sir.'

'Not as glad as I am, I promise, but thanks all the same. Found anything while I've been gone?'

Downes eased himself forward. 'Well, sir, there is a 'ouse. Just up the 'ill. Only about five minutes from 'ere. We got a torch.'

We set off. As we stumbled over odd bits of debris lying in the road Downes would occasionally shine his torch. At first there were merely excited shouts of protest, but then a bullet whistled through the air. We carried on in the dark while the five minutes extended to ten as we groped our way uphill. At the end of twenty minutes Downes signalled a halt beside a high wall.

'This is the place, sir.'

It was very dark. No lights were showing, but by standing in the middle of the road I could just make out, on the other side of the wall, the silhouette of the upper floors of a medium sized villa. Johnstone put down my case to flash his light on to a pair of gates about 7 ft high, set in the wall a few yards further up the hill and close to the villa. Downes was already there, and without more ado he lunged his whole weight against one of the gates, which yielded with a loud protesting shudder. Despite the blackness of the night the vague outlines of a drive and a garden could be discerned as we trooped through the gateway, our feet crunching on what seemed to be a big gravel sweep. Nearer the house it was possible to see through some trees straight down to the port below. Johnstone led the way round the house to some french windows where, but momentarily, he paused to fiddle the lock open and then we were inside.

' 'fraid there's no light, sir,' said Downes apologetically, 'but we found some candles.'

Moments later three or four candles were burning to reveal a good size salon, fully furnished, in French suburban fashion, and of more than customary comfort. Taking one of the candles I went out into the hall which, although sparsely furnished was agreeably clean for a house which could have been empty for some time.

'Care for a look round, sir?' offered Johnstone with the confidence of a professional estate agent.

Fatigue, hunger, and thirst: all were demanding attention but these two men had done so well it would have been churlish to decline. In agreeing to a conducted tour it soon became obvious that these two had spent much more time on their 'dekko' than they let on. However, the place would do for one night and if, by some hideous mischance, the owners returned we could always assure them that we would be gone by next morning. We set off round the ground floor; the dining-room was the right size with the right type of furniture — heavy, fumed oak, difficult to spoil — and a dozen matching chairs. There was also a study which would make an excellent office. Next to it was a lavatory wash place. Either the architect or the plumber must have been absent-minded when building the house — or perhaps one of them had a quirky sense of humour, because the lavatory cistern was housed in a cupboard in the study. At all events, this bizarre arrangement later provided some simple and highly rewarding amusement to the younger officers who would dart into the study, open the cupboard and pull the plug on unsuspecting visitors. The joke never failed.

Upstairs there seemed to be a considerable number of bedrooms, all fully furnished with bedding, and even sheets on some of the beds. By the time Johnstone — with a suitable flourish — threw open the door of the biggest and most comfortable bedroom I was beginning to have second thoughts about explaining to any returning owner that 'we would be gone in the morning'.

'Your room, sir.' He sounded as proud and pleased as if he had been going to sleep there himself.

Gradually the candles and the torch lit up the various parts of the room to reveal a large and obviously comfortable double bed, a high ceiling, ample cupboard space, and a washbasin with running water in the corner, all of which served only to crystallize my second thoughts.

'Well done, both of you,' I said. 'Now we'll go back into the town and get something to eat.'

From the doorway where he had been looking on Downes said quietly, 'No need to, sir.'

'What d'you mean? We've got to eat. You two must be as hungry as I am.'

By way of explanation Johnstone raised an arm slightly in the sort of dismissive motion used by schoolmasters dealing with particularly dense pupils. 'We got somethin' 'ere, sir, — in the 'ouse.' Still unsure that I had understood, he added, 'In the kitchen, sir.'

'Oh, —' I began, and stopped, discretion overcoming hunger.

'Shouldn't take long to 'ot up, when you're ready, sir,' he ended, making for the stairs.

In the previous nineteen days there had been an almost solid diet of bully-beef. It had been fried, made into a stew, eaten cold, hashed, every variety had been tried. Now was hardly the moment to show concern about the origins of any alternative. Once in the hall the sailors disappeared through a door presumably leading to the kitchen while I went to sample the comforts of the salon. It was a bit shabby, but that might be no disadvantage; it had an agreeable atmosphere. Ten minutes later Downes came in to announce that supper was on the table in the dining-room. In the piping days of peace this might have been the signal to go and wash the hands, but not this time.

Two candles on the table, and a big casserole exuding a heartwarming smell; civilized cutlery and china, a pleasantly shaped wine glass, all laid on a crisp white linen tablecloth. And, to top it off, an open bottle of wine. Sniffing proclaimed it not to be vintage, but not bad either. This time, however, conscience would not lie down.

'Where did you get this?' I asked.

Downes adjusted one of the candles on the table. 'Found it in the kitchen, sir, on top of the ice-box.'

'Open, like this?'

'The cork, sir, was what you might say, 'alf out.'

'And you gave it a bit of a tug?'

' 'ad to, sir. We didn't rightly know what it was.'

I was about to start in on a warning about pilfering when he continued, his expression becoming one of concern, 'After all this bombin' and minin' round the place the water might be dangerous to drink — don't you think, sir?'

He was deadly serious.

'You have a point there.'

'Yes, sir.'

'Any more bottles out there with their corks half out?'

'Dunno, sir. 'aven't 'ardly 'ad time to look.'

'Well you and Johnstone had better finish this one.' I handed him the bottle after topping up my glass.

'Thank you very much, sir.'

'Where's your food? Are you going to have some of this?'

I nodded towards the casserole in front of me.

'No, we're all right, sir. Got ours in the galley.'

'Good. Well, many thanks to you both. You've done jolly well. Now you slip along and get your food.'

'Aye, aye, sir, and thank you.'

Looking back, I can remember few more satisfying meals, partly because it was such a surprise, of course, and I was very hungry, but the stew itself was excellent; probably out of a carefully hoarded tin, but certainly not made in England. I was left with a general feeling of well-being at the end of the meal, however, which is easy to recall, even to this day.

By the time I had finished, both energy and curiosity about the villa had revived sufficiently for another walk round the garden in the dim light of a quarter moon. The grounds were rather bigger than I had at first thought. There was a decent level area immediately inside the gate to park a number of vehicles, plenty of rough lawn for storage of dinghies and other operational equipment, an all-round wall high enough to deter prying eyes and unwanted visitors, while the remainder of the garden was terraced down towards the harbour, giving a fine view of the port itself and, on most days, a distant sight of the historic island of Elba. The villa seemed almost perfect as a working and living base for the half dozen young operations officers who were due to arrive over the following few weeks. Somehow possession of the house must be legalized.

It was while all these splendid advantages were piling themselves up in my mind that I turned with some satisfaction to stare, once more, at the villa. Then I realized why the place was empty.

'Johnstone! Downes!' I shouted. From within came a muffled scraping of chairs, and shouts of 'Aye, aye, sir,' and then they were beside me. I pointed upwards.

'Look,' I said, 'there's no bloody roof.'

Large sections of the tiling had been ripped off, leaving the night sky plainly visible through naked rafters. Presumably bomb blasting.

'No, sir.' Johnstone was unmoved.

'Did you know?'

'Yes, sir.'

'Why didn't you tell me?'

'We thought as we could 'ave a better look an' fix it in the morning, sir.'

'Fix it? The whole bloody roof? How?'

He shrugged a little. 'Just needs a tarpaulin, sir.'

'And where d'you think you'll find a tarpaulin of that size in this place to cover that?'

Both sailors gazed earnestly upwards at the hole. Johnstone scratched his chin. 'Could be we could find one. Eh, Downie?'

'Could be,' agreed the 'poacher'.

'You know where there is one?' I said. 'Is that it?'

'Not exactly, sir.' Johnstone's tone was vague. 'But we could try. It's a fac', sir, the Jerries left a lot of gear sculling about when they scarpered.'

That they had something in mind seemed certain; such a pair were unlikely to be defeated by so trivial a matter as the lack of a roof. Not after the dinner they had just provided. Better perhaps not to think too much about it. Tomorrow was another day, and there was always the chance that we would find something else equally suitable. I would turn in.

'Well, good-night to you both, and thanks for the splendid meal. I did enjoy it. Tomorrow we might get the Commandant de la Ville to help us over the roof. We'll see.'

'Aye, aye, sir,' replied Downes. 'What time shake in the morning?'

'Oh, you needn't bother. I'm always awake early.'

'Tea at 6.30, sir?'

I gave in. 'Very good. Any time round then. Thanks very much. Good-night.'

The bed lived up to expectations, and I slept like a log until there was a knock on the door and Downes came in with a mug of tea. The fact that he had tipped most of the sugar bowl into it made it little the less welcome. Ten minutes later he was back with a jug of boiling water.

' 'fraid the plumbin's not up to much at the moment, sir.' As he was going out he glanced round with a cheerful grin, 'We'll 'ave a look after breakfast, eh, sir?'

'At the same time as the roof.'

'Yes, sir. Just like the roof. 's matter of fact Johnstone's up there now, 'avin' a look-see. Breakfast in about twenty minutes, sir?'

When I arrived down in the dining-room there were on the table two fried eggs, some French bread, and a good slab of unsalted butter. To-day such a menu may rouse no comment other than a warning that too many eggs are bad for you, but in 1943 things were infinitely more sensible. I tucked in.

Afterwards, on a further tour of inspection of house and grounds, the conclusions of the previous night confirmed themselves in the broad light of day: the whole property was precisely what we needed. The problem was still the roof, or lack of it. More than a third had simply vanished, and, try as I might, I could not share the confidence of the two sailors. From where could they hope to find a tarpaulin to cover that great gaping hole?'

Even if they were successful it would only be a temporary measure. The plumbing, too, appeared to leave a lot to be desired. A renewed search for another house would be easier and quicker in the long run than trying to make this one habitable, and the feeling was inescapable at that stage that any repairs by the two stalwarts might lead to trouble in the long run. A pity, but there was need for haste. Meanwhile it was best not to dwell on the inevitable struggle which lay ahead against the noisy hordes waiting, no doubt, in the office of the Commandant de la Ville.

Johnstone was clearing away the breakfast things as I explained my reasoning. He listened in silence as he stacked the cups and plates on a tray, pausing at the end only long enough to observe, not without a tinge of acid, I thought, that 'a better 'ouse would be bloody near impossible to find, sir.'

To disagree would have been cavalier so I told him that he and Downes were at liberty to continue the search themselves if they felt inclined, the only condition being that at no time was my suitcase to be left in the house unguarded. Meanwhile I was going to try once again at the Hotel de Ville. Fishing in my pocket I produced some money.

'You'd better have this,' I said, 'to go and buy some provisions.' He looked a bit surprised but took the proffered notes.

Walking down the hill towards the town I recalled that somewhere in the neighbourhood should be a British paramilitary signals unit: from there I might make a signal back to Maddalena. The truth was that I was funking the return to the Commandant's office, and therefore seeking some excuse for delay. It took another hour to find the unit; when I located them they were rather less than 300 yards from 'our' villa.

From the outside the place looked quite a lot more imposing than ours; it was modern, with a tidy garden and a pleasant patio overlooking the sea. Inside, however, there was a certain smug satisfaction in noticing that the furniture consisted, for the most part, of ration boxes to sit on, while army trestle tables did duty as both desk and dining table.

The Commanding Officer, Andrew Croft, in peacetime a well-known arctic explorer, now in uniform as a Major, and his staff were very hospitable, and after offering me all the help I might need, they produced a bottle of gin. Time flew by and just before noon I decided I had better return to the villa: there could be no knowing what those two sailors might be up to. As I was saying goodbye to my hosts at the door I picked up my cap from a radiator, and a thought struck me.

'I suppose,' I said to the CO, 'you've got a full tank of fuel for your central heating?'

He looked a trifle surprised at the question.

'D'you know,' he said, 'I've no idea. We've only just got in here from Calvi. No time to look.'

Privately I made a bet with myself that he would be disappointed, and hurried off 'home' to see what sort of system we had — if any. I prayed for something more antiquated, more primitive that didn't require sophisticated fuel. Then I reminded myself that we had decided to move anyway. On return there was no sign of either of the sailors. Immediately anxious about my suitcase I ran upstairs to the bedroom. All was well; it was still there, locked. But where the hell were Johnstone and Downes?

Just as I was getting up a good head of invective I heard something drop on a floor somewhere in the house: the noise seemed to come from above. Out on the landing was a narrow flight of stairs leading up to the floor above. As quietly as I could I crept up them, taking each stair gently. Half way there was a loud creak as the wood gave way under the extra weight. Downes' voice came in indistinct tones from

26

what sounded like somewhere much higher up. ''s all right, sir. It's only us. We see you come in through the gate.'

Quicky I mounted the remaining stairs only to find myself in almost total darkness. While feeling round for a light switch I remembered there was no electricity, and groped my way forwards until halted by a soft barrier which gave way when I pushed against it, but didn't yield altogether.

'Where are you?' I called.

''ere, sir.' Downes' voice was very close but I could see nothing. 'The other side of the tarpaulin. We done one side, sir, an' we won't be long on this one, if you 'ang on a minute.'

At my feet there was a sudden convulsion as the tarpaulin was raised just enough for Johnstone's head to appear under the bottom edge.

'Sorry, sir,' he said rising to his feet and lifting the whole thing on the back of his neck, 'I didn't 'ear what you said.'

'I didn't say anything, except to ask where you were. Now I'm here, though, where in the world did you find this lot?'

The tarpaulin convulsed once more to reveal Downes standing outlined against the sky, his feet planted on the joists while he struggled to manoeuvre the heavy material into place. He gave me a cheerful grin. 'From up 'ere, sir, we could keep a perfect watch on the gate. No one come in all mornin', and that's a fac', sir.'

'I'm very glad to hear it. But,' and I tweaked the material all round us, 'where did you get this?'

There was an awkward moment when I wondered if the silence which ensued might become a matter of 'dumb insolence' until Downes, always the one to exercise quiet charm round tricky corners, breathed rather than uttered the two words, 'Gash, sir.' He was gazing out over the rooftops as he added, 'It was going gash, an' there it was, you might say.'

You might indeed.

Johnstone came in from the other corner. 'What time would you like dinner up, sir?'

On my way down I couldn't avoid noticing that on the extreme edge of the tarpaulin there were some inscriptions: even though they were abbreviations they had a military air about them, and they were certainly in Italian.

There were two Italian anti-aircraft batteries only a few minutes walk down the road from us. I thought about them, and I thought about the tarpaulin, and I thought about the excellence of the salami as I ate my lunch. When I had finished I went outside and from the far end of the garden I inspected the roof, then I looked across to where I could just see the uncovered guns of the Italian batteries. It seemed improbable that the Italians could see our roof well enough to be able to raise their suspicions. In any case Johnstone and Downes had made a first-class job of covering up the tell-tale lettering. There was no longer any point in contemplating a move. Going inside I congratulated them both and went back to my paramilitary friends to send off my initial progress report to Maddalena.

From there I re-visited the Commandant du Port who obligingly dropped what he was doing with an alacrity born, I came to suspect, of a sense of despair at the size of the task ahead of him. He took me on a tour of the whole area. It seemed even worse than when I had seen it first only the day before. The basins were cluttered up with all manner of jettisoned war material, sunken craft, cranes which had been toppled in at the last minute by the Germans, bits of road blocks, some civilian cars, and just rubbish which had been thrown there. I asked again about mines. He said they didn't know much about where they might be, but a channel had been swept, was now well marked, and provided boats stuck to it there should be no disasters. The main problem was to clear obstructions from the water immediately alongside the jetties, and this was in hand by a mixed force of French military and port personnel. The quays had been mined by the Germans but fortunately, for reasons unknown, the enemy had failed to detonate them. After de-fusing the mines the French decided to leave them in place — one never knew in war these days, the Germans might be back. As we returned to his office the Commandant had cheered up enough to express the hope that a further three or four days should see the harbour in a fit state to allow reasonable working.

Later that evening, as I sat writing up a full report in what was now my 'office', the light started to fail but I decided I must continue as long as possible to use what daylight remained so as to conserve our stock of candles. I had just reached the point where I could no longer go on when the door opened, Johnstone came in and switched on the light.

'Sorry, sir,' he said with genuine concern, 'I just come in to do the black-out. I ought to 'ave told you, we found the mains disconnected so we just connected 'em up again.'

I laughed. They were hard to defeat, these two.

'Gettin' organized, gradual, sir. Downes has fixed the plumbin' so's at least the water comes out the taps,' he continued as he walked over to the windows, and closed the shutters. 'Not that it's very clean, just yet, an' I wouldn't advise *drinkin'* it, but it's better'n we 'ad before, which was the 'ose from the garden tap.' He slammed the last shutter to. 'So we're better off, ain't we, sir?'

'Who's the electrician, you or Downes?'

'Done a bit meself, in Civvy Street.'

'Well, it seems to me the pair of you shouldn't have much of a problem after the war.'

'Suits me, sir.'

'What does?'

'The war, sir, that is, if you take it the right way — an' of course, if you're lucky. Got to 'ave luck. What time supper, sir?'

When the report was finished I took it upstairs, locked it in my suitcase, which I hid behind a cupboard, and then went across to the basin and turned on the taps. From the cold tap a thick brown stream gushed out in noisy hiccups: when it cleared I washed. Nothing appeared from the hot tap.

On my way downstairs I went into the bathroom where the result from the taps was frankly discouraging. They appeared to have nothing to do with water. Closer examination proved that all piping had been severed just short of the taps, and the waste pipes had also been cut. The bath, it must be admitted, could claim to have a certain old world charm with its four iron-claw legs and brass taps; the whole thing rocked when I leant on it. Perhaps the owner had been about to have a new bathroom when the exigencies of the war had called him away, but I didn't really think so. I just wished he'd left it in a better state.

At the bottom of the stairs I met Downes coming to tell me that supper was ready. And there it was, on the table. Chicken. I prayed that they'd used the money I'd given them to buy it. There was also an open bottle of wine. Another one.

I was about to begin a serious remonstration when Johnstone came in. As the cook he had taken to staying in the kitchen. Now he wasted no time.

'The wine, sir. Sorry about that, but as I was sayin' earlier, sir, the water really ain't safe to drink. Got to let it run through the pipes a day or so, yet, before it's clean. An' I'm sure the owners of the 'ouse, they'd do the same if they was 'ere.' His closing words had developed into more of a question than a statement. Now he put the question direct. 'Wouldn't you say so, sir?'

'Yes, ' I replied, 'I dare say they would. But just in case they should have other ideas, go down to the cellar, lock it, and bring me the key. If we're worried about the water we can always boil the stuff we drink.'

The cloud which had been gathering on his face lightened. 'So we can, sir. Can't think why we didn't think of it before. Bring you the key, now, sir.' It didn't take much to realize that I was included in the 'we'.

He went out and I heard him conferring rapidly with Downes, then

29

both of them went down to the cellar where there was a lot of noise as the cellar door was banged shut, and even the key turning in the lock was to make itself heard. Afterwards I thought they came up the stairs rather slowly, and carefully, before Johnstone reappeared bringing the key which, with a slight show of formality, he put on the table beside my plate.

'Key of the cellar, sir,' he said quite unnecessarily, a curious expression on his face: he may have been trying out something new, like piety. It didn't last long.

'Thanks,' I said. I didn't care how many bottles they'd brought out of the cellar with them, they'd earned them.

'By the way,' I said, 'Looking at the bath just now I see it has been disconnected altogether from the water system. We shall have to find a plumber.'

'Yes, sir. Seems the froggies aren't too keen on washing. I'll 'ave a proper look in the morning.'

'Do by all means but I rather think it's more than either you or Downes can tackle — unless, of course, one of you is a professional plumber. The pipes have been cut and sealed.'

He made a funny little shrug as he picked up a plate. 'May be a way round it, sir.'

'Maybe,' I said.

That night I slept as soundly as usual but on waking at 06.30 I had a dim recollection of a dream connected with noise, an ugly scraping sound as of a heavy iron bench being dragged over paving stones. I dropped off again.

When Downes came in with a mug of tea about half an hour later I was still asleep. 'Many thanks, Downes. Just pop it down on the table by the window. I'll get up straight away. If you've got any hot water for shaving I would be grateful.'

'Comin' up in a minute, sir. Kettle's on the 'ob already.'

Getting out of bed I went over to the window to stare out over the sea towards Elba beyond which the sun was rising into a clear pale sky. In peacetime it would have been romantic; in war it meant simply that the two opposing sides could see more clearly to kill each other. Such sombre thoughts were banished by another knock on the door to herald Downes with the shaving water. I thanked him and asked him to let Johnstone know that I would be down ready for breakfast in a quarter of an hour.

'Better 'ave your bath, first, sir.'

I looked at him quickly. He was pulling my leg. 'Better have *what* did you say, Downes?'

There was not even the suspicion of a smile on his face. 'Your bath, sir,' he repeated.

'But, for God's sake,' I said, startled, 'there's no water, no waste pipe —'

'We managed to fix it, sir.' He was beginning to smile. 'Ready in a few minutes now.' And he was gone.

I swallowed my tea, and shaved, running through in my mind all the events and surprises of the past 24 hours. There seemed little risk of boredom at the rate things were going. Stripping off and wrapping a towel round my waist, I went along to the bathroom and opened the door. The bath had vanished. Only the sawn-off pipes remained as evidence that it had ever existed. Such was my astonishment that I remember (with embarrassment) looking behind the door in case by some miracle the room had changed shape overnight. I went out on the landing. No bath anywhere. I called down the well of the staircase to be answered by Johnstone peering up at me.

'What on earth's going on, Johnstone? Downes came up a few minutes ago to tell me the bath would be ready shortly. Well, the bloody thing's vanished — gone — it's not here.'

'I know, sir.'

'Then how the hell can he say it's ready?'

'An' so it is, sir.'

'What d'you mean — "so it is"?'

'It's ready — down 'ere, sir.'

'Where?'

I saw him shift from one foot to the other as he continued staring upwards. 'Outside, sir.' He swallowed, dipping his head as he did so. 'If you could come down, sir, I could show you.'

This was all beyond me; I went downstairs. Johnstone led the way across the hall; as we went through the drawing-room he turned his head slightly over his shoulder. 'We didn't want to burn the 'ouse down, sir,' he said. He opened the french windows and there, propped up on bricks with a fire burning brightly underneath, was the bath, iron claws and all.

As we came out Downes looked up from his position, crouched beside the bath where he was stoking the fire with small bits of wood. Close by him was a bucket of water. He dipped an experimental hand in the bath. ''ot enough now, sir. I'll just dowse the fire.' So saying he poured the bucket of water slowly over the fire. When the clouds of steam and smoke had subsided he again put his hand in the bath. Then he stood up, bent forward and put his hand right down into the bottom of the bath. 'Not too 'ot now, sir. Don't want to burn your ar—, backside, do you, sir?'

Meanwhile Johnstone had assumed his house agent's role once

again. 'Nice and sheltered in this corner, sir,' he said looking round the garden.

I was still mute with surprise and admiration as I suddenly recalled my earlier dream about ugly scraping noise. It had been no dream.

'But how —?' I began, when Downes anticipated the question.

'Simple, really, sir. Easier to carry the bath down 'ere. Now if we'd 'ave got the 'ot water upstairs, there wasn't no wastepipe to get it down again. We'd 'ave 'ad water all over the deck, sir. 'ere you're quite screened by the 'edge.' Like Johnstone a moment earlier, he looked round the garden, and waved a generous hand. 'Only got the seagulls, sir.'

Discreetly both withdrew into the house as I stepped into the water. The bottom of the bath was still pretty warm but that in no way spoilt the next fifteen minutes, memorable to this day, as I lazed in the warm water watching the light from the rising sun rippling on an almost flat sea, with Elba, looking even more alluring, showing through a gathering heat haze. We must stay in this enchanting place.

A day or so after legalizing the requisitioning of the house with the Commandant de la Ville no longer trying to escape, a signal arrived from the Naval-Officer-in-Charge, Maddalena, recalling me to report on the situation in Bastia, and to discuss future plans.

Above left 'Authentic picture of post-Captain looking for ants in his pants. St Florent, Corsica'. (Inscribed on back of original)

Above right SOIS 'on passage from Torre Annunziata to Naples'.

Below SOIS being decorated by the American Navy.

Left Lieutenant Tom Maxted, DSO, RNR.

Below Tom Maxted, 1980s in his own yacht.

Right Major Andrew Croft in 1943.

Below The type of rubber dinghy used on clandestine operations.

Left 'Prof' — Lieutenant Peter Sylvester-Bradley, RNVR.

Below (L to R) Lieutenant Paddy Davies, Captain Ken Carson, 'Skipper' Newton, Captain Dick Cooper, and Sergeant Arnold.

Chapter 2

THE SETTLING-IN PERIOD

Applying the principle of poachers making the best gamekeepers, Downes and Johnstone were left in charge of the villa. As a longstop safeguard, my paramilitary SOE friends from just down the road offered to keep a watchful eye on things. Beyond that there was only prayer.

The post of Naval-Officer-in-Charge, Maddalena, was to last only so long as it took to organize port facilities in Bastia capable of looking after the several flotillas of Allied coastal forces, and other ancillary craft mentioned earlier. As soon as such facilities became available the NOIC would transfer himself and all his staff north to the Corsican port, and his title would change to Senior Officer Inshore Squadron — SOIS, for short — a more aggressive-sounding appointment as, indeed, he made it become.

Filling the post was Captain Norman Vincent Dickinson, DSO, DSC. A little surprisingly he was a 'springer' (Physical Training specialist) of whom there weren't many by comparison with ordinary executive officers — torpedo, gunnery, navigation, or other specialists.

To look at there wasn't much springer-ish about him, except, perhaps, his lean frame and the lightness of his long stride. Somewhere about 5 ft 10 in (maybe 6 ft when standing up straight, which he didn't often do) he had fair, thinning hair, a ruddy complexion, tufts of hair on each cheek, and what might have started its career as a shapely aquiline nose until someone, or something, had been a bit rough: maybe it was boxing, after all, he was a springer. A good deal of the time he looked worried and for good reason. His command was composed of young officers, some still in their teens, all anxious to 'have a go', and, on occasion, given to arguing the toss, less than half of them being British. From the start he was both liked and trusted implicitly by all nationalities alike. He didn't mince his words although I don't remember him ever being dogmatic. In moments of concentration or difficulty he had a habit of rubbing his hands together lightly, letting his fingers interlace, usually just prior to lighting a cigarette (he was a heavy smoker). The initial impression may, sometimes, have been a trifle on the forbidding side, but better acquaintance soon revealed the quizzical dry humour, the reasoned decision, and, above all, the solid common sense. Among his immediate staff he quickly became known (never to his face) as 'Dick-o'.

When I reported to him after the first visit to Bastia a totally unexpected, but wonderful surprise was waiting. Up to September 1943 (the year of this chronicle) Maddalena had been an important Italian base for their MAS boats, the equivalent of the Allied Motor Torpedo- or Motor Gun-boats. The Italian capitulation resulted in these flotillas passing under the command of the Allies, where, it was hardly surprising, they became something of a Pandora's Box. To expect the officers and ratings of these boats to accept, to a man, such an about-face of loyalty from one day to the next was asking too much. As the NOIC pointed out when he took them over, it would be foolish in the extreme to expect them to go out and engage their ex-allies, or, even worse, their own compatriots at sea. What, then, was to be done with them?

In the middle of making my report he interrupted by holding up his hand. After enquiring in an oddly casual way about my plans — I had hardly any at that time — he went on to explain his predicament with the MAS boats. It was a bit puzzling until he suddenly suggested that I should consider them as a better alternative to the fishing-boat concept. Such a solution would kill two birds with one stone. He would be disembarrassed of finding some use for them; they would not be required, in any way, to be aggressive against erstwhile friends and compatriots, and the fact that they were fast craft should suit our clandestine role.

It was almost impossible to believe our luck, and I grabbed the offer immediately, subject, of course, to the approval of my 'master' in London, DDOD(I) Commander Frank Slocum. Of this I was not entirely sanguine: he wasn't always easy to convince of new ideas unless he had seen them in operation for himself. To him the safety of the passengers ('resisters') was, at all times, paramount. This proposal contained certain obvious risks of treachery — if one could call it treachery to change one's mind about accepting, overnight, that all one had been fighting for was quite wrong, and that now it was time to change sides. Given time, patience, and understanding that risk should evaporate, but it might take a long while to build real confidence between the MAS crews and ourselves. In the interim the risk remained.

As for the craft themselves, there were three types of MAS boat. The 120 ft copy of the German E-boat, fitted with diesel engines, the 60 ft torpedo-boat with twin 500 HP Isotta-Fraschinis, and the smaller version of the same boat, the 47 footer. To jump ahead a bit, we chose the 60 ft boat, and took out the torpedo tubes of some of them, raising their top speed from 37 to 47 knots. They were fitted with twin Graham engines as auxiliaries; these engines were supposed to be silent, and the claim was that they gave a speed of 6 knots cruising. Well, they were, and they weren't silent. Standing on the beach in an offshore breeze you couldn't hear them approach until they were almost on you; in an onshore light air they could be heard a mile or more off, a rather high-pitched whine. But more of that later.

All these details and specifications were sent off by signal to DDOD(I) with the blessing of the NOIC — and a fervent prayer from me. There ensued quite a bit of hemming and ha-ing to satisfy the natural caution of my London master but finally he sent both approval and good wishes. We were off.

The NOIC lost no time in summoning the senior officer of the Italian Naval Base to make arrangements for the boats to be sent up to Bastia after completion of what could only be pretty sketchy vetting of the crews: in effect this amounted to relying almost entirely on the personal judgement of the Italian Senior Naval Officer — and not much was known about *him* at that early stage. It was the best we could do.

During my short absence in Bastia more of the fishing-boats of what was known as the African Coastal Flotilla (the ones I had come out to command) had arrived to join 'SEADOG', the first to reach Maddalena. All were manned by volunteer naval crews, as they always had been. Now, mercifully, the operational role of the boats should no longer be necessary, although the officers and crews would have plenty of work from the newly-available Italian fast craft. Events were moving quickly in the right direction or at least they seemed to be: the matter of the reliability of our latest allies remained a bit of an open question.

Meanwhile I took the opportunity to have that yarn with Petty Officer Bates. We discussed the change of plan and decided that we would need a maximum of eight ratings as dinghymen, with himself in charge of them all: this allowed two dinghymen per boat with four operations per night. That would be our capacity; it was more likely that there would be two ops on any night which would allow the spare numbers to rest. We went through the list of ratings forming the ship's companies of the recently arrived fishing-boats, discussing each one's suitability for what promised to be rather a different type of operation.

Inevitably, the names of Leading Seamen Johnstone and Downes cropped up.

Pencil in hand, Bates gave a small airy wave of the arm before starting to write his list. 'We should have them, sir, I think.'

I said nothing, causing him to look up with eyebrows raised in query. Then he lowered his sights to inspect my shoes. 'Shouldn't we, sir?'

I nodded. 'I agree.'

Obviously relieved he glanced up again. 'They all right, sir? I mean up in Bastia.'

'As a matter of fact they've done very well. But I think you'd better come with me when I go back up north.'

His face lit up. 'Aye, aye, sir.'

On my final briefing from Captain Dickinson before returning to Bastia he instructed me to carry on digging in and, above all, to find living and office accommodation for himself and his staff; he wished to move up there with his growing fleet of coastal forces as soon as possible.

When Bates and I reached the villa a few days later things began happening quickly. Tom Maxted, the first of what was to become half a dozen operations officers — young RNR or RNVR lieutenants — arrived shortly afterwards. Permanent communication links were set up with both Maddalena, and DDOD(I) in London. For the next few weeks Bates, Johnstone, and Downes divided their time between receiving, unpacking, and stowing operational stores, rubber dinghies, firearms, and the like, and organizing the base itself into a more manageable form in and around the villa.

Although my new-found paramilitary friends (who, as already mentioned, turned out to be almost all members of SOE) were kindness itself, always willing to help out in shifting stores and providing the occasional pick-up truck or van (PU) the need to have our own system of road transport soon became imperative. But from where?

Before we could tackle this problem some half dozen MAS boats arrived from Maddalena, and their commanding officer reported to me. Curiously enough, he was not, himself, operational, although he had received orders to see that the boats were to be put at my disposal. With his young officers and ratings he was accommodated in a building which only a short while before (when they were fighting on the Axis side) had been occupied by other Italian naval personnel. The commanding officer informed me that he had brought six boats, the others were due to arrive a bit later. Would I like to inspect the first six? If so, when?

The following morning at 11.00 found me shaking formal hands with the Italian CO of the flotilla as he prepared for the inspection of his six crews, now all fallen in along the jetty with their backs to the water. Each crew of about eight ratings was separated from its neighbour by a gap of two or three yards. This made for a long walk, and was not really my form at all; it would have been easier to go round each boat while the hands were working, but, as I discovered then and on a number of subsequent occasions the Italians could be sticklers for formality.

The CO having provided a second, even grander salute, after shaking hands, led off to introduce the first of the young Italian Captains, all between about 25 and thirty. Yet another smart salute — a sort of abrupt shading of the eyes as if from a sudden blinding light — another handshake, and off we went to the next crew. Meanwhile the ratings remained rigidly at attention, looking smart and clean.

We were half way along the second crew when, just before we reached him, one of the ratings took a brisk pace forward, raised his arm palm downward in the Nazi salute, and said quite loudly, 'Heil Hitler!' There followed a moment of acute embarrassment for everybody, not least for the man himself: a bit sheepishly he looked round at his shipmates to see what they thought of what he had just done. Not much, it seemed. I moved a little closer to the man; he looked ordinary enough. Something had to be done, we couldn't stand there all day in a ridiculous sort of *tableau vivant*. Would it, perhaps, be good for morale if I pushed the man into the drink about two yards behind him? I turned to the commanding officer whose face was locked in horror. Discretion! Discretion!

'Would you,' I asked, 'Please tell this man that he is now supposed to be fighting on the *other* side — *our* side.'

The CO favoured me with an understanding shading-of-the-eyes, and then addressed himself to the offender. Under the ensuing avalanche of words the wretched man dissolved to become a greasespot, an effect not lost on his nearby shipmates. Further down the long line there were one or two other '*Heil Hitlers*'; each got the same impressive treatment which would have done credit to a Whale Island instructor. Not only was it an interesting experience but it also provided some sort of yardstick of reliability among the crews. Sadly, as we were to discover later, it did not eradicate altogether the unreliable elements.

The inspection completed, the CO invited me to take a glass of wine with him and his officers in their wardroom, and this I accepted gladly enough. The first essential was to get to know these new allies. On the way there he offered deep apologies for the erring sailors; in return I assured him that far from any offence being taken the incident had, perhaps, been a blessing in separating sheep from goats. Although comforted, he remained alert, watching his young officers while they drank their chianti in the somewhat austere atmosphere of a sparsely furnished wardroom. At first all was formality, conversation being stiff and in low tones. They were trying to find out what sort of animal they had to deal with, while I, on my side, was trying to do the same. Glasses were raised, and there were courteous small bows before each drink, like theatre 'business' before the star of the show makes his entrance. But there was no star. Gradually the conversation became freer, especially when I began telling them the bare bones of what they might be expected to do. No bellicose activity against either their compatriots still fighting on the other side, or their erstwhile allies, the Germans. Unless, of course, the other side started being beastly; then they would be expected to reply in kind — with interest. In proof of this peaceable approach we would be asking them to remove, to unship their torpedo-tubes, leaving only a couple of light machine-guns, and a 20mm cannon mounted in the stern to discourage pursuers.

At that stage it was not possible to go any further in explanation and they seemed quite relieved at what they had heard. The next thing was to have a good look at the boats themselves. This was arranged for the following morning, the CO choosing a young red-headed Lieutenant, a Captain of one of the boats, as my guide. He turned out to be a member of the well-known Triestine ship-owning family of Cosulich. Because of his wiry red hair he became known to all of us simply as 'Ginger'.

MAS 541, Ginger's boat, was all that one could have wished: minimum spit and polish, but everything neat, tidy, and well maintained, with good morale evident throughout the vessel. Even at that early stage the strength of character of the engine-room Chief stood out sharply. Capo Pulchri wasn't very big but he was, above all, a perfectionist, a quality we came to appreciate on more than one delicate occasion later on. He was also forever cheerful: except for his beloved engines life was a permanent joke.

It was Ginger who first told me that all officers and ratings serving in MAS boats were volunteers, rather like our own submariners. Surprised by this information, I asked him why, to which he gave a shy grin, shrugged his slim shoulders and said he really didn't know. It was like that; always had been so. Only when I knew them better did it become clear that they were generally considered in their own navy as being among the élite.

At the end of the inspection Ginger invited me into the diminutive wardroom for a glass of vino, gladly accepted. While he was pouring out the drinks my eye was caught by a small brass plaque mounted on one of the bulkheads. Curious, I moved across to read the inscription. The first words, in bolder type than the rest, were 'HMS *Fiji* '. The plaque commemorated the sinking of our own cruiser. When I turned back I realized that Ginger had been watching me. I asked him if he had been in command at the time. His embarrassment was minimal. Yes, he had been. He must have recognized immediately that in no way was I trying to criticise because he continued straight away with a brief account of the action, ending by saying that he had been very frightened. From his description of the event I wasn't surprised.

Not long after news came through from London that a First Lieutenant was being despatched shortly to help in the running of the African Coastal Flotilla (ACF), a nomenclature more paradoxical than it had been before. It did, however, carry on the tradition, as it were. Anyone who had ever come across the ACF had quickly learned that it concerned an odd lot of ginks who, generally speaking, meant well, but about whom it was best not to ask too many questions. However, back to our new First Lieutenant.

When he arrived he turned out to be a long, lanky peacetime geologist of some promise whose last civilian appointment had been in the British Museum, no less. Now he was a long lanky Lieutenant RNVR with good experience in destroyers behind him. Perhaps it was during this time that colour-blindness became apparent — I never asked him, although it was to have an important effect on his career.

To us, in the flotilla, he was never known as anything but 'Prof'. At first glance, for some odd reason, I was put in mind — and this is not meant unkindly — of Walt Disney's Pluto, in constant danger of appearing lugubrious until the sudden sparkle in the eye provided the lie. When he laughed, which, thank God, was pretty often, the whole place was liable to reverberate with the noise. His keen sense of humour was both generous and unfailing, although I was told much later that he could, at times, be quite fierce — just the right balance in a wardroom such as ours settled into being. On a personal note, many became the time when I had reason to be grateful for his lively intellect and common sense in solving problems. He didn't waste much time in putting me in my place, either.

Quite soon after his arrival I was summoned to Allied Forces Headquarters (AFHQ) in Algiers to plan a set of operations. Just before I left Prof asked permission to hold a mixed party — there were a few pretty Corsican girls around — while I was away. When I suggested that the date might be postponed so that I might not miss the fun he let out a bellow of laughter. 'But don't you see, the party's not for SOBs.' He was just two years younger than me. I have now forgiven him.

Due to his unfortunate tendency to colour-blindness there could be no question of him taking part in operations at sea, although it was so obviously the one thing he wanted to do. Eventually, in unexpected circumstances he got his wish on a memorable occasion which comes later. As an organizer, and wise counsellor to young and old alike, he was oustanding.

As if to redress the balance, the first operations officer to arrive was almost the exact counterpart to Prof. Tom Maxted (whom we have already met a page or two back) was a young (early-twenties) Lieutenant RNR I had known for some time and for whom I had asked. He had already proved himself to be a first-class Captain of a fishing-vessel working out of North Africa, and I expected him to do as well, if not better, in fast craft. And he didn't disappoint anybody. In those days Tom had two basic states of mind — asleep (or, at best, dozey) or, alternatively, very wide awake. To arrive at a mean seemed beyond him. Only two things really got him going: either an operation on to the enemy coast, when he would start with the planning and remain keen-eyed until he had secured alongside back in harbour; that was one thing. The other was the sight of a pretty girl; this was an event which somehow worked both ways; it didn't matter how old or how young they were, none seemed able to resist his charms. Maddening for the less fortunate.

Amongst the administrative problems solved on the spot by Prof was the engagement of a civilian cook called Maria. I was a bit apprehensive about his choice at the outset, because she was not altogether uncomely at 28 years of age in a largely male population, so that visions of trouble flitted across my mind. But I needn't have worried, such fears proved groundless. To her eternal credit Maria could, and did, make rations not taste like rations, and she was both uncomplaining and resourceful about providing meals at the oddest hours. It didn't take long, either, for her to show more all-round talents in pressing and ironing, washing, sewing on buttons, and later, on one never-to-be-forgotten occasion, acting as assistant motor mechanic. In appearance she had a quite dazzling jigsaw of gold fillings in her teeth, lots of black, black hair, and — wonder of wonders — hardly any moustache at all.

While all this was going on, NOIC Maddalena, now transformed into Senior Officer Inshore Squadron (SOIS) arrived in Bastia, and was comfortably installed in a house a few hundred yards up the hill from us. His office was located conveniently but, it has to be admitted, quirkily, in a nearby convent. He and his staff occupied one section of the building, the American Air Force another, while the nuns took up what was left. It was, as one member of SOIS's staff observed, odd sitting listening to the nuns chanting their devotions while planning

40

death and destruction to an enemy one could almost see out of the window. Such is war.

Tom and I, polite but inquisitive about how our new master was getting on, decided to call on him. There was another motive. Transport. We were careful not to complain outright as if it was his fault that we were at our wits' end about the problem but we went into some detail about it. As always, he was sympathetic, but said he was quite unable to help from official sources; he himself had no personal conveyance and would very much like to be able to 'get about a bit'. Further discussion threw up the notion of an approach to the Italian Army, who at that time certainly had less need of mobility than us. They, however, were stationed at Corte, miles away. More discussion ended in a carefully planned semi-official, verbal request to the Italian GOC, General Lazzarini (as far as I remember), that he would receive me as SOIS's representative. It worked. I was invited to go when I liked.

I cadged a lift to Corte, one of the four 'towns' in Corsica (excluding Ajaccio), situated slap in the middle of the island. The whole place seemed to be alive with green uniforms — but few vehicles were to be seen moving around. I had little difficulty in finding the General's office where I was received by the ADC, a long thin individual of about thirty with a wispy moustache and no chin that I could see. He was a Captain who wore an expression of permanent boredom, and had manners which varied between the casual and the positively offhand — even, as became evident, with his General. His only asset on this occasion was that his English was better than my Italian — and that wasn't saying much.

Once the initial introductions were over, and he was reasonably sure that I was who I said I was, namely the official representative of SOIS, he took me across to the officers' Mess and gave me a glass of wine while we waited for the General to turn up. He also informed me that the General would like to offer me lunch and after such an early start this was a welcome invitation. While we drank I thought how odd it was that only weeks earlier my hosts were fighting on the other side, and would have been glad to give me quite another sort of reception, in a POW camp.

We waited a good twenty minutes, carrying on a desultory, awkward conversation stuffed with halting banalities before discovering that the General, tired of kicking his heels for the British officer, had already gone into lunch. The news neither disturbed nor worried the ADC; there was, he said, plenty of time. At leisure we finished our drinks before making for the dining-room, a vast hall where a sort of running meal was being served to something more than a hundred officers. As I remarked earlier, the Italians can be sticklers for formality, and here

41

they were, at it again. As each officer entered or left the room he clicked his heels and made a jerky little bow towards the General. If the General happened to notice he bowed back, which kept him pretty busy and couldn't have improved either his digestion or his food. The ADC didn't bother with any such niceties as he elbowed his way through the passing officers towards the General's table where, with a nonchalant wave in my direction and a muttered reference to the '*ufficiale inglese*' he considered the introduction complete. The General was more polite, beckoning me to the vacant chair beside him. The ADC curtly advised an officer seated next to the vacant chair to move. I think he was senior to the ADC, but he moved all the same, leaving me to sit between the General and the ADC, an arrangement which obliged me to employ my inadequate Italian to maintain some sort of conversation with the General.

I had hoped that the ADC might act as interpreter, and this I think he guessed, for without further ado he turned away to concentrate his attention on the officer on his other side. He may have had little chin but he wasn't stupid. Meanwhile the atmosphere between the General and me could best be described as formal, and the conversation sluggish. What else could it have been?

He was a saturnine individual who never seemed to smile, but then he didn't have much to smile about; his command had withered to little more than a cypher, his troops had nothing to do, and he could only long for peace and the prospect of going home to his family. Instead, here he was, saddled with some fool ex-enemy officer who could barely make himself understood in frightful 'kitchen' Italian, and who was shortly going to remove some of his best transport. In the circumstances the General showed himself to be a tolerant man.

In the throes of wrestling with a mound of unruly spaghetti and the language problem I believe I got the message home to him that SOIS sent his compliments but also placed the highest priority on the need for transport. Between the endless little courtesy nods to the officers coming into and leaving the room, and trying simultaneously to eat his lunch — no question of enjoying it — he took a little time to reply. When he did he said that the ADC would see to my needs after lunch. It seemed to take a long time.

At last the General got to his feet. The ADC was still talking to his next door neighbour and affected not to notice until the General tapped him on the shoulder: even then he was at pains to finish his sentence before paying any attention.

Once outside I asked the ADC to interpret our precise transport requirements to the General — one three-ton lorry, two pick-up vans, and one private car. This was the moment to iron out any loopholes of misunderstanding: to pin down the ADC. The General played his part to perfection, giving instructions in short rapid sentences about which there could be no mistake before shaking hands, surprising me yet again with one of those odd little bows, a salute, and then a rapid disappearance towards his office. There was no opportunity to offer more than the most perfunctory of thanks, and a belated salute before he was out of earshot.

By now the ADC's expression was one of disgust and, as was to become apparent later on, not without reason. He led off towards the transport lines down the hill from the officers' Mess. There, together, we inspected what seemed like hundreds of vehicles — lorries, PUs, three-wheelers, all sorts — with few exceptions all in a state of disrepair or cannibalisation. A long search was needed to discover two PUs in good condition, and these were immediately earmarked for us. Of three-tonners, however, there were none except those in a deplorable state. As this was our most urgent need, I told the ADC as much, impressing on him that it was up to him to find one in good order and have it sent down to Bastia without delay.

I said I would give him a week, that should be ample. If at the end of that time a three-tonner had not arrived, I would get my 'Admiral' (SOIS) — an unofficial accelerated promotion seemed warranted for the occasion — to ring up his General. Unexpectedly, this approach made a satisfactory impression and he promised results with several 'va benes' for good measure.

Then we came to the matter of the car for me, and there was a marked change in his attitude. Sourly, he cast his glance round the lines of vehicles, mumbling to himself, clicking his teeth, and shaking his head. Here was a difficult problem, indeed. Must I have the car now? But of course, I replied firmly, how else was I to return to Bastia? Ah, but what was wrong with a PU? That would get me back every bit as well as a car. That was as maybe, I insisted, but it was not what the General had said I was to have. He had specified a car. The conversation came to a halt and the ADC suddenly turned on his heel and started slowly back up the hill towards the Mess. I followed. Just beyond the front door of the building three or four ordinary cars had been parked; the ADC led me up to a well-kept Fiat 1100 saloon. This would do fine, and thanking him I held out my hand for the key. He wasn't going to give up so easily. Opening the passenger door for me to get in, his mood seemed to change; he became airy and nonchalant. We should, he explained, just assure ourselves that the car was really in good repair. The General would wish him to do so. Any assurances that I was already satisfied were cut short when he slid in behind the wheel, started up, and moved off.

He was a good driver, there could be no doubt of that. For the next ten minutes he did his level best to frighten the life out of me; he could never have known how close he was to success. The back wheels were already spinning on the gravel with the acceleration as we went out of the drive, down a steep track where there was a sharp left-hand bend at the bottom. By that time we were going so fast that there wasn't a hope of rounding the corner without turning over, and I was bracing myself for the crash when, with a light touch on the brakes he continued straight on, hitting the grass verge with a loud smack before hurtling down a precipitous embankment and on to a level patch of roughish ground. Only then did I realize that my head had been striking the roof most of the time. On the far side of the valley a small cart track wound up the hill: this he took in third gear at maximum revs, to skid round a corner at the top, off the track and down through a clump of trees which he can only have missed by inches.

The 'Heil Hitlers' of the MAS boat inspection flashed across my memory: now, however, was not the moment to contemplate striking the driver. To keep silent didn't seem right, either. Distraction might work. 'She goes well,' I shouted, crouching lower in my seat. Out of the corner of my eye I saw a brick wall whizz by at enormous speed.

'No bad,' he conceded. 'But is small car. No fast like Lancia.'

I could only thank God and the Inspector-General of Italian Military Transport that it wasn't a Lancia.

The fragment of conversation had the curious effect of breaking not only his concentration but more important, his interest in the whole business. His mind was on other things as he slowed down and pointed the car once more in the direction of the officers' Mess. With only a small skid turn we halted outside the front door and he got out. I thought he was going to abandon me and the car altogether as he turned away but he seemed to remember something, came back, opened the car door and took out the ignition keys, by which time I had got out and was standing beside the passenger door. For a second he looked at the keys in his hand as though he'd never seen them before, and then with a return of the sour expression he came round to my side of the car. With a half-hearted salute (no bow) he handed over the keys.

'OK?' he asked.

'OK' I replied.

He gave a shrug of infinite disgust and looked at the Fiat.

'My car,' he said.

'Mine now,' I replied.

I went round and climbed into the driving seat. Letting in the clutch I leaned out of the window. 'Don't forget the three-tonner, will you?'

He heard but he was already walking up the steps of the Mess,

44

scheming, no doubt, how to acquire another car for himself.

*　*　*

By now Bastia was developing fast and filling up. British, Canadian, and American flotillas of coastal craft packed themselves into the jetty space as it was cleared of debris by the port authorities who were working very hard. Above our villa the French had established an anti-aircraft gun position, while on our other side the Italians had theirs. Most important as far as we were concerned was the arrival of two more operations officers. We had all been down to have a look at the MAS boats, and the beginnings of what was to become a mutual understanding and trust had been established between the Italian officers and their crews, and ourselves.

By this time, too, Prof had the wardroom well organized, and we were sitting at dinner enjoying one of Maria's excellent meals when she came in to announce between courses that a large lorry had arrived outside the house. It was exactly four days after my return from Corte. The ADC had kept his word, the three-tonner was ours. The news was greeted with considerable enthusiasm by all of us; abandoning dinner I went out into the street to inspect the prize. No more begging and borrowing of transport to move the operational gear from villa to harbour and back.

The night was very dark, yet to use a torch was to invite an immediate torrent of abusive threats from both French and Italian anti-aircraft guns' crews. Failure to extinguish the light instantly brought the more serious consequence of shots being fired indiscriminately into the night. So no torch. Once the eyes were accustomed to the dark it was possible to make out the silhouette of the huge mass of the vehicle. This was, indeed, just what we needed. Moving round from the back towards the front end I could see what appeared to be the driver still seated in the cab. Evidently he saw me for he climbed down to present what was recognizable even in that inky darkness as one of those eye-shading salutes. It was extraordinary, they never failed, even when there was small chance of them being seen; up came the hand to the forehead. Otherwise smartness of uniform, of deportment, movement, even of shaving, in the Italian army was nothing if not patchy. The MAS boat ship's companies were different. They were volunteers and proud.

Now the lorry driver fished in his pocket to extract a piece of paper which he pushed in my direction with the request that I should sign. It was, he claimed, the receipt which he had to take back to Corte with him. (For the ADC?) I asked him if he had eaten and he said no. Was

45

he intending to return to Corte that night? (It was well after eight o'clock.) Yes, he must get back to his unit; someone would give him a lift. I told him he had to eat first. He wriggled with indecision before good gastronomic sense prevailed, aided by the smell of Maria's cooking drifting out from the kitchen window.

Turning to go back into the house, there, leaning against the door post, watching proceedings with great interest was our cook. As we came to learn later, she had an insatiable curiosity in everything that went on round her. I asked her to prepare something for the lorry-driver and she hurried off inside in expectation of gleaning some new gossip over the food. It gave me the opportunity to cross-examine him about the monster vehicle. Was it, I asked, in good order? Oh, but yes, *Commandante*, in excellent condition, the best in fact that they had. Very powerful. Very good. In case of doubt he nipped back up into the cab and started the engine, stamping up and down on the accelerator to get her going properly. When he had achieved what he thought were high enough revs he opened the exhaust cut-out.

Italian battle philosophy incorporated the primitive belief — and took it seriously — that the more noise you made before combat was actually joined the more the enemy would be demoralized when the first shots were fired in anger. All their heavy transport vehicles were fitted with exhaust cut-outs for this very purpose. Years earlier it had worked well against the hapless Abyssinians. It had the added advantage of boosting the morale of the makers of the most noise.

My reaction was a standing leap in the air as the crescendo roar continued with the driver going on to full throttle. Desperately heaving myself up to the level of the cab I banged him on the shoulder. His face was wreathed in an ecstatic smile — white teeth gleaming even in the dark — as he shut down the cut-out and switched off the engine. The silence was almost painful.

'*Bene*' he remarked as he climbed down to earth: in congratulation he slapped the side of the lorry and kissed the tips of his fingers and thumb in appreciation.

It was while he was doing this that through the still-open door of the cab I thought I caught a glimpse of another figure crouched in the passenger seat. It didn't seem important at the time, perhaps he had been giving a lift to a chum. He slammed the door shut and we went into the house, he to the solicitous care of Maria, and I back into the wardroom to finish my dinner and to discuss the good news. We were getting down to some detailed planning when Maria came in to say that the driver wished to be on his way and could he have his receipt. He was close behind her, and produced a grubby piece of official paper which I signed and returned to him. He gave me a friendly salute and departed to leave us to continue our discussion.

Half an hour later Maria came in again to halt just inside the door-way wiping her hands on her apron and looking from one to another of us as if puzzling who to address.

To no one in particular she said, 'And what about the other one?'

Conversation ceased. The question seemed unanswerable. Not everyone in the room understood it in the first place, and those who did were no better off.

'What other one, Maria?' I ventured.

'The other Italian soldier.'

'Oh.' I glanced round in case someone knew something about the other Italian solider. No one said anything.

'I'm afraid I don't understand, Maria. What other soldier are you talking about?'

Her expression bordered on the pitying. 'The mechanic, Commandant. The mechanic.'

'Oh, him —' It seemed odd that she should be so forgetful. 'But he went some time ago. You fed him and then he left. Or is he back again?'

'No, Commandant, not that one.' She might have been talking to a five-year-old. 'He left. Yes. And he has not come back. This is the *other* one — ' sensing an interruption she added quickly, 'the *mechanic*.'

'I see. The mechanic.' A thought struck me. 'Where is he, this mechanic?'

'In the kitchen, Commandant. He stayed behind when the driver left.'

When I got to my feet Maria turned for the door leading the way to her quarters. And there he was. He wasn't dirty. He was filthy, with engine oil and car grease smothered on his hands, his face and in his hair, and he was wearing the dirtiest overalls in living memory. The shoes on his feet had no laces, and the leather had rotted with constant drenching in petrol and diesel oil. As I went in he was wiping a piece of bread round his plate soaking up the sauce remaining from Maria's delicious stew. When he saw me he stood up, not to attention, nor did he salute. He just looked apprehensive. He can't have been more than 5 ft 4 in and, at a guess, his age might have been eighteen but he looked only fifteen or sixteen. A subsequent bath revealed that he had fair hair, a paler skin than usual among Italians, and medium-brown eyes. His build was always slight, no matter how well Maria fed him.

'Who are you?' I asked.

'The mechanic, *Commandante*.'

'How d'you mean, mechanic? Mechanic for what?'

'The lorry, *Commandante*.'

47

'But the driver left over an hour ago.'

'Yes, *Commandante*.'

'Well, why are you still here?'

'Because of the lorry, *Commandante*.'

'But the lorry belongs to us now. We'll service it ourselves, and we won't be needing a mechanic. We drive these things without mechanics. D'you understand?'

Dumbly he listened, his expression changing from doubt to near despair. 'Yes, *Commandante*, I understand — ' he spread his hands and hoisted his shoulders in a huge shrug, ' — but this lorry — ' Despair became abject as he lowered his shoulders, his arms hanging loosely by his side.

'Well, what about this lorry? What makes it so special?'

'*Commandante*,' suddenly he was confidential, 'This lorry *needs* me.'

'Oh?'

'You see, *Commandante*, this lorry has only two gears.' He paused a second for effect before adding, 'Second gear, and reverse.'

Words almost failed me as I remembered the ADC. 'But good God, the driver said it was in excellent condition, the best that you had.'

'And so it is.' There was more than a hint of a smirk as he continued, 'You should see the others, *Commandante*.'

'How on earth did you get here with only one forward gear?'

'*Commandante*, when we started we had three gears going forward. That was at ten o'clock. Going down a steep hill something goes wrong. We are in third gear; we stop while I examine the inside of the gearbox and remove some parts. We still have two forward gears but now no reverse. Later we go uphill and again something goes wrong in the gearbox — and we have only second gear. But I manage to put back the reverse. After all, *Commandante*, there are moments when such a lorry may need to go backwards.'

'Damned lucky your second gear survived.'

'Yes, *Commandante*. Otherwise we should have had to arrive in reverse. And that,' he said gravely, 'would have been bad.'

He seemed quite relieved when I laughed. 'Well, it looks as though you've done very well to get here at all. You finish your meal and we'll talk again later.'

Prof was inclined to be more pleased than philosophical when he learned what had happened. 'At least,' he said, 'the bloody thing goes in both directions which means that we can use it to carry all the ops gear and the dinghies up and down to the base. It'll just take a little more time, that's all.'

Half an hour later, going out to the kitchen I could find no sign of the mechanic, and I asked Maria where he was.

'Outside, I think,' she replied, 'Working on the lorry. He's upset that it doesn't go properly.'

In the street the only thing to be discerned at all clearly was the mass of the three-tonner; the pavement between that and the house was in pitch darkness. However, when I called out a faint '*Subito, Commandante*' came from somewhere near my feet. Peering down, there he was, on his back in the road, grunting with the exertion of wrestling with some heavy object beneath the business end. The struggle continued for a minute or two, accompanied by a stream of whispered curses, until, with a sharp blow of metal on metal all sound ceased. Wriggling out the mechanic got to his feet, wiping his hands on the legs of his overalls.

'*Commandante*,' he said apologetically, 'I can do no more with that gearbox. She is *kaput*.'

'But you can't see a thing. Wait till daylight.'

'Eh! I can feel. I know that gearbox.'

It seemed more than probable that if he didn't know it nobody else would. That made good sense.

'Well,' I said, 'don't worry about it now. We'll see in the morning.'

'*Va bene, Commandante*.'

That he gave in so readily was a measure of his exhaustion. It had been a long and testing day even for a much older man.

'Meanwhile, we'll find you somewhere to sleep.'

He made a small bow and we went back to the warmth of the kitchen where I left him. Prof and Maria between them arranged a bed somewhere at the top of the house. Maria's motherly instincts were already hard at work on this slender young orphan of the storm. We might have a lorry which didn't work properly but at least we had a mechanic who knew about its insides; somehow we must contrive to hold on to him until all was in order.

First thing after breakfast next morning Prof and I went out to inspect our prize in the light of day. If anything it was even bigger than I remembered, so big that it was in danger of taking up more than half the road. And it was totally inert. The door of the cab was open and there, surprisingly, was the mechanic busy sorting out some wiring opposite the driver's seat. We gave each other good-morning and he went on with his work.

I called up to him. 'Is the gearbox mended, then?'

He didn't reply but climbed down to stand gazing at Prof as though trying to determine whether he represented good or bad omens. Never at a loss Prof gave him a loud and amiable '*buon giorno*' — the only two words of Italian I think he knew with any confidence.

'That gearbox is no good.' It was a simple statement of fact addressed to anyone who cared to listen. To ensure that we were suitably impressed the young Italian didn't look at either of us. Then out of the
corner of one eye he sized me up. 'But, *Commandante*, I have an idea
— '

'Oh? And what's that?'

From the care which he took in running grease-laden fingers
through his hair it was evident that he was considering his answer with
caution. 'D'you think, *Commandante*, you have two sailors, strong
sailors, you could lend me. Perhaps — yes, perhaps I could arrange
things.' Although his tone was light there could be no mistaking the
importance he attached to the reply.

'That depends on what you want them to do?'

'Well, *Commandante* — how shall I say it? — the gearbox is heavy.
More than I can carry.'

'But you said it's finished.'

'That, *Commandante*, is why I want to take it off.'

'Have you got a replacement for it?'

He looked at me as though anxious that I should not try to read his
mind. 'No, *Commandante*. Not yet.' His arm described a wide arc em-
bracing the whole neighbourhood. 'But I have been looking round.'

The innocence of the remark started bells ringing in my head: it
would be, perhaps, wiser not to probe. I explained the situation to Prof
who commented airily, 'I expect he just wants to get the thing off to
have a final look at it. Who knows? he may love it. Anyway I think we
should let him have the men. I'll get Bates to send up a couple of
ratings.'

When he reported to the villa a little while later Bates was accompanied by Leading Seamen Downes and Johnstone. While the introductions were effected the mechanic examined the two sailors closely,
weighing up their physical strength. In the end he smiled his approval.
I explained to them that they were there 'to give a hand with the heavy
work' under the instruction of the mechanic. Almost anything out of
the ordinary was enough to intrigue those two; the mere difference of
language would be the least of problems to any of them.

As I was about to leave I turned to the Italian. We couldn't go on
calling him 'the mechanic'. 'What's your name?' In mild surprise he
answered with a whole string of them. He was small anyway, and now
standing between the two sailors he looked very small.

'We can't manage all those,' I replied, 'you'd better be just Piccolo.'

He gave a light shrug and a shy smile. '*Va bene, Commandante.*'

The day was a busy one and there wasn't much time to worry about
Piccolo and the lorry, although after lunch I did go out to make sure

that all was going well. The place was deserted although evidence of some hard work was provided by the gearbox which now lay on the ground almost hidden between the front wheels. Looking through the open front gates I thought I caught a glimpse of the two leading hands and Piccolo walking up the road past the French battery quarters; momentarily they paused to look into the compound where the transport was parked and then they walked on. They seemed to be getting on all right, all very friendly, all very quickly. I shut my mind hastily and went back to work in the office.

Towards the end of the day I ran into Bates coming out of the front gates as I was driving in. I stopped to make enquiries.

'How did Johnstone and Downes get on with Piccolo today?'

'Oh, doing all right, I think, sir.'

'Can he possibly mend the lorry, d'you think?'

'Couldn't say for sure, sir, but I know he hopes to have it going in the morning.'

'Does he, now?'

'That's what he hopes, sir.'

'So do I. I think I'll go and have a word with him.'

'Oh, I shouldn't bother, sir.'

'Oh, why not?'

'Well, we invited him to have supper with us, sir, and he's probably down with them now. I mean seeing as he's been working all day with Johnstone and Downes, we thought he might like that. Seems like he knows his job, too.'

'I agree, Bates. I only hope he isn't too much of an optimist.'

'I don't think so, sir.'

'How did they get on with the language problem?'

'They managed fine. No trouble. Johnstone, he seems to know one or two words of Italian.'

Johnstone would know one or two words of any language.

'Well, good-night, Bates. Let's hope for the best.'

'Yes, sir. Good-night.'

When Maria came in to announce dinner later in the evening I pulled her leg gently about having lost her charge so quickly to the sailors.

'Oh, no Commandant,' she replied. 'He had a good meal before he went off down there.'

Piccolo might be young but he knew how to look after himself. He was still growing and needed all the food he could get. Over dinner Prof made a bet with me that the lorry would be running in the morning. I turned in hoping that he might win. When I went down to breakfast after a good night's sleep Prof was already at the toast-and-marmalade stage.

'Any news of the lorry?' I asked.

'Haven't dared to look,' replied Prof wiping his mouth, 'but I haven't heard any encouraging noises — like the grinding of gears.'

'We'll go and see after breakfast.'

A quarter of an hour later we went outside into the street through the back door. There was no sign of the lorry.

'That's marvellous,' I said happily, pleased to lose my bet. 'It must be mended.'

'Oh, I shouldn't be too sure,' replied Prof, 'someone might easily have taken the brake off and let the whole bloody caboodle career down the hill into the sea.'

He liked to keep a proper balance to conjecture.

For some reason we chose not to return through the back door, instead walking the few yards down the street to go in through the front gates. We both stopped in our tracks as we came face to face with the monstrous size of the lorry now parked a little coyly between two trees on the edge of the drive.

'Well, damn me,' said Prof quietly.

Piccolo was half hidden in the immense jaws of the open bonnet, as though he were about to be gobbled up for ever, while Bates, Johnstone, and Downes were loading dinghies into the back of the vehicle. Bates jumped down and came towards us.

'Is it mended?' I asked.

His smile provided the answer. 'Yes, sir.'

'When?'

There was a barely perceptible hesitation. 'Oh, a bit earlier, sir — in fact it's been done some time now.'

I paid Prof on the spot. In reply he produced a special line in Pluto smiles suitable to the occasion.

'Never,' he said, 'been happier to win a bet.'

'Nor I to lose one.'

We walked over to where Piccolo's feet were just visible as he disappeared deeper into the bowels of the engine. I tapped him on the leg and he started to wriggle backwards until, turning his head, he gave me a thin, rather uncertain smile.

'Well done, Piccolo. Well done, indeed. She goes all right, now?'

'*Si, Commandante. Va bene.*' There wasn't much enthusiasm behind the acknowledgement, but then he was lying almost upside down.

'How did you do it?'

He shrugged. 'Ma..' he said, and shrugged again.

'New gearbox?' I suggested.

A spanner fell from his hand down into the bottom of the engine and he dived after it. When he came up again he swung himself to the ground beside me.

'It goes, *Commandante*, it goes.' His tone bordered on the tetchy, as if he wished to dismiss further discussion. As a sop he added, 'Your two sailors are strong. The weight — it was pretty heavy. Without their help we could never have managed.' He ran a grimy hand through his hair.

While we were talking Prof had joined Johnstone and Downes: all three were busy arranging a transport programme for the day, and I walked round to join them. Addressing the two seamen I said, 'Well done, both of you. Between you and Piccolo you seem to have done a first-class job.'

'Thank you, sir,' replied Downes 'but it was Piccolo that did all the work. Bloody marvel, he was. Now we can get on with shifting stores.'

I was still curious. 'Tell me, what did he actually do? Mend the old gearbox or find a new one?'

There was a loud shout from Prof, 'Sir — I wonder if you would have a look at one of the new dinghies which has arrived with a large rent in the fabric. Perhaps you could tell me whether you think it's repairable.' He was standing by the dinghy assembly area. Prof never called me 'sir' without reason, and I took the hint. 'Very well, No 1,' I replied, 'Let's have a look at it.' I walked across the gravel to join him. From there he led the way into the garden out of earshot of the others.

'And what is all this in aid of, Prof?'

'Just an idea,' he sounded if anything, mildly disapproving. 'Don't you think they've had enough congratulations?' A bit puzzled by his attitude I said yes, I supposed so, and then we returned to examine the damaged dinghy which was certainly a write-off. As we were parting I told him that I would like him to come with me when I went up to see SOIS about an hour later.

I hadn't been back at my desk more than ten minutes before remembering that my parallel rulers were still in my car, and went out to fetch them. On my way back I met Piccolo coming out of the house, and I stopped him.

'I take it we shall be able to rely on the lorry. I mean she'll be all right for some time now, I hope.'

'*Commandante*, she should. She should. But one can never be sure with an old vehicle like that.' He was about to continue on his way when he changed his mind and walked towards me, stopping within a couple of feet of where I was standing. He looked at me earnestly, confidentially. 'What she really needs, that one, *Commandante*, is a mechanic.'

'So you said before, Piccolo,' I told him, 'But *how* are you to stay here? You'll be wanted by your unit in Corte.'

His hands which he had been wiping on a piece of rag fell to his sides and he turned to stare at the massive object of our conversation. 'They won't miss me,' he said continuing to stare a second longer before facing me again. 'And I would have so little to do.'

'You want to stay here, then?'

He nodded.

'You're sure?'

He nodded once more. 'Quite sure, *Commandante*.'

'But I can't pay you.'

'That doesn't matter, I get so little. Perhaps *Commandante*,' his eyebrows rose in query, 'you could feed me?'

'But, you must have pay from somewhere. You can't live on nothing.'

'No, *Commandante*.'

'And won't they court-martial you as a deserter if you don't go back to Corte?'

He gave me a surprisingly knowing grin. 'The *Commandante* can arrange these things.'

The *Commandante* was going to get himself into a hell of a lot of trouble if he wasn't careful. That seemed clear enough. Equally there was going to be even greater trouble if we had no transport.

'Well,' I said, 'I'll certainly try.'

We both understood the situation: we had done our best. He made another bow and went back to work, leaving me to puzzle out his salvation. It was hard to imagine the Italian army handing over one of its artisans to a foreign service, just like that. Presently Prof came in to remind me of our appointment with SOIS. Gathering the necessary papers together we went out to where the car was parked under a big tree on the far side of the drive; it looked diminutive beside the mastodon three-tonner. Piccolo dropped his work to open the big gates for us, and gave another abrupt little bob as we drove out and turned up the hill.

We hadn't gone more than a hundred yards or so when we had to stop. A huge lorry which I recognized as the twin of ours, was parked outside the French battery compound with several mechanics grouped round it; the road was blocked except to single line traffic coming down the hill. As we waited my eye was caught by the sight of yet another mechanic in the driver's seat of the cab; he was sweating and straining at some part of the machinery inside the cab, and revving the engine at the same time. There was an unexpected and awesome grinding noise as the shoulders of the man in the cab went into a convulsive effort. To judge by the handwaving of the onlooking mechanics his effort was wasted. At any rate the lorry didn't move. At that moment our road became clear and we advanced. As we drew level with the lorry the driver tried again, when the noise of snapping and snarling spur wheels and 'sprockets' became deafening, but not so loud as to drown out altogether the shouts of '*Merde*!' from the mechanics.

Prof's expression was as lugubrious as a camel at a funeral, and his voice was grave as he watched the performance. 'It looks, sir, as if they might have gearbox trouble, don't you think?'

'It does, Prof. It does.'

'Funny,' he said, 'It was going all right yesterday. I saw it.'

Chapter 3

THE FIRST
OPERATION AND
THE RED HOUSE

As a rule of thumb, twenty out of thirty days of the month were usable for clandestine transport ops: ten moonlight nights for the RAF who welcomed all the light they could get; and ten non-moon nights for us in sea transport, who welcomed all the dark we could get. First shot success for either service was by no means a certainty. There were too many imponderables: the weather, the enemy who could strike either at the resisters themselves, or at the 'vehicle' (aeroplane or ship). Lastly communications with the resisters were necessarily far from easy: too often these gallant people were on the run, or their W/T operator was too far away to be contacted, or, perhaps, he himself was on the run. The situation in occupied territory for all resisters was nothing if not fluid, making lightning changes the order of the day — or night.

By the end of November we were ready to go. The villa was organized, good communications with London had been established, the boats and crews were anxious to start. We reported our state of readiness, and promptly received, in return, our first operation orders: to land two men (usually referred to as 'Joes' for some reason I never discovered, by all British clandestine services) — anyway — to land two men on the night of 2/3 December some fifteen miles west of la Spezia. Great news. I went down to the MAS base to consult the Italian commander about choice of boat and crew.

Privately, as a result of careful observation during the previous few weeks, I came to the conclusion that 'Ginger' Cosulich was probably the most experienced and reliable among the young Italian Captains of MAS boats. This was in no way a slur upon his contemporaries, but rather because I had come to know him first and had worked with him more than his fellows. Fortunately the Italian commander now concurred in his selection for this first, all-important operation. Together we went off to break the news to him on board his craft. He was obviously delighted not just because he was to be the first boat to operate, but, as he said with relief in his voice, his crew had been sitting round too long doing nothing except routine chores. Now they leapt to work to prepare the boat.

The afternoon of the 2nd found Ginger and I poring over charts in his boat, plotting courses, speeds and times. At about 17.00 the two resistance members, accompanied by their conducting officer, Major Andrew Croft, head of the SOE unit in Bastia, and his Sergeant Arnold, came on board, and we prepared to cast off. As the lines were going out a messenger arrived in a hurry from the British Base commanding officer to say that the port was closed owing to the discovery of an enemy minefield at the entrance to the harbour. This hitch, coming at the last second when we were geared up for our very first operation, at the moment of truth, so to speak, of using the Italian MAS boats for this work, could be critical to the future. Accordingly, I nipped off to the office of the Commandant du Port to see if his advice might offer any better prospects.

Courteous as ever, he told me all he knew. That, so far, they had located one mine visually lying about 40 metres off the seaward end of the breakwater inside which the MAS boat was moored. The only suggestion he could make was that we should hug the breakwater right to the end on our way out, although he was careful to point out that that would not necessarily afford any protection against other mines known to have been laid in the same area. It wasn't much to go on, but it was something. Returning to the boat I told Ginger the news and asked him if he would be willing to try. With bland, if not unnerving enthusiasm he replied that he was under my orders. That settled that.

A few minutes later, in the now fading light, we cast off to grope our way on auxiliary engines, keeping close to the jetty towards the harbour entrance. A number of underwater obstructions, debris from German sabotage measures taken when they left, still littered the basin of the port. Many had edges sharp enough to pierce the boat's hull even at slow speed.

A rating appeared on the bridge to hand Ginger a small bundle; this turned out to be a curiously old-fashioned sort of flying helmet which Ginger now fastened on his head. Even in the dark my surprise must have been obvious for, without prompting, he volunteered a bit shyly,

'I never go to sea without my helmet.'

Puzzled, I asked him why.

'For good luck.'

Well — everyone is entitled to his private talisman.

'I hope it works now,' I said. He smiled agreement.

As we neared the end of the inner side of the breakwater and the harbour entrance I decided I didn't much care for the advice of the Commandant, and explained quickly to Ginger what I wanted him to do. As Captain of his boat he had the right always to refuse any order which he thought might hazard his craft. Now he nodded agreement and gesticulated with a series of wide sweeps of both arms to show that he had understood. When we were within fifty yards of the entrance auxiliaries were stopped and main engines started: with a deep growl we surged ahead and swung abruptly towards the shore side of the harbour. Gathering speed the boat circled in a wide arc as close inshore as possible, and then, once clear of the harbour mouth the helmsman put the wheel hard over and we headed out to sea. When on course I nodded towards Ginger's helmet, 'Seems to work.' He put his hand up to touch the lucky charm, nodded and smiled happily.

The sea was slight and the boat rode easily at our cruising speed of thirty knots: there was time to try to imagine what might be going through the minds of the Italian crew. Had we any more *'Heil Hitlers'* on board? If so, how many? Even the 'good' ones must be feeling a bit nervous. They weren't alone: we had had so little opportunity of creating any sort of operational trust. Now both sides were making their assessment, 'sucking it to see', waiting for the first incident. We didn't have long in doubt.

About half an hour out I went down by the very short ladder from the bridge, through the wheelhouse, into the wardroom — a matter of three steps and a couple of strides — to check again our course and timing. Coming up again into the pitch black night it took a few seconds to realize that there was now an extra man on the bridge, and that he appeared to be conning the boat from a small bridge wheel normally reserved for manoeuvring in harbour. There was no compass on the bridge to steer by: that was in the wheelhouse. Peering below I could just make out the dimly lit compass card and the conning wheel. The wheel was moving all right but there was no helmsman. I went over to this new figure, the bridge helmsman.

'And what,' I asked, 'are you steering by?'

In the dark I could sense rather than see him gaze at me as if I had gone off my head, at the same time I saw clearly his arm pointing into the sky.

'The stars, *Commandante*. The stars. What else?'

Quickly I summoned Ginger from below. 'Look,' I said, 'this chap says he's steering by the stars.'

'Yes,' replied Ginger, almost as nonplussed as the helmsman that I should find anything odd about it.

As gently as possible I said, 'But for heaven's sake, we're aiming at a pinpoint, not the North Pole'.

'H'm. Yes, but we always navigate like this.'

Under my breath I muttered, 'Not in this business' and went below to watch the wheelhouse compass. At the end of five minutes I returned to the bridge.

'Ginger, I'm sorry to upset your usual practice but please send the helmsman down to steer by compass. We are making a steady three degrees of easting on our proper course.'

For a moment I thought he might be about to argue. After a fractional hesitation he took the bridge wheel himself and told the helmsman to do as I asked. There was a rapid exchange between the two of them during the takeover, and then we were steering by wheelhouse compass, and Ginger abandoned the bridge wheel. To be corrected by a foreigner, a recent enemy to boot, cannot have been easy to accept. He took it very well.

In the next hour the only noise was the comforting drone of the main engines as we maintained speed. Then one of the look-outs reported pinpricks of red light on the starboard bow. They had, in fact, been visible for some time, and I wondered what they might be. Ginger, too, had been scanning them with his binoculars, no easy thing to do with the jolting of the boat; so far he had expressed no opinion about what he saw. More cries from the crew, '*Luce, Commandante, luce!*' By the urgency of the tones the crew seemed to be getting nervous.

'Any idea what they are?' asked Ginger.

'None. They're too far off to say for certain but they look like a couple of big fires ashore somewhere, or possibly a tanker.'

One or two members of the crew spoke to Ginger with many references to '*luce*'; after a minute or two of patient listening he turned to me.

'The crew wants to stop the boat.'

'What on earth for?'

'They say they don't know what the lights are.'

'Nor do either of us — yet — but we can't stop the ship for that. The longer we go on the easier it'll be to find out. Please tell them — no stopping.'

Ginger conveyed the decision to the nearest sailors who continued to peer anxiously ahead. But it wasn't the lights they were frightened of, as I suddenly understood. They were very anxious, however, about what this foreigner — me — might be up to. A series of extra bright flashes in and around the lights provoked a further wave of unease and nattering, obliging Ginger to ask once more if we might ease down. In explanation he said that once the crew knew what the lights were there would be no further worry. Reluctantly I agreed and speed was reduced to 15 knots; almost immediately it became plain that the whole display was the result of an air raid on la Spezia. Various among the more religious members of the crew crossed themselves as we resumed our 30 knots.

An hour later we stopped main engines and went over to auxiliaries for our two-hour silent run-in to the pinpoint. The main engines, the noise of which could be heard very often at a range of twelve miles, were frequently confused with the noise of high-flying aircraft, but we couldn't count on it every time. The enemy was not all that stupid. Although the auxiliaries were supposed to be silent they gave out a high-pitched whine, not readily identifiable with either boats or aircraft - unless, of course, you had experience of them. Then you knew quick enough. On the whole, and fortunately for us, enemy sentries seemed not to have been briefed about this; what they thought of us *if* they heard us is anybody's guess.

Now we steamed on at our maximum, a tedious 6 knots, watching the air raid as we went. There were many fires in and around the city and harbour, and once, when there was a particularly brilliant burst of tracer from several sources simultaneously, there was an involuntary shout of delight from the crew. Like watching Guy Fawkes night.

With almost painful slowness the silhouette of the coastline became visible, an unbroken panorama of cliffs and mountains which began to tower over us the nearer we got to our destination — the pinpoint. Although about three-quarters of a mile too far east our first move was to get in close to the shore where we would be screened by the sheer cliffs from enemy detection, inside the normal run of the inshore patrol vessels plying back and forth. About 400 yards from the beach we turned westward. Passing a village we saw the occasional flicker of light from a door being opened in one of the houses. The landing party was ready on deck when Andrew Croft and I made a quick check to verify our position, then we turned at slow speed towards the beach. Two hundred yards out we launched the rubber dinghy and the two resisters, the Major and Sergeant Arnold climbed down into it. Carefully the radio set was handed down to them and then they were pulling towards the shore. A gentle drizzle started to fall, reducing visibility; to forestall possible loss of contact we nosed our way in following the dinghy to within 200 yards of the beach, while the Major rowed on inshore. As we waited the drizzle turned to rain and the wind got up from the south: we had to keep manoeuvring with the engines to prevent being blown too close inshore. Half an hour went by before we saw a faint flash from the beach, an unscheduled signal that the dinghy was returning. By now, however, the wind was against them and progress became laboured so we moved in to intercept. When we picked them up the Major and his Sergeant were but sixty yards off the beach which was a measure of the resistance of wind and waves they had encountered. However, the resisters had been safely landed. That was the great thing.

Although he had shown signs of unease at having to take his boat so close in, at no time did Ginger complain. He could see and understand the necessity. To turn the boat round on auxiliary engines only to head out to sea was not easy. With no torpedo tubes and the main tophamper up for'ard she had a natural tendency to lie stern to a wind now slowly rising in strength. Once she had been brought round we started the most irksome part of all these operations — the slow but silent withdrawal from the pinpoint, requiring at least two hours of auxiliary motoring, the time necessary to allow the resisters to get clear of the area, and for us to avoid our presence becoming known to the enemy. At some future date we might need to use that same pinpoint again. Not a good principle, agreed, but sometimes that risk had to be weighed against the risk of missing the contact altogether.

Half an hour or so after our departure from the area visibility was down to about a hundred yards and the wind was blowing about force 4 straight into our teeth. In a MAS boat of such shallow draft progress became dismally slow; it was also uncomfortable. Built for speed, at a poor 6 knots she was wallowing laboriously.

Andrew Croft came up and joined us on the bridge. We were all wet and cold, and pretty miserable — until suddenly I remembered the 'self-heaters'. This must have been one of the best inventions of the war. It looked like an ordinary tin of soup. At one end, however, there was a small cap which, when removed set up a chemical process by which the kidney and vegetable soup content was at boiling point within thirty seconds. It was, however, essential to pierce the tin before removing the cap; one officer who failed to observe this rule caused the entire wheelhouse to be spattered with scalding hot soup from a bursting tin. Now we drank three cans of the soup with a marked improvement to morale.

An hour later, with the wind gusting to force 5 with an occasional 6, we reckoned our progress to be almost nil, and we decided that it was time to risk going over to main engines. The last thing we wished for was to be found five or six miles from the pinpoint at dawn. Keeping the revs to the minimum, compatible with not 'oiling up', the noise was not too bad. The boat immediately picked up to 15 knots, was easier to steer, and also more comfortable. Later we tried to increase to 25 knots but the slamming became intolerable, causing us to reduce back to 15. There was no question of steering by the stars now, the sky being completely overcast and heavy. The next five hours were wretched for everybody on board.

At 07.15, in the early light of the new day, we were all treated to a surprise. Land was sighted on our *port* side, with no sign of anything at all on our starboard hand where the Corsican coast should have been showing up. Fatigue fogged the mind. Surely, if we had been driven too close to the Italian mainland by the sou-westerly wind, we should be able to see Corsica to starboard? The explanation was not far to seek; it was also rather shame-making. We were on the wrong side of Corsica, having made too big an allowance for the weather during the night. Blushes over, we turned with some relief to run parallel to the waves (instead of flogging head-on into them) at a much increased speed. Only a quarter of an hour later we rounded Cap Corse to head for Bastia at 30 knots.

In the still indifferent light we observed two other fast craft likewise making for Bastia. For a moment we wondered whether they were friend or foe before identifying them as PT boats (the American MTB). Neither side challenged but they increased speed. Ginger raised an eyebrow in my direction and I nodded; it was what he wanted. Our torpedo tubes had been removed and we rode light against the PT boats weighed down with both tubes and armament. Their task was to fight, ours to avoid action. We left them comfortably at 47 knots. We were all tired but a good sound basis of mutual understanding and trust had been established. We never lost it.

★ ★ ★

Operations were beginning to build up to a rate which ensured that we were kept rather more than busy when a welcome signal arrived announcing the appointment of another operational Lieutenant RNVR. Certainly we could do with the extra help. Reading the signal through a second time I noticed that his age was given as 38. This could be a mistake for 28 — or he might be something special — or he might be quite unsuitable. Our average age, not including my own senile 32, was in the low twenties. I thought I knew the names of nearly all officers engaged in this particular work at that time, but I didn't know this one. Neither Prof, nor Tom had ever heard of him either. We waited with interest.

He arrived one evening without any warning from anyone, having apparently first gone to Maddalena. No one had told him we had moved. Prof shoved his head round the door just before dinner as I was finishing some reports.

'He's arrived,' said Prof.

I looked up. 'Who?'

'The new ops officer. Lieutenant Dow.'

He had spoken softly so I lowered my voice to little above a whisper. 'What's he like?'

Prof wagged his head from side to side in the lunatic manner he sometimes adopted when he wasn't sure of something, and grinned. 'I'll bring him in,' he whispered back, and vanished.

When a few minutes later Prof ushered in the new arrival he proved to be rather small, stockily built, with a lot of bristly hair beginning to go grey, a ruddy face, and pale blue eyes. Plainly he was tired after so much travelling and looked every day of his 38 years. When he apologised for being 'late' he spoke with a strong lowland Scottish accent. Coming round from behind my desk I shook his hand.

'Welcome, Colonel, you're just in time for dinner.'

Why I called him 'Colonel' I have no idea. But the name stuck thereafter. He blinked and looked a bit startled.

'Aye - sir.'

'Come and sit down, and have a cigarette.' I pushed a packet towards him and he helped himself.

'Aye. Thanks.'

'Care for a drink?'

'Aye. It's been a longish sort of day.'

I went out to the kitchen and asked Maria to bring us some wine. While I was away I had time to think, my God, he is old. When I went back he was sitting stiffly in his chair, staring at the opposite wall, looking, if anything, more grizzled than a minute or so earlier.

'Tell me, Colonel, what have you been doing up to now?' I asked resuming my seat behind the desk.

'Minesweeping.'

'Where?'

'Out of Liverpool.'

'And could you tell me what persuaded you to volunteer for this job?'

For a moment he looked away.

'It'll be a change,' he said in guarded tones.

'It should be that all right. What did they tell you before you left England?'

'Not much.'

We weren't getting along too well. Fortunately Maria came in at that moment. Putting the tray down on my desk she cast a swift gold-toothed smile at the newcomer. There was not a flicker of response, and she retired in what looked like a huff. I poured the wine and handed it to him.

'Your good health,' I tried.

'Cheers,' he replied and downed half the glass at a gulp.

'Did they tell you in London what you were coming out here to do?'

'Aye. Sort of. Landing operations, isn't it?'

'And picking up.'

'They mentioned that, too.'

'Have you ever been in fast craft? MTBs, that is?'

From his expression he appeared to consider this a trick question, and become even more cautious. 'No,' he replied slowly, and to remove any lingering doubt on the matter, added, 'And I don't want to, either.'

'I see.' I found myself beginning to wonder about this taciturn little man. 'Tell me, what sort of boats d'you think we're operating?'

His eyes opened wide. 'What sort — ? Why, *feeshing* boats.' Indignantly he drained his glass. 'That's wha' I was told in London.'

To gain a little time for thought I filled him up again before continuing. 'I see. Well, Colonel, you'd better get it clear that we are not operating fishing-boats any longer. We are now working from MAS boats — the Italian equivalent of our coastal forces' MTBs, MGBs and the like.'

'Oh.' He took a swig before peering into the depths of his glass while digesting this latest piece of information. When he looked up it was to fix me with a pebbly sort of stare. To emphasize the importance of his next question he spoke very slowly. 'An' wha' about the danger money?'

It was my turn to be baffled. 'Danger money? What d'you mean, danger money? Whatever for?'

His stare didn't waver as he pursued the subject. 'But I was informed there would be danger money – five shillings a day — in the fishing boats. The same as they get in submarines.'

'Good God. Who told you that?'

'They told me in London before I left.'

For the moment I could think of nothing to say. Someone in London had been filling the poor chap up with rubbish, or they'd been pulling his leg. While we sat, each pondering, he leaned forward and pinched one of my cigarettes. Well, evidently he wasn't one to lose his head in a crisis. I poured myself a glass.

At last try, then. 'Look Colonel, there has obviously been some serious misunderstanding. As I said just now, we do *not* operate fishing-boats, although those which have arrived and come up from Maddalena, we now use for accommodation. We *were* to have used them, yes, but thank God, just in time the MAS boats have been turned over to us, and we use *them*. That's the first thing to get clear in

64

Right Petty Officer Bates, 1943/44.

Below PT boat off Salerno, September 1943.

Left Warrant Officer Bates, DSM, Croix de Guerre.

Below Nearing retirement many years later: Her Majesty has a word with Lieutenant-Commander Jim Bates.

Right *MAS 527*, view of bridge layout and foc'sle.

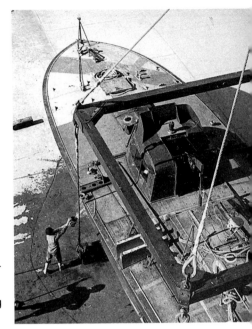

Below Tenente di Vascello Iappelli's MAS boat at speed.

Bottom *MAS 528*, showing recognition marking on foc'sle.

Above *MAS 563* showing 13.2mm machine-gun, and depth charges.

Below *MAS 558*, captured by the Germans at Varazze: subsequently sunk in April 1945 near Imperia.

Bottom *MAS 505*

your mind. And the second thing is —' and I left a pause for what I hoped would be dramatic effect '— the second thing is that there is *no* danger money.'

The dramatic effect was there all right, and it was instantaneous. Rising from his chair he stubbed out his cigarette, swallowed the rest of his drink, and said, 'Well — tha's simple. No fishing boats, an' no danger money. I'm away home.'

With that his pebbly stare turned to one of strong disapproval, and he made for the door.

'Sit down, Colonel.'

For a moment he hesitated, and I wasn't sure he would do as he was told. When he did he made it look as if it was a very temporary arrangement.

'Let us try to get this straight — ' I started, but he interrupted immediately.

'It's straight enough, already. There's no fishing boats an' no danger money. I've been made a fule of. I'm off, I'm telling ye.'

'Was it,' I asked, 'the danger money you were after, or work in the fishing-boats?'

'The two went together.'

'All right. Now listen to me. If you thought, or were led to believe that there was danger money attached to this job, then I agree you have been made a fool of. But there isn't any — and for a good reason.'

He was staring again. 'And what's that?'

'The work doesn't warrant it. That's why. It's a perfectly straightforward job, and simple. All of us are volunteers, agreed, but that doesn't make it dangerous. It's out of the rut, and just about as close to fun as you can get in wartime. There's no lack of volunteers. Understand that. Now — ' and I got to my feet — 'we've talked enough. We'll have some dinner — you must be hungry, and probably weary, too — so for the rest of the evening you can get to know the others a bit. You and I will have another talk tomorrow.'

He was thoroughly unhappy and made no bones about it, which was hardly surprising, if what he had told me was true. It was such an improbable story as almost certain to *be* true; as an invention it was equally unlikely. On the other hand it was hard to guess who could have filled him up with such nonsense. I escorted him next door where Prof, Tom Maxted, and 'Cuzzie' Cosens — another experienced young ops officer — were gossiping before dinner. I said nothing of the meeting just finished, leaving the new arrival to sit between Prof and Tom. Watching from time to time during the meal he seemed to be getting on well enough for me to imagine a glimmer of interest beginning to develop from his previous grumpy attitude.

Prof was always an excellent talker, and with the occasional exercise of his more ghoulish wit usually managed to conjure a laugh from even the very dour. On the other side Tom was recounting one or two of the more amusing operational incidents. After dinner I contrived to catch Prof's eye; he and I then repaired to the office where I told him what had gone on earlier.

True to form Prof came straight to the point. 'D'you want to keep him?'

'We need him,' I replied.

'Not the same thing. We need another ops officer, right enough, but does it have to be him?'

'Oh, no. But I have a feeling — '

'Exactly.' Prof cut me short; perhaps he sensed that I might be about to waffle. 'So you do want to keep him.'

'I don't know about that. All I am sure of at the moment is that he won't be any use if he's going to have a permanent chip about fishing boats and danger money. Did he mention anything about it at dinner?'

Prof shook his head. 'No. He didn't say very much really, although I did get the impression that he still isn't too happy. The only thing I did was to tell him that we could have a yarn in the morning when I would show him round.'

The best answer seemed to be to return Lieutenant Dow to store with a rude message to whoever had been responsible for his original briefing but nothing could be decided that night, so we agreed to resume in the morning.

When I came down to breakfast Prof was already circling the table arms outstretched like an old vulture with an empty bowl in his hand. As I sat down he swooped on the cornflakes, then the sugar bowl, before settling himself, ruffling his feathers into a comfortable position, in front of the milk jug. He did the same thing pretty well every morning and it never failed to amuse me.

'Well,' he asked, splashing the milk lavishly in and around his plate, 'what are we going to do with your Colonel? Made up your mind yet?'

'Not yet. It depends largely on him.'

'It doesn't, you know, unless he opts firmly to go home. It's up to you — to decide whether you want to keep him.'

'Maybe you're right, Prof, but I don't care to have to admit it at breakfast.'

He bobbed his head up and down and grunted in amusement. 'Sorry — sir.'

'All right. You bring him along to the office at nine — and this time you stay and listen.'

'Aye, aye, sir.' He gave me a suspicious look and reached for the toast.

On the dot of nine o'clock there was a knock on the door and Prof and the Colonel came in. I waved them to chairs, preparatory to addressing the Colonel directly.

'Now you've had time to sleep on our conversation of yesterday, have you made up your mind what you want to do? D'you want to go home?'

For the first time a half smile flickered in his eyes. He spoke slowly, carefully. 'Well, it seems daft to come all this way to do a job and then go straight home.' So far so good. He waited a second before adding, 'But I'd like to know a wee bit more about what I'd be expected to do. I mean what's my part in such operations? There really are no feeshing vessels?'

'There are, but I wouldn't use them while we've got the MAS boats. Does that put your mind at rest?'

Again the trace of a smile. 'Aye. No fishing vessels.'

'As far as your job would be concerned you would be another operations officer — like Tom Maxted, or young Cosens — you've spoken to both of them — or like me. We all go to sea landing and embarking resisters in or from enemy territory.'

Immediate doubt showed in every line of his face, the protest came out quickly in very north-of-the-border tones. 'But I couldna dae tha!'

'Why not?'

'I wouldna know how.'

Prof, who up to then had said nothing, leant forward in his chair and said quietly, 'There's nothing to it, you know. No magic.'

The unexpected corroboration seemed to have a calming effect. His next question was a genuine enquiry not a protest. 'But would I be expected to talk to these resister folk? I haven't a word of a foreign language, you understand.'

Step by step, between us, we took him through a typical operation while he listened attentively in silence. At the end he shook his head sadly and shrugged his shoulders.

'I couldna' do tha' ', he said.

'Why not?' I asked.

'Oh, I'd need a lot o' practice first.'

We couldn't help laughing.

It wasn't so amusing, however, to hear Prof saying, 'But, my dear man, you don't seriously expect you would be let loose all by yourself *without* practice. Then he turned to me. 'The CO will probably take you himself. Won't you — sir?'

There were times when I went off Prof.

'You can come with me tomorrow night.'

Relief was at last beginning to dawn in the Colonel's mind.

'You mean I really don't have to go off by myself for some time yet? Is that it?' He was actually smiling.

'That', I said, 'is, indeed, it. One thing must be understood, however, if you decide to stay then you stay for good. We can't afford to waste time training someone for them to leave immediately they're fully trained.'

'Aye. I understand that,' he said.

'Well? Yes or no?'

'I'll stay, if you'll have me.'

★ ★ ★

One morning towards the end of 1943 the telephone rang on my desk and Prof, who happened to be in the room, answered it. He put his hand over the mouthpiece as he passed the telephone to me. 'It's the CO of the PT boats — Lieutenant-Commander Barnes. He says he'd like to speak to you personally. Something confidential, he says.'

'Hallo, Commander,' I said, 'What can I do for you?'

The voice at the other end was slow but purposeful.

'Good morning. I wonder if you could spare me a few minutes of your time for a little talk? Something's come up.'

'But, of course. You can't give me any idea of what it's about, can you?'

'Well, right now, I guess it's better not. Not on the phone, that is. Would it be too much to ask you to stop by my office during the day. I'd sooner talk here if you don't mind.'

'By all means. I'll be with you in half an hour if that's convenient.'

'Fine, Commander, much obliged. See you later.'

And he rang off.

'Urgent?' asked Prof.

'I've no idea, except that he's asked me to go and see him today, so presumably it must be fairly important. Probably something to do with the next series of ops that we're planning.'

Our relationship with the American flotilla, which arrived after us, had always been excellent. On several occasions Barnes had kindly lent us boats, especially when we were engaged on ops for OSS. They had proved themselves to be kind, hospitable, efficient, and good company to work with. One could not ask more.

Half an hour later I presented myself at the American PT base offices down in the port, and was shown in straight away to the CO's office. He was a young-looking Lieutenant-Commander whose reputation of professional competence and skill had preceded his recent arrival with his flotilla in Bastia. Now he sat behind a desk almost bare of papers, very smart in well-pressed uniform, and keen and alert of eye. He made me feel quite inferior, although I'm sure this was unintentional, for he was a very polite officer who always did his best to make one feel at ease. During the preliminary exchange of courtesies I got the odd feeling that he was a little embarrassed by what he was about to say. The opening question did nothing to dispel the impression that something awkward might be on its way up.

'Tell me,' said Barnes, 'd'you know a place called the Red House?'

I could only shake my head. 'No, I can't say I do. But should I?'

'I can't answer that question, Commander. I don't know whether you should, or not.'

No clues, so far, as to where we might be going.

'Could you,' I ventured, 'please tell me something about it?'

'Why, sure. But I'm surprised you don't know about it. It stands only a couple of hundred yards from your front door, just off the main road going down the hill.'

'Sorry. I'm afraid I still can't place it.'

'No matter.' He picked up a ruler on the desk to tap the palm of the other hand with it prior to fixing me with a look of what I thought might be latent suspicion. Quite disturbing. 'It's a whorehouse,' he announced.

'Ah.' I breathed a sigh of relief. 'And you think I *should* know it. Is that right? Nice of you to recommend it.'

The ruler waved a firm negative. 'No, no, that's not what I meant, at all. I am certainly not recommending it.'

'Oh, I'm sorry, Commander. You mean I should keep away from it? Avoid it? Bad reputation, and all that?'

'No, no, no.' The ruler waved vigorously. 'Nothing about the *place* — '

'Oh, — I'm being very dense. I thought you wanted to talk about the Red House. You mean you don't?'

Carefully he put the ruler aside. 'No, I don't.'

There was a moment's pause before he continued. 'I would like to talk about your *sailors*.'

'Oh, I see. Not the Red House. My sailors, then. Right.'

In a gesture of some impatience he leaned across the desk. 'Your sailors *and* the Red House.'

'Both at once?'

'Right. Both at once. You got it.'

I breathed a trifle easier. 'I'm not surprised if they go there, if that's what you mean, Commander. I expect yours do, too?'

'Sure. They all go there, I guess.'

'No harm in that, surely? Keeps everyone happy.'

He gave me a wry look. 'Not my men, it doesn't.'

Oh, I'm sorry to hear that. My sailors get there first? Is that it?'

'Yeah. That's it. Your men are *always* there first.'

'Well,' I said, 'we should be able to stop that pretty quick by stagger-ing hours of shore leave. I mean if your chaps are a bit slow off the mark, say, we could give them six o'clock to eight, and mine from eight to ten, or something like that. Easy, and fair — surely?'

Instead of agreeing, as I had hoped, he leaned once more across the desk, so that there could be no doubt about the seriousness of the next question. 'Commander,' he said, 'do you have two sailors — just the two I wish to speak about — called Johnstone and Downes?'

Oh, God. The Heavenly Twins.

I replied with caution. 'I think I do, as a matter of fact.'

Barnes did the best he could to soften the blow he was about to deliver. I think he was embarrassed, and now, on hearing those names, so was I.

'Well,' he said, 'what I have to say does not come easy. I don't like to complain about someone else's men, especially when they belong to another country.'

I could only hope whatever they had done was not as bad as he made it sound. 'I shouldn't worry about that — we're not over sensitive, you know. Could you tell me what is the complaint about these two?'

'Sure. I'll do that. In a nutshell, my men tell me that your two men are running the joint.'

'Good heavens, Commander, you astound me!' (Surely, on such oc-casions one may be permitted one lie.)

'Yes, sir, running it.' He picked up the ruler again as if in warning that there was more to come. 'And not only that. They also keep my men *out* of the place. Can you imagine that?'

I couldn't; it didn't seem to make sense. 'If,' I reasoned, 'my chaps were really running the place, wouldn't they wish to welcome all the custom they could get? More customers, more money. Surely? If your men really wanted to get in I can't see two British sailors stopping them. I mean you've got hundreds of them. It doesn't seem logical, somehow.'

He was very calm and quiet. 'Commander —' he looked straight at me, 'your sailors keep my men out with a *tommy-gun*.'

'What, *all* of them?'

'No. Not all. Those who pay are allowed in.'

'Well, I don't know,' I paused to absorb the full awfulness, 'wouldn't that be pretty fair? I mean don't your chaps expect to pay?' I hurried on before he could answer. 'But the tommy-gun — that's another matter, altogether. Are your men sure about it? I mean, possessing arms not officially issued is a very serious crime in our book.'

'My men are sure about the gun. There's no question.'

'Right, Commander Barnes, sir, I will deal with it.'

'Many thanks for dropping over.' He rose to his feet and extended a hand. 'And the other one takes the money,' he added to cross the final t.

When I returned to the villa and told Prof what had happened I really thought he would be ill laughing: his shoulders heaved and shook, he swayed from side to side with great guffaws. Tears streamed down his long face. He was quite helpless.

There was, however, the other side to it. 'I know it's bloody funny, Prof, but we could be in a bit of trouble. If ever there was a court-martial offence this is it.'

'Exactly,' he replied, wiping his eyes. 'That's half the fun really. What d'you propose doing about it?'

'We have no option. There's only one proper course.'

'What, run them in?'

I nodded, and he continued, 'And that will mean a bloody awful rumpus ending, I suppose, in a court-martial right in the middle of the operational period. And they're our best dinghymen.'

'You don't have to tell me. With Bates they are our best men all round. It's a real sod.'

Now he became serious. 'Is there really no way round?'

'None that I can see. It's gone too far. Too many people have become involved. If they are not run in and anyone, especially the Americans, get to hear that we've done nothing they won't keep quiet about it, and the next thing will be our heads on the block. That's certain.'

With a brief chuck of his head Prof reached for his cap, clapped it down over his brows, and made for the door. 'I'll go and get 'em now.' With his hand on the door-knob he turned, 'D'you want me there as a witness?'

'No thanks, Prof. I don't want any aiding or abetting.'

'I'd love to be there, all the same.'

'I daresay.'

'OK.' He shut the door behind him.

He didn't leave me long to consider the problem; presumably both men had been already in the grounds. There was a knock on the door, and Prof put his head round the edge to announce 'Leading Seaman Johnstone, and Leading Seaman Downes reporting, sir.' The two of them advanced into the room to stand in front of the desk; each was

71

carrying his cap, as they stood more or less at attention. From the door-way Prof raised his eyes heavenward and left. I didn't waste time.

'You both know the Red House, I take it?'

Instantly, each in his separate fashion, became wary. Downes became wooden, while Johnstone leaned forward slightly balancing like a boxer, on his toes. Like his stance Johnstone's reaction was light, ready to spring in any direction. 'The Red House, sir? You mean the house just down the hill from 'ere, sir?'

'I do. Yes.'

'Well, sir, we know it — ' he gave a sidelong glance at Downes who didn't react — 'That is, in a manner of speaking.'

'What manner of speaking d'you mean?'

'It's a place we go to sometimes, sir.'

'It's a brothel isn't it?"

'Yes, sir.'

'Where did you get the tommy-gun? From the armoury?'

I might have been accusing them of stealing the Taj Mahal. Johnstone's expression of horrified disbelief would have done credit to any of our finest actors. 'Tommy-gun, sir? Did you say — '

'Tommy-gun, yes. And you both know perfectly well what I'm get-ting at. I'll give you the facts. The Americans have complained...'

They stood silent and expressionless as I went over what Barnes had told me; it was as if I was talking about something that had nothing to do with them at all. At the end I said, 'You both realize that this is a clear court-martial offence?'

Downes, the specialist in conciliation, now threw in his bit. After a series of big swallows when his adam's apple flew up and down rapid-ly, he assumed a pained look. 'Court-martial, sir?'

'Yes. Court-martial.'

'Because of the tommy-gun, sir?' He made it sound as if we were discussing a water-pistol.

Both appeared scandalized at what I was saying.

'Amongst other reasons, yes,' I said. 'All the charges would be serious.' I ticked them off on my fingers. 'Drawing a weapon from the armoury without permission. Using the gun to extort money. Assisting in running a brothel. Being absent without leave — I suspect. And I daresay KR & AI can dream up a number of other charges. Now tell me why you shouldn't be court-martialled.'

They stood silent in front of me.

'You admit the charges are correct?'

At this point Johnstone rose half an inch on his toes; he was going to make a fight of it. Politely, of course.

'Put like that, sir, we can't, neither of us, argue.' He sank back again.

'But it wasn't like that, sir.'

'Oh? Then what's your version? And it had better be good.'

He twiddled his cap round in his hands, inspecting the inside for inspiration, before looking me straight in the eye. His voice was earnest and solemn. 'That woman 'as been done a great wrong — '

'What,' I interrupted, 'are you talking about? What woman? What's she got to do with it?'

'*Madame*, sir,' he pleaded. 'Her that owns the 'ouse.'

'Right. Now let me make it plain that we are not concerned with the owner of the brothel, or with any wrong that may have been done to her. We are talking about you two drawing a gun from the armoury, and using it to extort money. That the place of extortion was a brothel is, for the moment, incidental. Leave everything else aside. Now — what is your explanation? — if you have one.'

Downes had been watching intently. Clearing his throat, purging immoral thoughts from the atmosphere, he started, his gaze levelled just above my head.

'It was like this, sir. Some time ago — musta bin weeks now, I suppose — we was comin' up the 'ill from town when we met *Madame* goin' the same way as us an' carryin' some 'eavy baskets. Me and Johnstone, we give 'er a 'and, and in gratitude, like, she arsks us in for a drink. Seemed quite natural to us. Oh, yes — there was some ladies there, too.' He lowered his glance for a second to see how I was taking all this; evidently what he saw wasn't too encouraging, for he hurried on, 'An you know 'ow it is, sir.'

'I'm prepared to guess. I don't wish to hear about the young ladies. Go on.'

'Well, sir, afterwards me and Johnstone got talkin' to *Madame*, an' she told us she was in trouble with the Yanks — the American sailors, sir.'

Thoughts of future stringent disciplinary action had been waning quite steadily; now they flew straight out of the window. 'Oh? What sort of trouble? I should have thought the local madam would have been more than a match for the Americans. Or has she broken the law, too?'

'Oh, no, sir. What 'appened was, they used to go to 'er 'ouse in a group, grab the girls, and then not pay.' A dramatic look of anguish flooded his face. '*Madame* said she could see ruin starin' at 'er, sir.'

'And what had that got to do with you two? Did you ever bother to find out if she was telling the truth?'

'Oh, yes, sir. We did, sir.' He was full of righteousness, and getting down to fact; he had it all worked out now. 'We was there a coupla nights — I mean *Madame* arst us to be there, sir. That's what it 'ad to

73

do with us, if you see what I mean. We was there when along come four or five Yanks, sir, an' they did exactly — but exactly, sir — what *Madame* 'ad told us. Just made a set for the girls, an' no payin' at all.' He drew himself up. 'Didn't seem right to us, sir, it didn't.'

'So you went off, and without any permission from anyone, you drew a tommy-gun from the armoury. And after that you set up a tollgate at the door. Isn't that what you did?'

To the righteousness was now added aggrievement. 'Well, sir, like it was, it just wasn't fair, sir. Was it, sir?'

'Very gallant, I'm sure.' They had to be taken down a peg; I made a pause before the next question. 'And what was your share of the evening's takings?'

Both looked horror-struck, regarding the question as patently below the belt in its unexpectedness.

'Our *share*, sir? We just took the money for *Madame*, sir.'

'So you've just admitted, but how much did she give you for doing so? That's the question.' At once I changed my mind. 'No, don't answer that, either of you. The amount had nothing to do with the charges. What matters is that you have admitted standing at the door taking money.'

Such was the evident relief at not having to divulge the sordid business arrangements that when Johnstone spoke there was more than a suspicion of a smile round his mouth.

'Yes, sir.' He was back up again, balancing half on his toes.

'And the American sailors were angry, were they?'

'Yes, sir. At least some of 'em was and some wasn't.'

'Who were the ones who weren't?'

'Oh, those who'd be'aved fair. They'd paid all right — beforehand, like.'

'So there were some who paid?'

'Yes, sir. They was usually the ones who'd bin floggin' their cigarettes and PX stores down on the jetty. They could afford it, sir.'

'Did you get any other perks besides a share on the evenings you were there?'

'No, sir, except an odd glass of wine, and — ' He stopped.

'And?'

'Well, sir, really nothing more — from *Madame*, that is. Sometimes the girls —'

'Yes, yes. I understand. But never mind about the girls. It's bad enough already. Where's the tommy-gun now?'

'Back in the armoury, sir.'

Doing my best to subject them to an intimidating stare I spoke slowly. 'Very good. That's all — for the moment. You can go now. One of you is to present my compliments to the First Lieutenant and ask him to speak to me. Until I send for you again — possibly, I must warn you, about a court-martial — neither of you is to go near the Red House. You are both to remain within the grounds of the villa.'

They trooped out. What a mess. On reflection, perhaps the biggest surprise was that nothing of this sort had happened before. By and large I saw no reason to disbelieve what they had told me. A few minutes later Prof came in agog to know how it had gone. I gave him a summary of the interview. (The following is the gist of our subsequent conversation.)

His comment was brief. 'A bit of a bugger, h'm?'

'Quite a bit of a bugger, as you say.'

Neither of us spoke while we considered what we realized *should* now happen. Prof was the first to begin putting thoughts into words. 'Supposing there is a court-martial?'

'Then we should lose our two best dinghymen; something we simply can't afford to do, Prof.'

'There'd be some pretty dirty linen to be washed, too, wouldn't there?'

'Indeed. Very dirty.'

'And it wouldn't only be ours, would it?'

'You mean the Americans?'

He nodded before I added, 'And the gallant *Madame* herself could also be called.'

A great shout of laughter went up as he put his head back to let the noise out more quickly. 'My God! Of course — *Madame*.' He gave an awful leer. 'Almost worth risking the court-martial to hear *her* evidence, don't you think?'

Ridiculous as the idea was it provoked more constructive thinking. Prof became serious. 'A court-martial is certainly not — in this instance, anyway — going to help the war effort, or Allied relations. It could also embarrass the Americans.'

'Assuming some of 'em would be called as witnesses.'

'That's just the point.' Prof's right eyelid twitched fractionally. 'Alas, they would have to be called.' There was a second's pause, and his eyes looked heavenward as he added, 'Unless — unless — '

'Prof, I know what you're thinking. And it's quite scandalous — '

'And what's wrong with that if we can hold on to our dinghymen?'

He was right, of course, but there was one other thing which still worried me. 'You know, Prof, I can just see a faint possibility of killing two birds here. If we could use this situation to encourage our American cousins to stop their troops flogging all their bloody PX stores along the jetty beside the boats, that would be a real bonus. It would make our sailors very happy: *they* don't do it because our rules against it are much too strict. Besides they've got very little to flog.'

As I spoke he was nodding agreement. 'And the Red House?'

'Oh, that still stands. As you've already pointed out we may be able to squeeze quite a bit from that. The essential bit, in fact.'

Prof cocked an eyebrow. 'And the illegal withdrawal of the tommy-gun from the armoury?'

In silence we stared at one another.

'On second thoughts,' said Prof, 'it might be better if you were to go and see Barnes right now.'

I rose from my chair. 'Come on, Prof, *we'll* go and see him.'

As a result of the interview which followed, the Lieutenant-Commander (to his eternal credit) was sympathetic enough to opine that a court-martial of the two British sailors could cause unnecessary damage to Anglo-American relations. And we opined with him.

Chapter 4

GORGONA

Shortly before Christmas the American communications experts decided that the tiny island of Gorgona, some fifty miles to the nor'-nor'-east of Bastia, should be 'captured' and used as an observation post against enemy shipping going in and out of Livorno, and, to a lesser extent, Spezia — although the latter was quite a step further up the coast. I was asked if one of my boats could be made available.

Mid-December of that year showed the moon at its most brilliant phase: we would be right out of line with our usual dates of operating with *no* moon. For this operation, once they were ashore the Americans were hoping for all the moonlight they could get in order to find their way round the island more easily. The quicker they could actually see any opposition there might be the quicker they would be able to deal with it. The plan was to use a total 'invading' force of twelve men, to capture or otherwise deal with such enemy as they might find, and then to leave six men on the island to operate the Observation Post, before returning to Bastia.

Our own intelligence on the island was pretty sketchy. Since the Allied arrival in Bastia our boats of all sorts had passed quite close to the island on numerous occasions with no signs of opposition. Some did say there was a German garrison, others that they were Italians. No one knew for certain. The only indisputable fact was that there existed a fairly large penal settlement on the east close to the diminutive port.

Ginger and his *MAS 541* were chosen for the op. Together we studied the charts, to conclude that the only real obstacle might be the size of the port being inadequate to take the MAS. To overcome this we decided that we could, if the weather was kind, perfectly well ferry the troops ashore in dinghies, and then leave the boat alongside the outer wall of the breakwater. That, the Americans agreed, was quite acceptable.

The evening of the operation came. Ginger and I waited in the ward-room of *MAS 541*. Time ticked by until, according to the schedule, the Americans were late in arriving on the jetty. We decided to go up to the bridge from where we could keep a look-out. At that early hour of the night everything was unexpectedly dark. I could just make out a few crew members moving round the upper deck, lashing down dinghies and generally preparing for sea. On the jetty there was nothing to be seen except a pile of what looked like rubble or, perhaps, coal some fifteen yards away. I must have made some tetchy remark about being kept waiting; from out of the pitch-blackness a disem-bodied voice replied in a rich southern drawl, 'But we're right here.' A second later this was followed up with, 'Waiting for you, Commander.'

'Where?' I couldn't see any sign of soldiery.

Up from the jetty a young lieutenant vaulted on board to come up to me and point in the direction of the heap of rubble. 'Right there,' he said. 'Can't you see? That's us.' Putting his hand up to the corner of his mouth he called ashore. 'OK Colonel, the boat's ready for us.' In response there was a muffled word of command which I couldn't catch.

Then a strange thing happened. Like some giant sinister flower the heap of rubble began to blossom, opening out large petals which started moving about. Each one separated from its neighbour, seemed to take on the untidy shape of a leafy artichoke balancing on its own truncated stalk. It was quite unnerving to watch until the shapes revealed themselves as members of the long-awaited boarding party.

I had never seen an American commando in 'combat dress' before. Seen at close quarters as they came on board one could only marvel that they could move at all, so weighed down were they with guns, hand grenades, ammunition clips, canteen equipment, groundsheets, bedding rolls secured about their person. How they could fight while cluttered up with all that impedimenta was hard to understand, and yet they had proved themselves splendidly again and again in battle in a war which was nothing if not mobile.

There was also a quantity of communications equipment and general stores to embark. Prominent, I felt sure, on the stores list would be lavatory paper. It seemed to be an inflexible idiosyncrasy of the American armed forces that whilst they were prepared to put up with a surprising amount of discomfort, much of which would have been considered intolerable to our own forces, the one thing without which the Americans were miserable in the extreme was an ample supply of what we thought of as 'luxury' lavatory paper.

For them, none of that rubbish about 'smooth side for the officers, rough side for ship's company and the edge for the midshipmen'. It was soft all the way, for officers and GIs alike. True democracy in the 'toilet department'.

Ginger, too, was astounded by the spectacle of the fully-equipped American commando; he was worried by their number. '*Ma* — ' he said, 'how are we going to get them all on board?' In an attempt to anticipate the problem the torpedo tubes had already been unshipped and their space taken up by landing equipment (rubber dinghies, etc). The space below decks allowed for two or three officers in the wardroom/charthouse, while aft there was little more than shelter space for a couple of men. For'ard, in the foc'sle was the crew's quarters.

To make more room the three torpedo ratings were put ashore; as well as giving a little more space it also lightened the boat. The American officers were asked to go below into the charthouse, while the enlisted men crowded round the former torpedo mountings. In this fashion Ginger and I were left in peace on the tiny bridge, to get on with the navigation. It was, by chance, a full moon, there was no cloud, the sea was flat calm, and there was no wind as we eased our way out of harbour. Happily, by now, the enemy minefield had been located and a wider safe channel swept through it.

We were in no hurry, not wishing to arrive before 22.00 by which time we reckoned the island would have settled down for the night. Normal prison discipline demands 'lights out' pretty early and would be doubly likely to save electricity which, as we were to discover, was a precarious commodity on such a small island: on the alertness of the problematical garrison we would just have to take our chance. Who could say, they might be friendly?

Once clear of the harbour and the swept channel we switched over from auxiliary to main engines at a speed of just over 20 knots. The night was quite perfect, and we invited the American officers to join us on the bridge. There were three of them which made the space crowded but nobody minded. One was tempted to wonder if their thoughts could be anywhere but with such a perfect sea. To be engaged in aggressive pursuits in these surroundings seemed wrong; it would be so much more appropriate if we stopped to enjoy the beauty and tranquility of the night. War seemed a long way off and terribly stupid as the moon's reflection was shattered into a myriad small sparkling lights from the waves.

Capraia, an island about double the size of our target, Gorgona, lay about half way along our route. In the silvery light it showed up well to add to the romantic atmosphere of the occasion. Two hours after leaving Bastia we went over once more to our silent auxiliary engines. There might not be much of a garrison on Gorgona but there was no sense in advertising our arrival through the deep roar of the mains. To knock any vestiges of capriciousness from our minds, twenty minutes later an aircraft was heard approaching, and we stopped the boat; the phosphorescence of our wake could give away our presence. It came right over the top of us at about 1,000 ft, and the night was so clear that we could see the glow of the red-hot exhausts of the twin motors as it went by, flying very fast. When it was safely away from us we resumed our leisurely way, coming up to the southernmost tip of Gorgona, and proceeding up the east coast, close inshore. Not a light, not a sound from shore disturbed the calm of the night.

The American officer in command of the party was also the local head of OSS, and his presence could only be interpreted as an indication of the importance attached to the operation. He was serving in the rank of full Colonel and his name was Russell Livermore. Only a little later he was to become a helpful friend. On being informed that we were within about ten minutes of our destination — the minute harbour — he ordered two of his men to lie flat on the foc'sle, and four more to line the landward side of the craft, all being armed with tommy-guns, and ready to open fire at the first sign of trouble. The Colonel was taking no chances.

It was not easy to spot the mouth of the harbour which was lying in shadow but when we did we stopped the boat about a cable's length from it while we lowered a rubber dinghy discreetly into the water. An American Captain with an Italian name, who not surprisingly spoke fluent Italian, then slid down into the dinghy. He was armed to the teeth and cradled a tommy-gun in his lap while I pulled ashore. On the trip in I remembered the six American soldiers still on board the MAS, all with their guns pointed in our direction. For peace of mind I stopped thinking about them, concentrating instead on the hope that there would be no opposition to our arrival. We were then in the deep shadow of the rocky cliffs dominating the harbour: whilst covering fire should be a source of much comfort by day, it does not have quite the same appeal in the dark when the gunners cannot see what they are supposed to be protecting.

As we rounded the short breakwater we found ourselves in the tiny harbour. We could see nothing, but suddenly there was the noise of many hob-nailed boots running over cobbles towards the jetty we were approaching. Then there were shouts, friendly or hostile it was difficult to determine; they weren't more than twenty yards away, at a guess. Meanwhile I realized we were silhouetted (to the shouters) against a background of light open sea.

To my companion I said, 'I think you'd better say something to them.'

He remained quite silent while the shouting became more insistent, and recognizable as Italian (thank heavens) and not German. 'Say something,' I pleaded with the Captain. 'Go on.'

At last he spoke. 'What shall I say?' he asked.

'Anything. Anything you like. Ask them how auntie is — but something in Italian.'

A bit tentatively he called out, '*Buona sera,*' not very loud, but evidently loud enough.

There was an immediate chorus of response from the crowd which was just becoming visible as we approached to pull alongside the stone jetty. Friendly hands came out of the night to help us as we groped our way up the ladder let into the stonework. At the top we were surrounded by a milling crowd of vociferous men who slapped us on the back in an amiable boisterous way. There was just enough light at those close quarters to see that none of them was in any sort of uniform; they were, therefore, probably fishermen. The question then arose, did these friendly people understand whose backs they were slapping? In the dark, for all they knew, we could be either German or Italian. We should have to 'suck it and see'. Turning to one of the crowd I told him we were Americans and British. The news was broadcast to the others by a shout louder than anyone else's, and we were treated to renewed and rather harder slaps on the back, with much use of '*bene, bene*'.

Time was passing and I suggested to the Captain that the MAS should be called up to enter harbour. With his now fluent Italian he was almost totally submerged in the excited fishermen but he managed to shout his agreement. Flashing the pre-arranged signal out to Ginger I saw him move the boat ahead at the same time as he acknowledged the signal. With great skill he brought her in to lay her gently alongside the inner side of the breakwater: there was barely room for him to turn the boat round, so small was the harbour.

The American Colonel and his men assembled on the quay preparatory to carrying out their part of the operation. Lanterns and torches had been produced among the local inhabitants and by their flickering light the scene resembled a bit out of a modernized 'Flying Dutchman'. With some difficulty, owing to the enthusiasm of the locals who wished to savour to the full this excitement, the Colonel eventually got his men going up the cobbled street into the town. The crowd was divided by admiration of these supermen of American soldiers and the chance to chat to the MAS boat crew: the youngsters followed the soldiers while the elders remained with us.

I posted one look-out in the small tower on the end of the jetty and

81

two more on the jetty itself. We had no wish to be taken by surprise by some passing enemy patrol boat. Visibility out to sea was excellent; by the light of the moon we could see up to about four miles.

An hour went by peacefully: no sounds of strife from the interior of the island. Then a gentle puff of wind came in from the north-east. Ginger and I were seated on the sea wall, gossiping, as we watched the rippling of the water approaching the island like some secret messenger of the gods speeding to warn us of lurking danger. Neither of us said anything at the time but our vigilance increased and there was little surprise when half an hour later, the first zephyr changed to a smart breeze blowing straight into the harbour mouth. When the boat started to surge alongside the wall with the slight swell, I thought the time had come to warn our American friends that they should be prepared to leave at short notice, or else, if the weather worsened and they still hadn't completed their task, they could remain on the island while the boat put to sea and searched for more hospitable shelter. Ginger and I agreed that I would go and try to find the Americans while he remained with the MAS, ready to sail if the need arose, at any time.

From the knot of islanders gathered on the quayside I sought a guide, explaining that, owing to the deterioration in the weather I wished to find the Americans as quickly as possible. This produced a hubbub of suggestions and advice from half a dozen voices. There was, however, one louder and more insistent than the rest. He was wearing a sort of Rupert of Hentzau hat which I took to be a form of badge of office — which, indeed, it turned out to be — and to eliminate further competition he grabbed me by the arm, propelling me towards the village centre. As we went he stated with some pride that he was a prison warder, and that he *knew* the Americans had gone to the apartment of the prison governor.

This theory had, at least, the basis of likelihood behind it as in an earlier discussion the gallant Colonel Livermore had told me that he 'guessed we will pick up the governor somewhere along the line'. Who should know better the way to the governor's apartment than one of his own warders? He was in good training, my guide. Although wearing heavy hob-nailed boots he was as nimble as a goat over the uneven, unlit cobbles, and the rough-hewn steps as we climbed up through the village 'main street'.

All the time, through a barrage of trivial chatter I was listening hard for any sounds of battle or shouts of surrender from my friends or the enemy, but the whole island was as silent as the grave; we were the only ones making any noise at all. Not even a dog barked. Five minutes later we arrived outside a large modern block of what looked like flats, an incongruous sight in this wild backwater. The guide halted at the foot of a wide flight of steps leading up to an imposing front door. One could only suppose it had been built by the Fascists as yet another tribute to *il Duce*.

'The governor's apartment', said my guide in a hoarse whisper, and ran up the steps. If the Americans were here they were keeping remarkably quiet about it. I followed up the steps through the front door, into a large hall; by our torches I saw a staircase straight ahead, and a lift shaft — but no lift in it — to the right. (The money runs out even in dictatorships, apparently.) We climbed to the first floor where there were four smart front doors giving on to a gallery; circling the gallery, the guide stopped in front of a pair of doors, larger and more imposing than the others, with a big brass knocker on one of them.

'The governor,' announced the guide in tones suggesting that he really ought to bow in respect. Instead he pressed the bell at the side of the doorway. I heard no answering ring the other side of the door: neither did he, for after a few seconds he pressed it again. Then he slapped first his thigh and then the side of his head, pointing an index finger at his temple to indicate his own stupidity. No electricity, no bell ring. He seized the doorknocker and beat three times with it. The echo reverberating round the big empty hall was enough to rouse the whole block, but there was no response from the governor's apartment as we waited in silence, straining our ears for some sign of life. Not a sound.

We were simply wasting time. Not only were the Americans not here, nor, apparently, was the governor. Irritated by this needless delay I was about to turn away when there was a faint rattling of chains from within the flat, bolts were being drawn and then, very slowly an inch at a time, the doors started to open to reveal a totally unexpected and touching scene taken straight out of some mid-Victorian drama.

A small girl of about six, certainly not more, dressed in a full-length white cotton nightdress, pigtails down her back, stood just inside, the doorknob in one hand, a candle in the other, staring up at me eyes wide open in apprehension. She said nothing: just stared. Behind her in a single straight line were four more girls ranging in age between about ten to fourteen years, all dressed the same in long white cotton nightdresses, all holding candles, all wide-eyed in fear as they looked between the guide and me, and back again. For some long seconds no one moved and no one said anything. The tableau *vivant* of the 'Unexpected Visitors' was perfect.

As gently as I could I explained who I was before asking the all-important question, 'Could you please tell me if some American soldiers have been here. Or, perhaps, if they're still here?'

There was another lengthy silence before the smallest and youngest shook her head from side to side very slowly. From her expression and the way she did it there was no means of knowing whether she was saying that she hadn't seen any Americans or whether she hadn't understood the question. One of the elder girls came to the rescue.

'No Americans have come here,' she said firmly.

'Then, perhaps, your father, the governor is here?'

There followed a general shaking of heads before one of them recognized the guide who had been standing in the shadows outside the door. She addressed him by name and when he answered, all of them joined in a babble of exchanges too rapid for me to follow. The guide, seeing that I had lost the conversation, then translated it into simpler Italian. He was nothing if not polite.

'The young ladies say they don't know where the governor is, but their mother, the wife of the governor you understand, would very much like to see you.'

'The governor's wife wants to — But she doesn't even know that I'm here, let alone who I am. What do they mean?' I began to feel wary.

'They say, *Commandante*, that perhaps the governor has returned and is now with his wife who is ill.' It was more of a plea than a suggestion.

Alarm bells rang louder in my head as I felt the ground slipping from under my feet into one of those farcical situations which defy all control.

'Tell them, if you will, that I am concerned only with finding the American soldiers who I thought might come here because I know they wish to see the governor. Since they are not here I will now leave. My apologies to them all for having disturbed them.'

As I was struggling in Italian anyway no interpretation was needed. Their united reaction was a wail of protest.

'But our mother is ill. Please come and see her.'

'I'm sorry, I'm not a doctor. I can do nothing for her.'

But, yes, *Commandante*,' was the chorus. I was not best pleased to notice that the guide had joined in in support. 'Please come and see her. She is very ill.'

Knowing it to be the folly of weakness, I reasoned that sometimes the longest way round was the shortest way home, and I gave in. Perhaps she was really ill; perhaps I could have some medicine sent to her later on. Anything to avoid a row.

'All right,' I said, 'take me to her on the strict understanding that I cannot stay long.' Time was beginning to rush by but two minutes wasn't much one way or the other.

The door was opened wide and I was ushered into the hall to be led by two of the elder girls down a long passage of parquet flooring at the end of which they stopped outside a door. One of them knocked, to be answered from within not by any dulcet tones, but by a low-pitched sepulchral wail bidding entry. One of the girls went in and I could hear a hasty whispered conversation which terminated abruptly with the door being opened wide and an invitation to go in.

It was a large room by any standards, and it needed to be, most of the available space being taken up by one of the largest beds (including that of Were) I have ever seen. And in it was one of the largest women I have ever seen. She was rolling ponderously from side to side, moaning and groaning in distress. But of the Americans or the governor there was, alas no sign, past, present, or future.

Before I could say anything she started. '*Commandante* I am ill.' The bedclothes heaved like waves in a rough sea as she rocked back and forth. 'Please, you must find me some medicine. My husband is not here—'

'*Signora*,' I explained, 'I am not a doctor. I cannot help you. I will tell my American friends about you. If you could tell me where your husband is we might arrange for some medicine for you.'

'The governor, my husband, is not here, *Commandante*. My children —' she cast a glance at the eldest girl standing quietly in the background — 'my children will have told you already.'

'Indeed, they have, *signora*, but you must have some idea as to where he is. Please tell me.'

'*Commandante*, I am very ill.' She was turning up the volume. 'Can't you see? I must have an injection. Can't you give me one?'

Why, so often, was I inflicted with such demented conversations? For a fleeting second I was tempted by the obvious vulgarity. I remembered Nanny and my manners just in time.

'*Signora*, I can do nothing for you unless you tell me where the governor is.'

'He is in prison, *Commandante*. Now my medicine.'

'In prison, did you say? But who—?'

'He locked himself in, *Commandante*, for safety.'

'Thank you *signora*. I will go there immediately.' Turning to the guide I said, 'Come on, off we go to the prison. I can do nothing for the *signora* now but we'll try to arrange something when I have found the Americans.'

Bidding the governor's wife and family a hasty but definite farewell we left in a candlelight procession of the children. As we got to the front door I could still hear the governor's wife moaning about her need for treatment.

Once outside I said to the guide, 'Now, my friend, quickly does it,

85

back to the jetty.'

'To the jetty *Commandante*? But you said to the *signora* that you would go immediately to the prison, No?'

'Yes I did,' I replied, 'but I've changed my mind. I now wish to return to the boat so let's get going.'

'*Subito, Commandante, subito*,' he said, 'but first please, I must tell my wife.'

'For God's sake —,' I protested, when he interrupted.

'But *Commandante*, she lives on the next floor above. I must tell her.'

'Very well, but run.'

I knew that there was every chance that in the dark I would lose my way back to the ship without this obtuse man.

'Please, *Commandante*, to come with me. Then she will believe me.'

I ran up the staircase after him but by the time I got on to the next floor he was already opening his own front door. His wife, candle in hand, met him in the hall. He gave her a perfunctory kiss, then whirling round he made a proud gesture with his arm, in my direction.

'And look! Look who I have with me. A British officer!'

She looked, and what she saw sent her hand to her mouth as if to stifle a scream. Who could blame her?

'Quick,' the guide said, giving his wife a shove towards the bedroom, 'get out the champagne.' She bustled through the open doorway to the bedroom and I watched, fascinated against my will, as she rummaged round in the bottom drawer of a large cupboard and finally, after throwing out an odd assortment of clothes, produced a magnum of Italian champagne.

The guide and his wife were jubilant — they had waited years, they said, for just such an occasion as this; we must now drink the champagne to celebrate the Anglo-American arrival.

This time I really did protest — vehemently — explaining that we could come back later. I made my way determinedly out of the bedroom and into the kitchen, but the guide was before me. He rushed over to the kitchen table and seized an enormous fish which was lying on some newspaper.

'This fish, *Commandante*, my wife and I present it to you. It is a very good fish — see how it shines even in the candle light. My wife will cook it for you.'

'No, no, no,' I shouted. 'No certainly not. There is no time. Please tell your wife that I am not being rude but please no champagne and no fish. Just take me back to the jetty.'

The guide was nonplussed by this show of apparent obstinacy; but not for long. With a sudden sweep he picked up the fish and the magnum of champagne and held them aloft.

'*Va bene*. To the jetty we go, *Commandante*,' he announced, and kissing his wife on the top of her head, he made for the door where he turned to add for the benefit of the world, 'It's very important. The *Commandante* must find the Americans.'

Too right, he must.

We ran most of the way back to the jetty with twenty valuable minutes wasted, except for the meagre intelligence concerning the governor's hide-out. If I could find the Americans reasonably quickly I could at least save them from the experiences which I had just suffered. As we went I could not help conjuring up in my mind the picture of the governor's wife and family receiving the Americans.

The wind had shown only a slight increase and the boat was still riding easily with Ginger very much on the *qui vive*. On the jetty I learnt from bystanders that the island garrison consisted of somewhere around ten Italian soldiers, all past their prime, who, on hearing of the American arrival had beaten a hasty retreat up into the interior of the island and were believed to have taken refuge in an ancient disused fort on top of the island's highest point. For the second time I found a guide: my original one was now making merry with the crew of the MAS boat, the champagne flowing.

My new guide and I set off at a brisk pace inland towards the believed scene of any action there might be. He was, like his predecessor, a loquacious man, but his conversation was limited — limited to an interminable complaint about the shortage of food on the island. '*Mangiare, mangiare*' all the way up the path. I had little breath to spare, at the pace we went, for any but the tersest compassion. Twenty minutes hard going brought us to our goal where we found one or two locals who had come up to see the fun. From them we learnt that the Americans had left with their 'prisoners' about five minutes earlier going down by the so-called road. We had missed them by taking a short cut up one of the many paths. Down we went, by the same short cut, and a few minutes later caught up with the Colonel, who was bringing up the rear of his party. He told me there were eight prisoners and I asked him to hurry his men down; this he obligingly did. On the way I asked him if the Italians had shown any resistance.

'Oh, no,' he replied, 'At least not aggressive resistance. The first trouble we had was to find them. They're all old men, and they bolted, as soon as they heard we'd arrived, up to that castle we just left. When we got there, godamnit, they wouldn't open the door. Barricaded themselves inside. Would they come out? Hell, no. We told them they wouldn't get hurt, but it made no difference. Finally we had to break the doors down. There they all were in the cellar, scared to hell. In fact

— I don't mind telling you, Commander, — they were so scared that some of 'em had behaved in a very childish manner.'

Now these unfortunate 'old men' — I suppose their average age was around 42 — were being hustled down the hill to they knew not what fate.

As soon as we arrived alongside *MAS 541* the whole eight of them were shoved down into the forward compartment of the boat, the crew's quarters, under the foc'sle, with two or three American soldiers as guards. I asked the Colonel if he was going to 'pick up' the prison governor, and I told him where he was, and also about the governor's wife.

'No, I guess not this trip,' he replied, 'I can't stand too many frightened men at once. Bad for morale. And, I guess too, that the lady'll keep until we have time to come back.'

This was just as well, as the boat was beginning to surge awkwardly with the increasing sea. No time was lost; the Colonel gave orders to leave one officer and six enlisted men, plus a radio set, to hold the island, and the remainder embarked. Ginger had dropped an anchor in the middle of the diminutive harbour, in order to haul the boat's head round on leaving, but now the anchor was fouled under a rock. In the increasing swell the hemp cable parted but at least we were pointing in the right direction and just squeezed through the narrow channel. Once more the painful business of running on auxiliary engines for an hour, in order not to reveal our presence in the area to any inquisitive patrol.

When we were clear of the island there was time to relax a little and at this moment I noticed a smell, as of fish and chips. Going aft I opened the engine room hatch and was immediately assailed by the full aroma. I went below and there was the Chief Engineer, a splendid ebullient character, by name Capo Pulchri, busily grilling the remains of my huge fish, on one of the exhaust manifolds.

'Eh, *Commandante*,' he said 'What a fish! We've eaten half, and now we eat the other half.'

'And the champagne?' I asked.

'Eh, *Commandante*,' he laughed. 'We never drink at sea.'

He turned to look at a gauge. 'All gone,' he said over his shoulder.

When I returned on deck Ginger seemed so glum and taciturn that I asked him if anything were wrong. He shrugged his shoulders in some resignation.

'The soldiers,' he said, 'they are all being sick down for'ard. My crew are upset.' I could well imagine they were.

'That's war,' I replied. 'Let's go over to main engines.'

If Capo Pulchri hadn't finished his cooking that was too bad. The roar of the mains always provided a certain indefinable sense of comfort and security, and, if the weather was reasonable, the boat was a lot steadier. We cruised along gently at 27 knots, and I hoped the soldiers would feel better — but we were going to be much too early to chance a return to our home port. The French and Italian shore batteries at night were a trigger-happy lot, their principle being to shoot first and risk questions later. Our principle, therefore, was to enter harbour only in daylight, except in emergency.

The 'self-heaters' were shared out on the bridge, and for once, we were able to impress our American cousins. They had never seen it before and bombarded me with questions on how the trick was done. I had no idea; to me the only thing that mattered was that we enjoyed first-class, really hot soup when we most needed it.

Long before dawn we had to revert to auxiliary engines to avoid being off Bastia in the dark and so at the mercy of our own shore batteries, who were particularly touchy since a flotilla of E-boats had come down the coast quite recently to lay another minefield off the harbour mouth. On that occasion not a shot had been fired, the shore batteries being confident that the E-boats were part of our own forces. Next morning there had been an inquest and the battery control officers had received a well-earned 'bottle' from SOIS. They weren't going to be caught out again.

We ran into heavy rain squalls which made the hours of waiting the more tedious until the first glimmerings of dawn provided the signal for us to head homeward on main engines. To 'clear the fluff' we increased a prolonged burst of full speed, finally securing alongside at 07.30.

When the for'ard hatch was opened the prisoners were allowed on deck; eight more miserable, dishevelled men would have been hard to find in the whole Mediterranean area. Tired, hungry, seasick, cold, and far from home, it was hardly surprising that they were frightened stiff of their American captors, most of whom were so young, fit and well-armed. With a charming show of old-world courtesy Colonel Livermore thanked Ginger, his crew, and me for our help in the 'capture' of the island.

As he stepped ashore he turned. 'I guess,' he said, 'we'll have to go back and get that governor soon. I'm sure the Commander here can't wait to see that lovely little lady, the governor's wife, again. So long, boys.'

* * *

One of the more exasperating occurrences in Bastia was the frequency of electricity cuts. Perhaps it was inevitable that these should happen either when we were in the middle of dinner, or when we were about to sit down to eat; it was, after all, the time of maximum load, when so many stoves and ovens were in use, a factor which tended to increase irritation. The cut might be either confined to the sector or it could be general, when the whole town was blacked out.

Candles were hard to come by if sought over the counter in a local shop, even at inflated prices. Somehow Maria managed to produce enough on most occasions but I heard unofficially that the resources of Messrs Downes and Johnstone were being called into play more frequently with the passage of time.

Sitting working at my desk one evening just before dinner the lights quite suddenly went out. I was in the middle of writing a longish report which, for once, was going unexpectedly well, making the interruption that much more aggravating. In order to avoid worrying Maria who was busy getting dinner ready I shouted for Piccolo. A minute later he came in with a lighted candle.

'Piccolo,' I complained, 'this is too much. Every time one is doing something important the lights fail. What is it this time, town or sector?'

He went over to the window, drew back a corner of the blackout and peered around the horizon.

'Sector, *Commandante*. In the next door sector there are lights.' The imperfections of the blackout were accepted as inevitable in a town of so many nationalities: only when there was an air raid alert were strict measures applied; these usually meant someone at the power station pulling the main switch.

'Well,' I said, continuing to be unreasonable in my annoyance, 'do something about it, Piccolo. Do something.'

I felt rather than saw him looking at me discreetly, trying to judge whether my wrath might be directed against him, personally. Having satisfied himself that it wasn't he gave me a half smile, bobbed his head a few times, and muttered one of his inevitable '*va bene, Commandante*' before leaving the candle on the desk and disappearing.

There were no more power cuts for another three or four days. When the next one occurred a group of us was sitting round the fire gossiping after dinner. Maria was quickly on the spot with candles. More out of fun than anything else I asked her to send Piccolo in to see me, simply to pull his leg.

'He just went out, Commandant. At least I think he did,' she replied. 'He was there in the kitchen when the lights went out, but he —'

At that moment the lights came on again and she never finished the sentence. I got up and went over to the french windows and, easing my way round the curtains, opened the door and went outside. Not a light was to be seen in our sector, although none of the other sectors seemed to have been cut off. Returning inside I went through to the kitchen calling once more for Piccolo. He re-appeared quickly enough from the direction of the cellar.

'Hullo,' I said, 'Did you fix this?' indicating the lights.

He looked a bit nervous. 'But you said, *Commandante*, that I should do something.'

'I did, indeed. And now well done. Tell me how you did it.'

He was a modest youngster who liked to be told when he had done something well, but he had more than a touch of the conjuror's reluctance to reveal the magic of his tricks. Now he spread his hands, pulled down the corners of his mouth and shrugged.

'Come on, Piccolo — I'd like to see. Show me.'

'If the *Commandante* insists,' he said. 'But we must go to the cellar which is very dirty.'

'Lead the way. The dirt won't matter.'

There was a minor honeycomb of cellars under the house, most of them full to overflowing with an odd assortment of stores. Threading his way through to the corner of one of the rooms, he now pointed to a black metal cover on the wall. To me it looked like an ordinary junction box which, indeed, it was until he took the cover off. Then there were obviously more wires than usual crammed into the space. One cable in particular was odd in that it went from the box, out through the small ventilating window high up in the wall. To this Piccolo now pointed.

'That's all, *Commandante*,' he said.

'But where does it go to?'

'Outside, *Commandante*.'

'I can see that. But where to after that?'

He pulled a face and shut the box, to lead me in silence out into the garden, round the house to the little window we had just seen from the inside. Sure enough, there was the cable coming up from the cellar to crawl across a path and into a clump of bushes. Continuing on to the garden wall we could see the cable coming out of the bushes and thence up to and right over the wall. As far as possible it had been concealed in its final leap.

'And from here where does it go?' I asked.

Piccolo stood on tiptoe, and pointed to a house standing remote from its neighbours some distance away.

'Into the cellar of that house, *Commandante*.'

'Do the people who live there know about this?'

'No, *Commandante*.'

'But,' I protested with visions of civil actions from our neighbours, 'they'll soon find out, surely. They'll see the cable leading into their cellar.'

'I have buried it all the way.'

'Is it safe?'

'If their fuses are good, yes, *Commandante*.'

'You don't think we should offer those people over there in that house some form of reciprocal arrangement when their lights go out?'

Momentarily he was horrified, and then he laughed.

'No, *Commandante*, I don't.'

'Who are they? D'you know?'

'It is the house of a very rich banker, *Commandante*.' Leaning towards me in a confidential manner he added scornfully, 'A collaborator.'

'A collaborator?' I asked. 'With whom did he, or does he still collaborate? On whose side is he, or was he?'

Piccolo threw up both hands. '*Commandante*, I don't know. They just told me he was a collaborator and that was enough.'

'And who were "they" who told you?'

'Oh, Johnstone and Downes, *Commandante*. They said they knew.'

They would.

* * *

A little under a fortnight after our expedition to Gorgona Island, Colonel Livermore returned to the charge in a telephone call.

'Say, Commander,' he said, 'you remember that little lady you were so sweet on?'

'You mean,' I replied, 'the one you were so unkind to in refusing to go to her rescue?'

'I guess we both mean the same girl. Now, however, I think we really do have to go to her assistance.'

'Oh? Has she died?'

'Not so far as I'm aware. There wouldn't be much we could assist her with if she had died, now would there?'

'We could always bury her.'

'I hope that won't be necessary, Commander.'

'So do I, Colonel. Very much indeed. I can't wait to introduce her to you. Was that all you rang me about?'

'No, not quite. I wonder if we could have a word about something which has just come up?'

An hour later we met in the office of SOIS's Staff Officer (Intelligence), a young Lieutenant RNVR, by name, Paddy Davies. In a short space of time he had earned a reputation for the concise accuracy, and sometimes eccentric manner, of his briefing, supported on both counts by a sound knowledge of naval and air intelligence of the area. His style was his own.

Once I remember a senior Commander RN with a formal, not to say stuffy, approach being briefed by Paddy concerning a certain stretch of enemy coastline which the Commander intended to reconnoitre with his specially trained team, for the purpose of gathering further information useful in case of future landing. As fast as Paddy produced information the Commander plied him with more questions, many of them pertinent, some not at all. At last all possibilities appeared exhausted and the Commander was about to leave when he had another sudden thought. Pointing to an area remote from the original, he said, 'And what about here? What are the known defences at this point?'

Paddy leaned down close to the Commander's finger on the chart, then he looked up, contriving a suitably grave expression. 'Sir,' he said, '*that* place — well — sir, have you ever seen down the inside of an 88 mm at close range? I mean all that sophisticated barrel lining which they have developed in the last year or so?'

Torn between suspicion about just where he was being led, and the fear of missing some fascinating tit-bit the Commander offered an uncertain 'No'.

'Well, sir,' Paddy's polite confidential air was at its best, 'if you go to that place you will be looking down the barrels of sixteen of them. Very close indeed.' He made a slight pause before adding with professional solemnity, 'Could be interesting, sir.'

There were no further questions.

Now sitting in that same office I listened while Colonel Livermore explained to Paddy and me that his signallers had lost contact with their team on Gorgona. It had happened with no warning of trouble, causing them to feel anxious that there might have been a German raid on the island in which all the Americans we had left there might have been killed or captured. The Colonel asked Paddy if he could throw any light on the situation. Had there been any known enemy activity in the area within the past week? Consulting a file of signals in front of him Paddy shook his head slowly. 'H'm. Nothing here.' Continuing to read he reached across the desk to press a buzzer. 'I'll get Alice to bring in the most recent batch.'

Alice was an ATS girl who acted as his secretary. There were no WRNS in Bastia. Fair-haired, blue-eyed, and generously built, Alice was — as Paddy loved to remark — 'always willing'. Whenever he said

93

it Alice never failed to blush. As if through second sight she came in carrying a sheaf of signals in one hand and her notebook in the other. Seeing us sitting there she volunteered a smile in our general direction and handed the papers to Paddy who started to glance through them quickly.

'Still nothing,' he said, 'No, nothing here at all.' Putting the last signal on top of the pile he looked up. 'I'm not trying to be too optimistic, Colonel, but I'm fairly confident that we should have heard something if there had been trouble in the area. I say 'fairly' because one can never be certain. The Germans don't tell us much, after all. Looks rather as though you might have rather a pleasant run up there in one of ACF's luxury speed boats.'

'That is exactly what I was hoping to hear,' replied Livermore. 'If we get no further word in the next 24 hours, the Commander, here, and I will go right on up there. He has a girl-friend waiting for him.'

In fact when it came to it the Colonel opted to remain behind in Bastia: in his place he sent four American officers and a quantity of wireless equipment. With me came a fairly recently arrived addition to the pool of ops officers, a young sub-lieutenant, RNVR — Ranald Boyle — almost straight from Eton. A Scot, he had a fund of amusing stories about his countrymen and was to prove himself imperturbable in moments of difficulty.

Because there had been no further news from Gorgona before we left Bastia it had to be assumed that there might have been some untoward incident on the island: for this reason we were obliged to go through the same tedious silent approach, using the auxiliaries for the final hour and a half run in. None of us believed anything was wrong but that didn't mean we could take risks.

There was no moon and we arrived a couple of hundred yards from the harbour entrance at 23.00. This time when I pulled into the mouth of the tiny harbour, it was to be hailed from the jetty in good round American terms by one of the officers left behind from the previous operation. He told me that he and his little band of brothers had been expecting us for some nights — ever since their transmitter had burnt out.

Ten minutes later the MAS entered harbour and started to discharge passengers and stores while we listened to the local gossip. It seemed that the Gorgonians had been very friendly, at times almost embarrassingly so, to the Americans; for some reason, not immediately apparent, they 'had it in' for the governor and wished to see the back of him as soon as possible; a wish echoed in an anguished plea from the governor himself. If, he explained, the Germans or the Italians came to know that he had stayed on when the Americans took over, the inference would be that he had changed sides, and he would then be in mortal danger should the Germans plan a raid. Furthermore, he added, his wife was ill and needed medical attention — as if one could forget.

To get the governor on board the MAS was easy; he simply couldn't get there quick enough, abandoning both his children and his ailing wife in his haste. The lady, herself, was another matter altogether. Her bulk, quite apart from the appalling state of her nerves and general health made her a most unwieldy cargo to shunt around. Eventually, to the accompaniment of much moaning and groaning from the lady, and shouts of advice and encouragement from helping hands and bystanders alike she was shoehorned down into the wheelhouse to join her wretched husband. Meanwhile Ginger was filled with consternation, remembering all too vividly the aftermath of transporting the Italian garrison on the previous trip. Alas, his worst fears were fully realized, and noisily, too. In an endeavour to lessen the havoc in his boat Ginger drove us all home at breakneck speed, the roar of the main engine exhausts effectively drowning any wails or complaints from the passengers in the wheelhouse.

To everyone's satisfaction, on our return to Bastia the governor was removed with commendable speed by the Colonel's men who then set about a rigorous interrogation, ending with a long term of internment for both husband and wife. When, at last, the governor found himself safe from German retaliation behind the protection of American barbed wire he spent the remainder of his internment making a damn nuisance of himself to anyone willing to listen, and to quite a few who weren't.

Chapter 5

CHRISTMAS DINNER AND THE FIRST OPERATION TO FRANCE

As mentioned earlier one of the official orders which we did our best to observe was the embargo on barter between members of the flotilla, officers or ratings, and the local civilian population. Unlike our American friends, we didn't really have much to offer, other than cigarettes and a small supply of sweets, but the practice, if allowed to continue led quickly from the personal to commercial enterprise, and that was where real trouble began. So, no barter. This didn't mean that the occasional personal exchange of a packet of fags for a bottle of wine, if discovered, was immediate cause for court-martial, but anything more was at least frowned upon.

Today that may seem a pretty pedantic outlook, especially in war-time when there is a natural tendency to abandon the niceties of living in favour of the practical; but hard experience proved the wisdom of the principle, time and again. It came, therefore, as a pleasant surprise when Petty Officer Bates formed up to me a couple of weeks before Christmas, with a request that I might help in finding a turkey for the ship's company dinner on Christmas Day. If no turkey were available, any other feathered friend would do. What I should have done was to invite Maria, our endlessly resourceful cook, to use her talents. Instead, I volunteered personally to do what I could.

By lucky chance Captain Dickinson had invited me to accompany him on a visit to a Corsican family some twenty miles up in the hills to the south-west of Bastia. The opportunity seemed heaven-sent; with a little tact, money, and luck I should be able to supply the answer to Bates' request.

Three days later SOIS and I set out after an early breakfast. It was one of those soft pearly mornings, ideal for driving up through the pine-clad mountains. Rose pink columns of jagged rock towered up to

Above A group of MAS boats showing their graceful lines.

Below *MAS 532* — sunk 30 April 1943 in 'Narrows' by air attack (*IWM*).

Bottom Camouflage adopted experimentally by *MAS 558* (*IWM*).

Above Bastia harbour in 1944 (*IWM*).

Below Bastia Harbour 1943/44.

Bottom Damage to part of the harbour installations after the German withdrawal in 1943 (*IWM*)

Above Further German destruction in port installations in 1943.

Below Bastia, Old Port, British MTBs 1943.

Bottom More enemy damage to Bastia in 1943 (*IWM*).

Left Captain F. A. Slocum, CMG, OBE Royal Navy (*IWM*).

Bottom left Lieutenant D. N. (Paddy) Davies, RNVR, Staff Officer (Intelligence)

Bottom right Paddy Davies today.

the delicate blue of the sky before reaching down to bury themselves in the foundation of dark green conifers through which the road twisted and turned upwards. Here and there, as if to round out the whole picture-postcard effect, patches of snow obscured the rock face while the yellow of a tall poplar stood out in sharp colour contrast to accentuate the massive green of the pine forest. The atmosphere could scarcely have been more peaceful. War seemed a long way off.

To add to the other-worldly effect the 'road' over the last five miles of our journey frequently dissolved into no more than cart tracks, making it difficult to know which one to choose. We were now travelling through more open but still mountainous country with broad stretches of grassland to vary the scene. Herds of sheep and goats could be both seen and heard by their bells as they grazed on the higher pastures. It was, indeed, from one of the shepherds that we learned the route over the final mile to the farm.

Our hostess, Anne-Marie, we had met previously at a drinks party given by one of the local dignitaries in Bastia. From the moment she met him she thought SOIS was pure bliss. Lots of girls did. But he was a cautious man: that, I reckoned, accounted in large measure for my presence on this occasion. Anne-Marie was fair, medium height with a good figure, and aged about 25. At that first meeting, she had appeared extremely chic, wearing *rue de la Paix* clothes as only French women know how. And she was *very* pretty. Her conversation was both quick and lively, and, gifted with a natural *joie de vivre*, she laughed a lot. A comfortable sophistication completed the array of talent.

Now, as we drew up in the courtyard of the farmhouse she appeared on the balcony running round the inside of the rectangular building. This was another Anne-Marie. Gone was all trace of finery and chic clothes. In their place she was dressed from headscarf to thick, coarse-wool stockings and clod-hoppers, in unrelieved black, everyday peasant dress. Taken completely by surprise, for one unnerving moment I thought, perhaps, there might have been some tragic event in her family. Then she smiled and we were all shaking hands.

'Don't look so horrified,' she exclaimed. 'Up here, at the farm, I have to dress like this. It is our home, and we all dress the same. Mama does and so do my sisters, when they are here. It is the custom. We would be considered very immoral if we wore our Paris clothes.' She looked from one of us to the other and smiled a big welcome. 'I am so glad you could come. You have no idea how lonely it becomes up here, all by myself.'

'You have no one here at all, I mean to look after you?' the Captain might have been talking to his own daughter, he was so shocked.

'Oh, I have the men's wives; they care for me while the men are supposed to tend the sheep.' She laughed. 'But you can see how lazy the men are; they just gossip all day. Seldom do I have anyone to talk to, except about farming.'

We wandered round on a tour of inspection. It wasn't a farm at all in the English sense, consisting of a building enclosing three sides of a square, the fourth being open for the passage of animals, humans, carts, and vans. There were no tractors. Anne-Marie occupied a relatively modest section of the premises. As in a number of other Mediterranean farming districts all the farm workers, men and women alike, were dressed in unrelieved black woollen garments — the same as Anne-Marie; only some of the children wore coloured clothes.

In moving round the countryside one of the more curious features was the number of derelict or near-derelict houses to be found, some of them in improbable places, others right beside the main road. There seemed no reason for them. When I asked Anne-Marie about them she shrugged as if the answer were obvious.

'The general explanation is really quite simple', she said. 'When a building starts to show its age, or perhaps it needs some major repair, this is treated as sufficient reason to abandon the old in favour of building one or more new houses. If there is any further use for the old one it is used for storage. It's the custom.'

Although it might have seemed wasteful to us it was clearly logical to those who lived in a country with so much spare land.

Lunch was ample, if not a feast, with generous quantities of lamb — quite delicious, too — as the main course. The wine was of the region and not as rough as might have been feared. Time passed all too quickly in an atmosphere which, but for our uniforms, was completely divorced from the war. Indeed, the conversation was concerned with pre-war times, people, and places, so that it was only at the last minute that I remembered to ask about the possibility of obtaining a goose or turkey for the sailors from one of our hostess's tenants. Anne-Marie was immediately desolated; poultry was the one thing she could not offer although she gave the names of two farms near Bastia where she was sure they raised chickens and turkeys. It was a start. Reluctantly, we left, SOIS twinkling at Anne-Marie, and she at him. It had been a very happy day.

Reality was all too quickly restored on returning to Bastia where a signal had arrived summoning me to Algiers for the monthly operational conference.

The next morning I cadged a lift off the ever-obliging American Air Force who were flying a poor demented Staff Sergeant down to Algiers for medical treatment. He arrived at the aerodrome in a straight-jacket, in the charge of a doctor, a calm young man who advised me to take no notice of his patient; advice which was not so easy to follow when the patient developed other ideas. For some reason the British naval uniform seemed to intrigue him, and he demanded my attention from the moment we boarded the Dakota.

Shortly after take-off he invited me urgently to look down at the water beneath us as we headed south along the east coast of the island. Evidently I didn't do so with enough enthusiasm because he soon started to shout, 'Commander, water. Look at the water. Look at it.' This went on for some time and there seemed no way of stopping it when, without warning, we hit some form of air disturbance with a large hole in the middle of it. The result was impressive. The Sergeant on his stretcher was catapulted into the air while the doctor and I clung to the metal benches running down each side of the aircraft.

The 'drop' — for that is what it felt like — seemed a long one at a smartish pace before we fetched up in some normal air when the Sergeant came down to hit the floor with a resounding thwack. The pilot must also have been awed by the experience because he came aft shortly afterwards to apologise — although how he could have been expected to avoid the invisible he did not explain.

I had hoped that the incident might end the Sergeant's obsession with water and the British uniform, but not so. After a further half hour of shouting, even the doctor's nerves began to fray. Fishing in his bag of tricks he produced an instrument like a horse-syringe which he filled to capacity with some liquid. Then, with a reassuring smile in my direction, he held up the fingers of his free hand, 'Five minutes — maybe less,' he said, and stabbed the needle into the Sergeant, pressing the plunger to its full extent. About sixty seconds later the patient was using the last of his conscious energy in a final shout of 'Water'. Then peace reigned. The doctor smiled again; and so did I.

The business in Algiers took rather longer than usual and I could not get back to Bastia until three days before Christmas. The morning after my return I met Petty Officer Bates in the garden of the villa.

'I was wondering, sir, if you'd been able to do anything about a turkey for the Mess.'

A turkey. My God, I had forgotten all about it, in the press of travel and conferences of the past few days, and immediately confessed as much to Bates. He smiled sadly.

'It's all right, sir. We'll manage with rations and what we've already got,' he said.

I thought for a moment. I had let them down and something had to be done.

'I'm terribly sorry, Bates. There's only one thing I can suggest, and that is, that you chaps should have a go at seeing what you can find for yourselves. Time is so short.'

He brightened visibly.

'I think we might manage something, sir.'

'Good. But there is one condition.'

'Sir?'

'That whatever is found shall be paid for, and I will pay you back. That must be clearly understood.'

'Aye, aye, sir. Thank you very much.'

Later I told Prof what I had done. His reaction, as usual, was entirely practical.

'You were quite right of course,' he said, 'and I think the result may be quite entertaining.' And then, smiling malevolently, he added, 'If you don't mind court-martial.'

'Well, Prof,' I replied, 'if it comes to that, now that I've told you, you can attend alongside me in the dock.'

Christmas morning came, and with it the traditional invitation to call on the Petty Officers' and Seamens' Mess (the two were rolled into one) at midday. As Prof and I walked down the hill at five minutes to noon he started to snigger.

'What's so funny, Prof?'

'I was just wondering,' he replied, 'what today is going to cost you. I hope you're feeling rich.'

Petty Officer Bates was at the door to welcome us with a 'Happy Christmas', and I was relieved to see he was beaming with every sign of being a very cheerful man. As we walked into the Mess Prof's eyes were darting round on a tour of inspection; then he nudged me and hissed in my ear, 'It's going to be *expensive* — Sir! Look how they're all grinning.'

For the next half hour an amazing variety of drinks was offered to us; we drank them down as slowly as we dared. At one point I managed to get Bates on one side.

'Tell me about the Christmas dinner, Bates.' There was a rich smell of roasting fowl of some sort floating round the room.

'Fine, sir. Couldn't be better. Thanks very much.'

'What did you manage to get?'

'Like to have a look, sir?'

'Is that wise, Bates?'

He was still smiling. 'Oh, I think it'll be all right, sir.'

In the kitchen were three chickens and one good sized turkey roasting in the ovens, and a mass of spuds and other vegetables cooking on the stove.

I could only congratulate him. 'Well done, Bates. You seem fixed up pretty well, and I'm very glad.'

'Thank you, sir.'

'You let me know tomorrow how much —

'Nothing, sir.' In an embarassed little gesture he waved me to silence before adding, 'Didn't cost us a penny, sir.' Seeing my continual astonishment he smiled his confidence. 'Promise, sir.'

'But how — ?' I asked, alarm beginning to take over.

He gave me a long searching look. 'Well, sir, Downes is a country lad, as I expect you know. He managed it, you might say.' There was a slight pause before he confided, 'There won't be any backlash, sir.' And there wasn't.

* * *

Shortly after Christmas orders came for us to carry out our first operation to France, a welcome change in the routine of operating on to the Italian coastline and the peripheral islands.

The increased distance posed a new problem; instead of the usual run of between thirty and a hundred miles from Bastia to the pinpoint we were having to stretch this to 150 miles — a round trip of 300 miles in a single 'night'. To accomplish such distances meant two things: shipping extra fuel tanks in the form of big plastic mattress-like bags, and lightening the vessel as much as possible by cutting down on crew members. Ginger and I agreed easily enough on just how this was to be arranged; when he was fighting on the side of the Axis, MAS boats had often had to use extra fuel tanks. He didn't like having to do it, it made the whole boat more vulnerable, but that had to be accepted.

On the morning of the operation a signal arrived from London giving the exact pinpoint where one parcel containing money was to be swapped for another parcel containing information and documents, the recipient and giver at the other end being a member of a resistance organization who would expect us between 02.00 and 02.30. The general location of the pinpoint was not far from Cavaliere, well inside the waters between the French mainland and the Iles d'Hyeres. On plotting the pinpoint precisely on a large scale chart it was immediately evident that the position given in this latest signal did not correspond, by some 1,000 yards, with that given in the original orders from London. An operational top priority signal was whizzed off pointing out the discrepancy, and asking for clarification. This was by no means the first time such a thing had happened. The resisters in the field normally used map co-ordinates while we used latitude and longitude. While in theory there should be no difference, in practice there often was. The business of reconciling the two was seldom easy owing to the hazards of communication between the 'field' and the headquarters in London. It was always essential to remember that the average resister was liable to arrest at any minute unless he kept himself mobile, ready to move at any time, and quickly. This applied particularly to wireless operators.

Ginger and I made arrangements to sail at 18.00, leaving ourselves a margin sufficient to take things steadily at a 'low' cruising speed thereby conserving fuel, and, we hoped, giving us a more comfortable ride. These turned out to be but pious hopes, not plans, a frustrating but fairly common occurrence.

At that time there was an acute shortage of petrol in the island owing to tankers being sunk, the increase with every day of the war, in operational requirements, so that road transport was hard put to cope with the many demands made upon it. For this reason we, in the flotilla, had taken to using the three-tonner as a form of tank-wagon to refuel the boats.

When Ranald Boyle, Petty Officer Bates and I got down to the boat at 17.30 it was to find a distracted Ginger pacing up and down the deck, twirling his helmet in his hand. As soon as he saw us his arms began moving in circles of dismay while he bemoaned the non-arrival of the fuel which had been ordered: it was, he said, now so late that the operation would have to be postponed.

This was something which simply could not be allowed to happen. At the appointed hour of 02.00 next morning a resister was going to take the considerable risk of trying to reach the pinpoint unobserved to collect funds which would allow his 'réseau' to continue functioning. He must not be let down.

Ranald, accompanied by Bates, raced back to the villa with an urgent message to Prof to find out what had gone wrong. Not only had we to refuel the normal tanks but also the extra plastic containers which through their awkward shape and pliability took time to fill. The situation didn't look promising.

In much quicker time than expected Ranald returned to report that the three-tonner had fractured its back axle: Piccolo was working frantically to replace it, and Prof sent the promising message that he thought the lorry would be alongside within twenty minutes. It seemed hard to believe that anything could save the day in spite of Prof's optimism.

Almost to the minute his word was justified although the fuelling did not actually start until the moment when we should have been slipping for sea. We all worked flat out for the next fifty minutes, cans being filled and emptied, pumps thrusting near to bursting point, and the extra tanks gradually inflating into their final clumsy shapes.

While we had these monsters on board no smoking was allowed in any part of the vessel.

At 19.00, an hour late, we sailed. As Ginger donned his helmet I turned to him, 'We'll have to cut the usual procedure. Get her on to mains as soon as you can.'

Even after the weeks of work together he was still apt to take such remarks literally. Now he gave me a sharp glance of enquiry. 'You mean, *Commandante*, we go on mains immediately? Full speed? From the start? We make a big wash, and maybe —' he stood sideways on the bridge, his eyebrows raised, pointing at the boats lying ahead and astern of us — 'maybe break the other boats?'

In spite of the seriousness of the moment it was impossible not to smile. There was no doubt he was ready to give the order.

'No, no, Ginger. Not immediately. We *don't* break the other boats. We go past them on auxiliaries, as always. I mean *after* that. We've got to go a bit if we're to make up lost time.'

Fastening the strap of his green helmet under his chin he nodded with a brief smile of relief, and ordered the auxiliaries to full ahead; he took the boat wide of the jetty and on reaching the end swung sharply towards the harbour entrance, at the same time switching over from auxiliaries to mains. Our normal exit looked pretty tame by comparison with the way in which we shot out this time. We increased quickly to let the boat skim comfortably over a glassy sea at 30 knots on our way to Cap Corse, the northernmost tip of the island. By the time we turned the corner, altering course from approximately due north to due west towards the pinpoint the engines had used up a sufficient weight of fuel to allow an increase of speed to 35 knots; this we maintained for the next three and a half hours. The swell was just enough to make the plastic fuel tanks wallow awkwardly on the deck as they became emptier: occasionally this would cause the whole boat to lurch off course to one side or the other, a tendency which diminished as we progressed, until finally we rode easily, the then empty tanks being rolled up and stowed amidships.

Protection against wind and weather on the bridge of *MAS 541* had been reduced to a minimum, partly to cut down the silhouette and partly to give an all-round clear field of vision with no possible 'blind' spots. After three and a half hours of driving at that speed we were thankful to shut down the mains in exchange for the gentle breeze created by the altogether humbler auxiliaries.

The coast we were then approaching was new ground of which we had no previous experience. Such intelligence as we possessed suggested that enemy patrols both at sea and on land would be German (as compared with the Italian coast where both Italians and Germans operated). Some recent reports indicated that German vigilance in the area had increased in recent weeks, but it was a hell of a long coastline to watch over effectively, with more and heavier demands being made by the High Command for additional troops to be sent north against the threat of certain Allied invasion. As far as the French were concerned the tide of war had changed sufficiently to make it unlikely that their navy would have much inclination to help either side — if, indeed, they had any operational craft available. That was not to say that French land security forces would turn a blind eye to our 'reception committee' of that night. For their own safety all resisters were obliged to treat their own police as hostile at that time, apart, of course, from the individual policeman or gendarme known to be sympathetic.

At the end of two laboured hours of approach at 6 knots we sighted land: if anything, we were a little early having more than made up for lost time. It was only just after midnight. To identify our landfall was not easy owing to the formation of heavy ground mist to obscure long sections of coastline: when eventually we succeeded, we were about a mile too far south, with still another hour's run in to the pinpoint. As we steamed up the gulf formed by the Iles d'Hyeres to port and Cap Camarat to starboard the sea settled down to a glassy calm in which the noise of the auxiliaries became, to us, sitting right on top of them, far too loud for peace of mind. It was not a new experience; it happened always on such nights, and we never got used to it.

Nearing the pinpoint we reduced to 3 knots while Bates and I prepared the rubber dinghy for the final leg inshore. In such patchy visibility distances were difficult to judge with any accuracy; rather than err on going in too close where we would be heard if not seen from the shore we stopped the ship at what I estimated to be about 750 yards from the beach, and there last minute instructions were confirmed. Ginger would keep the engines ticking over while we were away. Ranald was to keep a careful check on the time; if the dinghy were not back at the MAS by 04.30, or he could not actually see her returning, he was to give the order to return to Bastia — and go.

Pulling inshore Bates and I were glad of the exercise; the night may have been fine, it was also chilly. It wasn't long before I realized my guess of 750 yards was badly adrift — it could well have been double that distance, making us arrive at the pinpoint exactly ten minutes late at 02.10. Even so, we should have seen at least one signal by then. We were, of course, looking at the first of two possible pinpoints, waiting about 100 yards from the shoreline. There was no signal. At the end of twenty minutes we decided to try the other pinpoint about 1000 yards to the east. As we paddled along parallel to the beach we were caught in the headlights of a car on the road, as it came towards us. For a second or two it seemed as if we might have been seen but it was only the result of the road being at right-angles to the beach. The car passed going quite slowly.

At the second pinpoint we waited for a further full twenty minutes, approaching to within a cricket pitch of the beach. Still nothing. Perhaps neither of them was right. Perhaps there had been a mistake. Quietly we moved further east into the next bay. Only the occasional car hurrying along the coast road broke the silence of the night. (A small crumb of comfort was provided by the fact that we could no longer hear the whine of the MAS auxiliaries.) Something had gone wrong but we could not afford to be at fault for lack of effort. We returned once more to the first pinpoint, and waited tucked in close to the jetty where the 'reception party' was supposed to be. In the dark the vague forms of shoreside villas could just be made out, but not a glimmer was to be seen.

Without warning a searchlight blazed out from somewhere just above our heads, its beam focused in the direction of the MAS boat. Three times the light came on in a prolonged flash before it was extinguished finally. It made me jump a bit.

'Could you see the boat, Bates?'

'No, sir, nothing.' Such was his temperament that he paused before adding, 'I wonder why they did that, sir? Funny they didn't keep it on. Didn't seem able to make up their minds, perhaps.'

The time was creeping by at a disturbing rate. It was 4 o'clock already. At 04.10 we gave it best. There wasn't all that much time left before the MAS would, if Ranald obeyed his instructions, push off back to Bastia. We headed the dinghy out towards her and started pulling hard. We hadn't gone more than a few yards when a light appeared in one of the villas beside the jetty. We stopped. The light went out, and nothing further happened. We were becoming pushed for time and pulled briskly away from the beach in the general direction of the MAS: visibility was still poor in patches. During his long wait Ranald had had time to realize that my earlier guess at the distance between boat and shore was much underestimated; as the time drew near when he had orders to leave he took the sensible and, as it turned out, very fortunate decision to move in to try to meet us. He could hardly have judged it better. Our hopes of finding him before the deadline of 04.30 were fading fast when suddenly there was the MAS bearing down on us. Five minutes later we were on our way home, disappointed and still worried at the failure to make contact with the resisters, and wondering what had gone awry.

The sky was already beginning to lighten after only an hour's run on auxiliaries: we were closer than usual to the coast to go over to main engines, but that couldn't be helped. We could do without the attention of enemy air patrols. At 35 knots we ploughed our way homewards until at 08.40 we were once more off Cap Corse. Ginger was about to make the final alteration of course to the south when he spotted what appeared to be a fishing boat some two miles offshore on our port hand. By gesture he queried our next move. I nodded towards the fishing vessel. Anyone fishing, or pretending to fish in such a good observation spot was worth investigating. Who could say that the enemy were not trying to play the same game as us?

Only a superficial glance was needed to reassure us that the boat was, indeed, what she purported to be; a mound of nets and a very fair catch of still lively fish were strewn around the deck. However, the unusual engine-room orders had brought the chief engineer up from below to see what was going on; in no time at all he was doing a brisk trade with the fishermen who were delighted at the instant business; they wouldn't even have to land their catch. When we got under way again we had enough fish to feed the entire crew for a couple of days. A minute or so later I thought some of the gilt had been taken off the gingerbread when one of the main engines flatly refused to start. But the captain wasn't in the least put out. 'We'll return on one engine,' he said lightly. As soon as Capo Pulchri, the chief engineer, had gone below, he turned to me and touched the helmet still on his head before giving a shy smile. 'My helmet, *Commandante* — if one of the engines had failed six hours ago where would we be now? As it is we have some fine fish as well as good luck.'

* * *

For a week or more I had trouble with my hard-won Fiat 1100. She was reluctant to start in the morning and when eventually she did so there was no life in the motor; on the hill up to the villa from the harbour I had to change down to second and crawl up. Piccolo had taken first this bit, and then that, to bits; he filed, he cleaned, he burnished, and he cursed but there was no improvement. After yet another morning of fruitless endeavour he came to me with a face as long as a boot.

'Eh, *Commandante*, she is tired. She is tired and soon she will die altogether. There is no means to make her go again as she used to.' He shrugged in desperation, his fingers spread wide. 'I have no spares. She is finished.'

'Can you get any spares from Corte?'

When he had some embryonic plan in mind, about which he hadn't quite made up his mind, either he would hunch his shoulders a little, keep his arms close to his sides, and spread his palms wide, or — a more positive sign — he would shoot out his lower jaw and push his head forward, eyebrows raised. Now it was the jaw movement. 'Better to have a new engine, *Commandante.*'

'Of course. I quite agree. Let us, by all means have a new engine. But from where?'

His expression became blank. '*Commandante,* there is one —'

'Where?'

'In the town.'

'Who has it?'

'It's in a garage. A private garage.'

'Are you intending to steal it?'

He looked shocked. 'No, *Commandante,* not to steal it. I just know where it is, that's all. I have been looking round. It is the only one. Maybe they'll want £50. Maybe more.'

'Out of the question. We couldn't possibly afford that.'

The car was not on our official establishment, and any repairs would have to come out of our own pocket.

'I know, *Commandante.* That is what is troubling me.' The problem was clearly causing him a lot of personal agony.

'Well, Piccolo, we shall never find out unless you ask, so why don't you nip off down there and see what you can do?'

'*Va bene, Commandante.*' Glad to be shot of such a tiresome conversation he turned on his heel, a suspicion of a smile indicating that he had already worked out some form of answer. How far Messrs Downes and Johnstone featured in it would only be revealed by time. Later in the day I did see him briefly when he was stubbornly non-committal. The owner was away, he said, and he wasn't prepared to deal with underlings. He would try again next day.

Over the following few days there was too much going on to worry about the car beyond fretting at its miserable performance each time I used it. Somewhere in the background I guessed that Piccolo was not being idle in furthering the cause of the new engine; it was best to leave him alone to get on with it.

Coming out of the house after breakfast a morning or so later I looked for the car to go down to the Base, but could see only one of the PUs in the drive: of the car there was no sign. Perhaps Piccolo was out testing it again. I was about to get into the PU when the Fiat swung in through the gates, Piccolo at the wheel. He hadn't seen me. Pulling up sharply enough to make the gravel fly he got out, slammed the door and then, standing hands on hips he started to curse. What he said I have no idea, but whatever it was wasn't strong enough to express what he felt. With a quick lunge forward he opened the bonnet and spat in the engine — twice — before slamming it shut again to stand glaring hostility at the whole car. He hadn't moved when I walked up behind him.

'Any news about the other engine?' I asked.

He spun round and looked embarrassed. 'Eh, *Commandante*, this car —' He flapped an accusing hand at the offending vehicle. 'And they want £60 — for the new engine.' In his anger he spoke through clenched teeth. '£60! *Commandante*. It is a scandal.'

'Could I, perhaps, be of some help in bargaining?'

For some reason the very idea sent him into headlong retreat. 'Oh, no *Commandante*. No thank you very much.' He reflected a little before adding, 'If I may have the morning off, please.'

He was so upset at what he regarded as his own failure, poor Piccolo. I told him to take off whatever time he needed.

'The car will be all right to take down to the Base, *Commandante*, but please may I have it back again this afternoon? At two o'clock.'

There was nothing further to be done although from his last remark he appeared to have some plan in the hatching.

The remainder of the forenoon I spent with Tom trying out a new lightweight wooden dinghy fitted with a specially silenced $1\frac{1}{4}$ hp Stuart Turner petrol engine which we hoped would make our inshore work easier in the coming months. The boat was, in fact, all that we could have wished, proving surprisingly fast and manoeuvrable for its diminutive size, and, more important still, a good little seaboat.

We returned to the villa late for lunch but in high good humour. As we ate Prof came in and sat down next to me.

'I gather,' he said, 'that Piccolo had quite a bit of a row with your car this morning.'

'Yes, he did. It was spectacular while it lasted. I didn't know he could get into such a rage.'

'Did he tell you he would like to have another go this afternoon? He hopes you won't mind using one of the PUs for the next two or three hours.'

'Yes, he told me he'd like the car at two, but what I can't fathom is why he thinks he'll have any more success this afternoon than he did this morning. However, it's up to him.'

In the office a pile of work was waiting to be dealt with, and for the next hour or so I just got on with it. Small though we were as a unit there was always more administration than seemed reasonable, despite Prof's invaluable contribution.

Taking a break I lit a cigarette and wandered over to the window to look down on the harbour where the sun's rays were reflected in the water, the boats, British, Canadian, American and Italian, bobbing gently alongside the jetties. What a place it must have been before the war; what a place it might be to come to after the war — once all the débris had been cleared away. Perhaps a short stroll in the garden might be pleasant before resuming work: on exiting into the garden through the french windows, however, I was met by an astonishing sight.

In the middle of the drive was the Fiat with all its doors open and the bonnet completely removed. That was all right. The rest was very strange. From the space where the engine should have been Piccolo's head and shoulders were protruding vertically, and he was holding both arms above his head. Above him, standing straddled with one foot on each mudguard was the cook, Maria, holding one end of a stout wooden pole, the other end of which was resting on the roof of the car; slung, by chains, between the two ends of the pole was the engine (a new one, I hoped) which Maria was lowering slowly down to Piccolo's waiting hands. Bizarre as was the sight it was certainly matched by the conversation.

'More right, Maria. More still. Now lower. Come on. Now further back. Lower. No, no, you've got it wrong. Up again. Can't you see? Now down. Down. Too far. Up!'

Undoubtedly heavy though the strain was, Maria still managed to giggle.

'Eh, Piccolo, you are a monster. D'you think I can hold this thing for ever while you look up my skirts? Lucky I am wearing some drawers.'

'Maria! Look what you are doing. I do not care about your drawers. Now lower the engine — straight. Straight, I said. Don't wobble. So. Good. Down. Hold a second. Good, now I've got it. Go on lowering gently.'

Maria was sweating as Piccolo gradually sank out of sight, guiding the engine skilfully on to its bed. Finally from ground level he called to her to let go. It was safe for me to let them know I was there. Maria was so surprised she almost fell off the car.

'Eh, Commandant, you make me jump,' she gasped and giggled again. 'You see, I have become a mechanic.'

'Strong woman, more like, but well done.' More softly I added, 'I'm glad about the drawers.'

Her hand flew to her mouth, 'Commandant, you heard, then?'

'Not really, Maria. Come on, I'll give you a hand down.'

I took her extended hand and she jumped down beside me. The ground shook as she landed: she was a well-built lady. From beneath the car Piccolo shouted.

'Come on, Maria, what have you done with all those bolts I gave you?'

'On the front seat,' she replied. 'Now I must get the Commandant some tea.'

Red in the face from embarrassment and still letting go the occasional giggle she disappeared into the villa.

From the side of the car, looking down into the engine I could just see the strain on Piccolo's upturned, sweating face as he lined up the engine on its seating. He was, as usual, smothered in grease and grime, although now mixed with the strain was an element of dour triumph.

I tapped the top of the engine. 'New?'

'New, *Commandante*.' He even managed a smile.

'How much?'

'One pound,' he replied, starting to wriggle out from under the car. When he got to his feet I gave him a close look to see that he wasn't just pulling my leg.

'One pound, did you say?'

He nodded. 'Yes. One pound, *Commandante*.'

'But that's ridiculous, Piccolo. You said they wanted sixty when I asked you before.'

'So they did, *Commandante*.'

Whenever he found himself in difficulties, especially if others might be involved, he confined his remarks to the minimum; an old head on young shoulders.

'Well, why only one pound now?'

'We had to *buy* it, *Commandante*.'

'So I understand, but why for only one pound?'

'The *Commandante* will know that it is not allowed to requisition from a civilian without official permission. The rules say so.'

'What are you talking about, Piccolo?'

'We do not requisition the engine *Commandante*. We buy it. For one pound. We have a receipt. It is very easy, and very legal.'

He was at his most taciturn as he fished around in the depths of his overall pockets.

'Here, *Commandante*,' he said, proffering an oily piece of paper, 'is the receipt.'

And so it was, exactly what he claimed, a receipt for £1 in payment for one 1100 cc Fiat engine. The signature was an illegible scribble but the name of a local garage was printed on the heading. The easiest course would have been to leave well alone, to accept the situation and be grateful, but while I was reading the receipt Piccolo volunteered another piece of information.

'If we go to the French authorities, *Commandante*, to requisition, this will take too long, and who knows, *Commandante*? — perhaps they also would like the engine, and so we never get it.'

There was much wisdom in what he said. Was there perhaps too much? Could it all be his?

'Quite right, Piccolo, You've done well. But tell me, how did you come to know all these rules about requisitioning?'

He looked round for some avenue of escape, and finding none subjected his shoes to an intense study, wiggling his toes round inside the bursting seams.

'Eh, *Commandante*,' he breathed, 'we had to have the engine.'

'Yes, indeed, we had to have it, but that doesn't tell me *why* you got it so cheap.'

He took a deep breath and rushed his next words. 'The owner was frightened, *Commandante*.'

'Frightened? Why? What of?'

He fixed me with a stare, defying contradiction. '*Commandante*, he was a collaborator.'

'Oh.'

From somewhere a thought occurred while we took time for reflection.

'He couldn't, I suppose, be the same as the one from whom you sometimes steal our electricity?'

'No, *Commandante*. Another one.'

'I see. And how did he like the pound you gave him?'

Up to then Piccolo had been careful: now a look of relief spread over his whole being. He knew he was on much safer ground, and he laughed happily. 'He liked it very much, *Commandante*. He said "thank you".'

'Just one more thing, Piccolo. Who went with you to buy the engine? Who provided the pound?'

Once more he became very serious. 'Johnstone, *Commandante*. He knows about collaborators. He made sure we got it cheap, too. It is a good engine. Quite new.'

And, as he said, very legal. The receipt proved it.

★　★　★

We were given almost no notice to make a fresh attempt at reaching the resistance group in France. They were in a bad way and needed help urgently. It caught us on the hop. Those MAS boats not undergoing maintenance repairs were all scheduled for operations that night; not one could be made available. Only one hope remained: an appeal to our faithful American standby, Lieutenant-Commander Barnes. As always, he offered immediate co-operation by calling in one of his best PT boat Captains, Lieutenant Steele, a young officer with a lot of experience behind him. The three of us went over a plan of action there and then.

Returning to the villa I told Petty Officer Bates what was afoot, and that we would take the new wooden dinghy instead of the usual inflatable one. Apart from wishing to prove the efficiency of the new dinghy in practice (we had done enough trials with the boat to be satisfied with its performance in most types of weather) we had the problem of overcoming the noise factor when using a PT boat. Whereas the auxiliary motors of the MAS boats made a loud whine on still nights, the PT boats had no auxiliary motors, relying, instead, on the heavy muffling of the underwater exhausts of the powerful Packard engines. In calm weather this form of silencing worked well; the Americans could lie-to confident that they could not be heard except at very close range. In even a slight swell, however, things were very different. With the rolling of the boat the exhausts were brought above the waterline to make a noise like a couple of giant bulldogs fighting under water, and they could be heard at an uncomfortably long range.

Our wooden dinghy should provide the answer to noise. We could leave the PT boat much further from the beach while motoring inshore without a sound, using the tiny Stuart-Turner. In the unlikely event of an engine breakdown we knew from experience that we could pull the rigid hull of the wooden dinghy faster than the inflatable.

The Met report was far from brilliant when we sailed at 19.00, but this was nothing unusual as it was compiled by the flying boys and many miles from our operational area. With the ability of the PT boat to make the final approach to the pinpoint at more than twice the speed of the MAS boat auxiliary engines, we were able to sail an hour later than on our last attempt.

The standard of comfort of Lieutenant Steele's boat was, indeed, luxurious by comparison with that offered by the much smaller MAS boat (no adverse reflection on the latter): spacious flats (accommodation) below for both men and officers, proper electric cooking facilities, good heating arrangements, all made for a comfortable ride in a boat about 12 ft longer than its Italian counterpart.

Bates and I loaded the dinghy amidships and lashed it down securely to prevent any movement en route. Leaving harbour we wedged ourselves into snug positions at the back of the bridge where we could enjoy the unaccustomed treat of being passengers for the next hour — until we reached Cap Corse — where we would be altering course out to the west.

Having made the turn Steele and I went below into the charthouse to make last minute checks on our course and timing so as to arrive at the pinpoint at 02.00 next morning. I was pleased that despite the short notice and lack of craft we had been able to meet this particular commitment: without knowing the full facts it appeared that the group at the other end were in considerable difficulties and needed all the help they could get.

Coming up on deck some twenty minutes later it was noticeable that the boat was moving quite a bit and throwing up heavy bursts of spray from the west-sou'-westerly wind and sea. Although the ride may have been easier than if we had had to take the weather bow-on, ten minutes later an inspection of the dinghy showed at least a foot of water slopping about in her. While we were baling her out the spray continued to come over us in sudden deluges. We made a search for some form of tarpaulin or other cover but none was available, our only hope lay in the weather easing up as we progressed. I blamed myself for failing to foresee this hazard from the moment when we had first received the boat. It was a problem which had never worried us with the inflatables which were carried normally upside down until the moment of launching. You cannot turn a motor dinghy over without up-ending the petrol tank, too, an unpopular move in any circumstances, especially at sea.

Steele was pushing the PT boat along at a steady 25 knots into weather which, far from abating, was throwing up heavier spray and giving ever greater movement to the whole boat. Again Bates and I went aft to bale out the dinghy: this time where was even more water in her, and it was clear that we should never be able to start the engine when we got to the other end: but no matter, this certainly would not preclude us from pulling ashore in her. Indeed, if the wind maintained its direction it would carry our engine noise away from the beach to allow us to make a closer approach.

Unhappily over the next hour there was such a deterioration in the weather conditions that Steele asked if we should continue. As the current jargon had it — was our journey really necessary? It was necessary, all right, but there would be no hope whatever of arriving anywhere near on time, if at all. We had already had to ease to 20 knots, and further speed cuts seemed inevitable.

By 22.30 wind and sea had reached force 5 to 6 and were still increasing. There was nothing for it but to abandon the operation and hope that the reception committee would realize the impossibility of operating in such conditions in sufficient time not to risk their necks by going down to the pinpoint to start flashing their torch signals out to an empty sea. That was the main hazard of such operations — once the taxi had left the garage there was no means of communication between the taxi and the intended fare until and unless the fare was picked up.

By the time we arrived back in Bastia at ten to three next morning there was a full gale blowing which lasted for the next 36 hours. A whole month had to go by before we could try yet again.

★ ★ ★

At the beginning of 1944 Bastia, in common with an increasing number of theatres of war, had become thoroughly cosmopolitan as far as the Allies were concerned. British, Canadian, American, Free French, and Italian forces jostled each other in a friendly (and sometimes not so friendly) effort against the common enemy. Such a minestrone of nations, each with its proliferation of authorities and personalities, required a single strong hand to keep firm control and give clear but tactful direction.

This brief account of those days would be incomplete without recognition of the gratitude we all owed to the one man who succeeded so well in the role of keeping that essential control. SOIS, 'Dicko', 'Sir', 'Master', 'Uncle Richard' (much later), Captain Norman Vincent Dickinson — by whatever name he was, or became known — I never heard anyone express anything but fulsome appreciation of the fact that he was there in charge of us all.

That said, what of the man himself? In this narrative there are a good few anecdotes in which he features large but the one which made me laugh the most is worth telling, I think. Beneath an exterior which, wholly unintentionally, could be on the forbidding side there was a receptive mind. Not always, let it be said: time wasters were never welcome unless he wished to gossip, and he could, on occasion, 'let his hair down' quite a long way.

Just after breakfast one morning the telephone rang in the office which was, fortunately, adjacent to the dining-room. Swallowing the last of my coffee I answered. The voice at the other end was crisp.

'SOIS speaking.'

'Sir.'

'I've got some Frogs who say they want to see me. Can you come up in half an hour and interpret.' This was an order, not a question. 'I've no idea what they want. You'll have to find out.'

'Aye, aye, sir. Half an hour —'

'Yes. 'bye.'

A typical SOIS telephone conversation.

When I reported to him he was sitting crouched behind his desk, gently rubbing his hands together in concentration as he went through the overnight signals. He glanced up to see who had come into the room, said nothing, and went on with his reading. A minute or so later he looked up, and gave me a wintery smile.

'Sit down, and have a cigarette,' he said, pushing a box towards me across the desk. 'The Frogs should be here in a few minutes.' Once more he went back to his reading, while I sat silent, smoking. There was a knock on the door which he seemed to ignore. The chap on the other side knew the form, evidently, for, after a ten second interval he came in. It was Charles Buist, the young Lieutenant Staff Officer (Operations), a very able and likeable chap.

'The French are here, sir.'

SOIS shuffled all his papers on one side, and heaved a sigh. 'Right. Show them in one minute.' Charles disappeared and SOIS turned to me.

'I don't know who these chaps are but I think they are some sort of commando lot who want to get up to some skulduggery. Right up your street, I should think. Anyway, if you'll interpret we'll soon find out.' There was a second hesitation before he added, 'Incidentally, I have a slight hangover. That chap Tufty Forbes makes a most nauseating and dangerous cocktail. He made me drink four in a row last night.' ('Tufty' Forbes was one of the British MTB Captains.)

There was a further knock on the door. SOIS 'Dicko' looked up as if expecting the door to open: when it didn't he glared, and drove his clenched fist into the open palm of the other hand — an extension, perhaps, of the usual palm-rubbing needed for concentration. Seldom had I seen him look so unhappy.

'Come in.'

When the door opened a truly remarkable vision stepped into the room. A Capitaine de frégate of the French Navy in his ordinary monkey-jacket is striking enough, but the one who now stood just inside the doorway was scarcely credible. In addition to the usual uniform, he was wearing white, brilliant white, spats reaching just below the knee, aiguillettes on one shoulder, a sword-belt round a coat which was not designed to carry it, a pair of immaculate white gloves, and a sword — a serious looking affair more like a rich man's heavy-duty cutlass, really.

SOIS was struck completely dumb: he tried to say something but words failed him as the gallant Commandant gave one of those remarkable French salutes. Raising his arm forward in a wide arc as though about to present a 'Heil Hitler!' he appeared to change his mind at the last split second, bending his elbow to bring his open palm to temple level, and hold it there for so long that SOIS moved to rise from his chair to give an answering salute. At that moment the Commandant brought his arm down to his side smartly, to stand to attention.

'*Mes respects, Commandant! Capitaine de Frégate Vieux-Martin.*'

'My God!' SOIS spoke quietly. 'What he's just done simply isn't possible. Who the hell is he?' His shoulders were hunched as though against a gale of wind.

'He's a *Capitaine de frégate* — a Commander to us — and his name is Vieux-Martin.'

'Well, please ask him never to do that again. I can't stand it.'

Horror still showed on his face as he shot his first direct remark to the Frenchman; it was, in fact, just such as he used to any of us on his staff, the sort we had come to accept as a term of friendship. Boring away, fist into palm, he stared straight at the Commandant.

'Well, you toad, and what do *you* want?'

For a fraction of a second the Frenchman flinched; in that same instant the appalling thought whisked through my mind that he had understood. Then he beamed a smile of enormous charm, made a little formal bow, and repeated his opening phrase —

'*Mes respects, Commandant.*'

It was the smiles that did it.

Captain Dickinson rose to his feet, came round the desk, and held out his hand in greeting; he, too, was now smiling. The contrast against his former glowering expression was so marked that the Frenchman was caught a bit off balance. As they shook hands SOIS took the Commandant's elbow and escorted him to a chair; passing close in front of me he whispered, 'He didn't understand, did he?'

I shook my head.

As he sat down the Frenchman removed his cap to reveal a pate as bald as a bladder of lard. Carefully he disposed of the fearsome sword, laying it close beside him as if he might need it any second. SOIS turned to me, 'Now ask him to what do I owe the honour of this visit? But first apologize to him that I cannot match the splendour of his rig. Also tell him that, bizarre as it may seem to him, I left my sword at home when we went to war.'

The Frenchman enjoyed the English humour. 'Please tell your Captain that I have never killed anyone with my sword but that I am glad to have brought it with me so that I may call upon him with proper honours due to him.'

The initial shock over and the niceties exchanged, it was apparent that they were beginning to like one another especially when Vieux-Martin explained the real purpose of his call. His plan was to conduct a series of bold raids against the enemy coast, using his not inconsiderable commando unit of Moroccan troops. Very alarming they were, too, when they weren't being seasick, as I was to find out on practice runs. They were so damn difficult to see in the dark, and they knew that.

Subsequently Vieux-Martin (that was not his real name; he belonged to a well-known aristocratic family most of whom had to stay in Occupied France) — subsequently he proved himself a very courageous fighter who, like so many of his kind, was to be killed in action some four months later. His first meeting with SOIS remains unforgettable.

Chapter 6

OPERATIONS FOR THE OSS

The local head of OSS, Colonel Livermore, he of the Gorgona operation, rang me up on New Year's Day to ask if he might 'drop by' for a chat. This approach was the normal style adopted by those with either something unpalatable to say, or some hairbrain scheme to unfold. The Colonel's attitude when he arrived was so obtuse that it wasn't clear which it was to be. He hedged about, metaphorically shifting from one buttock to the other while he made up his mind. Eventually he got round to it.

'Commander, I haven't come here to talk just platitudes — 'he paused for a good look to see that I was still listening '— but I find myself in a difficulty...'

It looked like the unpalatable.

I was wrong. For some time his organisation had been in communication with a more than ordinarily powerful group of Italian resisters. Radio contact was, however, irregular and difficult, and, what was worrying him most, lately they had admitted that they might have to get out of the country, or at least go to ground indefinitely if enemy counter-espionage got much closer to them: they were already very close.

There was nothing out of the ordinary about this type of situation, it was happening all the time throughout enemy-occupied territory. Now, however, the Colonel had received an urgent *cri de coeur* in the form of a message from the group asking for a boat to be sent to pick them up that very night from a beach just south of Orbitello. To add to the problem the signal had been couched in such terms as to give grounds for suspecting the group might already be under enemy control. In these circumstances the Colonel had doubts about the wisdom of risking a boat. He was seeking my advice. Really there wasn't much that one could offer, but I agreed to send a boat if he was prepared to take the chance. Forewarned, in such a situation, is forearmed, and I was grateful that he had been so frank.

Further discussion only served to reveal rather more about the group than I cared to learn, but it seemed to ease his mind. We tried to make it a practice among the ops staff not to know more than was absolutely necessary for good communications between boats' crews and passengers. The one thing we sought to avoid was any indication of the identity of our passengers. In the event of capture we couldn't give away what we didn't know. During our conversation, although he avoided revealing all the names of the group the Colonel mentioned one — the son of one of the most important figures on the Italian political scene at that time — and from that one name his serious concern became understandable. He was, indeed, on the horns of an uncomfortable dilemma. In exchange for these confidences I could only repeat that we were ready to have a go at the operation.

While we had been talking the Colonel had, apparently, been doing some hard thinking. With a polite smile he rose, picked up his cap and moved towards the door. With his hand on the door handle he said he would make one more attempt to get in touch by radio with the group in the hope of obtaining more evidence on which to base an assessment of the situation 'in the field' (at the other end). He would call me.

Late in the afternoon he rang to say that he had no further news, and, therefore, we could stand down for that night.

Somewhere about teatime next day one of the Colonel's young officers turned up at the villa to report that a new signal had now been received from the group. If anything this one was more worrying than the first. They claimed to be in greater danger than ever and must be lifted out the country without delay. By itself that was just the sort of information to expect as the preliminary move in setting a trap for us. But they had said more, and whatever that was apparently provided the Colonel with enough reassurance for him to warrant sending a boat that night. There would be between eight and ten people to bring off the beach. That meant two dinghies.

While I was beginning to consider which boat to use the young officer told me that, in view of the importance of the operation which involved some well-known Italian personalities, the Colonel had, off his own bat, approached Barnes for the loan of a PT boat. It wasn't that he didn't have confidence in the performance of the MAS boats — more often than not they were more reliable than the PTs — but he feared that one of those to be embarked might be recognized by a member of a MAS crew. It made sense.

In their last signal the group had given map co-ordinates of the pin-

119

point from where they wished to be picked up. A quick check against an Admiralty chart showed plenty of open water with the pinpoint about two-thirds of the way along a sandy beach several miles long. There didn't appear to be any easily recognisable landmarks, the countryside in that particular area being flat for some distance inland; the hills in the background were too far away to be of much use, navigationally. On the ordnance map roads seemed few and far between, indicating that the group were hiding in some nearby farmhouse, if they were there at all.

Lieutenant-Commander Barnes chose one of his best captains, Lieutenant Boebel in *PT 214* for the operation. Together he and I discussed the drill for the evening, setting the time of sailing shortly after 20.00. Meanwhile, up at the villa, Petty Officer Bates was warned that he would be coming with me, and that he should prepare two dinghies, and draw the usual weapons.

During a last-minute conference on board *PT 214* just before sailing, OSS stated that there had been no further news from the group, but that they had made closer study of the last messages and had concluded that, on balance, they rang true. We were advised, however, to exercise more than the normal caution. (An odd sort of warning when you came to think of it, rather as if we weren't always on the look-out for trouble in enemy territory.) The password consisted of my asking the first member of the group I might see, in Italian, 'What is your name?' The answer should be, 'Giuseppe.'

It was just after 20.15 when we sailed on one of those perfect Mediterranean nights, with no wind and not a ripple on the water, all very much to be desired in peacetime against a romantic setting, but we preferred to have rather less idyllic conditions, a little offshore wind from the pinpoint and some modest waves to beat out a swish on the beach to drown the noise of our approach. But you can't have everything.

On the way I explained to Bates that the organizers were not a hundred per cent sure of the sort of reception we should get; in no circumstances, however, was he to become aggressive unless given the word, or fired upon first.

'And how many did you say there are, sir?'

'There should be ten.'

For a moment he weighed up the information.

'Shouldn't be difficult, sir. Both guns are loaded, and there's several spare clips.'

Bates seldom displayed emotion, but there seemed, at that moment, a slight hint of hope in his voice that there would be a bit of a fracas at the other end. On more than one occasion there had been signs that he, in common almost certainly with the Heavenly Twins, believed that our role as taxi-drivers of the anonymous wasn't aggressive enough.

PT 214 rumbled steadily along at 25 knots for the next four and three-quarter hours, causing one to reflect again on the sheer idiocy and waste of war — not just the one we were fighting. Any war. The heavens shone and twinkled in all their brilliance, as the boat's wake drew an elegant phosphorescent line across the black satin sheen of the ocean. Civilization really hadn't advanced very far ...

At 01.00 the Island of Giannutri was about five miles off on our port beam to warn us that we were within twelve miles of our destination: it was time to reduce to 15 knots. Contrary to what we had believed the closer we approached the pinpoint the more useful became the silhouette of the mountains in the background. It was an exceptionally clear night enabling us to fix our position accurately over the last two or three miles of our approach at a speed further reduced to 7 knots.

Plumb on time, from exactly where we expected, a pale blue bright light flashed out one long and one short, twice, in our direction. A good signal, but was it a good sign? The next twenty minutes would tell.

The ship was stopped some 200 yards from the shore line. While waiting for the repeat signal Bates and I lowered the dinghies into the water. Again came the bright blue flashes, and we climbed into one dinghy, towing the other one. Bates sat in the stern with a tommy-gun across his knees, giving me the occasional correction of course. When we were within 40 yards of the shore the light flashed on, straight at us, and stayed on until I swung the dinghy round and waved vigorously for it to be extinguished. In the welcome darkness Bates brought the tommy-gun to the ready, holding it close to his side.

'What do they think they're playing at?' he muttered. 'Trying to tell the whole countryside we're here?'

'Get the other dinghy alongside,' I replied. 'We'll separate now, and go in, in line abreast. Keep about 20 yards between us.'

With a quick snatch he brought the other boat up to us, jumped into it, and was pulling away, all in one continuous movement. As he went he called, 'Tommy-gun's at your feet, sir.'

'Thanks. We'll go in stern first over the last twenty yards.'

'Aye aye, sir.' He was already paddling gently in, one eye on me, the other on the beach.

Twenty yards or so out I swung the dinghy round to go in stern first; if there was to be trouble better to face it than get it in the back. Obliquely I saw Bates do the same. Seconds later we ran into surf; it wasn't big but it was unexpected. I stopped paddling and with an oar sounded for depth. We had about four feet of water under us, and about 15 yards to go to the beach. A rubber dinghy is light enough to be awkward to handle in surf, and so, grabbing the painter I jumped into the water. Bates did the same and together we waded towards the knot of people we could now see standing huddled together ten yards up the sandy beach. When the water was knee-deep we stopped, tommy-guns in hand.

'What is your name?' I called in Italian.

There was no answer. I called again. Waiting for the reply I sensed rather than saw Bates edging over towards me, while the seconds ticked by.

'Shall I let 'em have it, sir?' whispered Bates.

'No, wait.'

A third time, very loudly now, I challenged.

It must have been a further two seconds before a voice, full of uncertainty, called 'Giuseppe.'

Wading the final few yards to dry land we dragged the dinghies clear of the water, and I walked towards the group who had made no move since we first saw them. I was still clutching the gun, just in case.

A figure detached itself and approached.

'English?' it asked, in Italian.

'Yes, English,' I replied.

This let loose a babel of voices, all speaking at once, with one, louder than the others, repeating over and over again, 'Compli*ment*... compli*ment*... Compli*ment*...'

Closer to they were countable. There were six, all told. Bates, still unconvinced, always wary, stood waiting. I turned to him. His tommy-gun was covering the group all the time.

'You take three, and I'll take three.'

'Aye, aye, sir.'

To the resisters as a whole I said, 'All right. Let's go.'

With a rush they surged forward down the sloping sand to launch themselves bodily into the grounded dinghies, four into one, and two into the other. I swear I heard the noise of Bates sucking his teeth.

'All right,' I said with more patience then I felt, 'now you can all get out again.'

Even in the dark their gestures of astonishment were clear.

'But — but *why* — ?'

Poor chaps, clustered tightly together in their anxiety to be off, they looked a sorry bunch sitting there high and dry, waiting for some miracle to transport the rubber boats into the sea. They needed some persuasion.

Clumsily they stumbled to their feet and climbed clear so that we could get the boats back in the water; there we divided the passengers into two groups of three and led them like trusting sheep until they were wet up to their knees; then we let them scramble inboard. To push the dinghies, now heavily laden, back out through the surf was not easy, and Bates and I found we were up to our chests before we could get back inboard again. By that time the passengers had disposed themselves 'comfortably', two sitting on the thwart from which the boat had to be rowed, and one in the bows. Shoving and grunting in the dark they were finally re-seated so that I could start pulling out to the waiting PT boat. On the way, the large bulky figure seated in the stern almost right facing me, leaned forward and gripped me firmly by the shoulder.

'Compli*ment*, *Capitaine*, compli*ment*!' He was smiling broadly, and repeated the phrase every few seconds to make sure that his appreciation was not forgotten. It didn't make pulling any the easier even if it made him glow with delight, which was the apparent effect.

We had been away from the beach about two minutes when I became aware of the smell of a heavy, and I judged not very expensive scent; mixed up with it somehow was an equally heavy layer of rum. The combination was quite objectionable. Behind me, from what seemed the direction of the smell a voice suddenly burst into song. Loudly, too, and in impeccable English.

'Yo, ho, ho, and a bottle of rum — Jesus Christ — oh, Jesus, we're off — we really are — OFF.' There was a lot more in similar vein, accompanied by what felt like a good deal of arm-waving, from the same source. Whoever it was, was demonstrably drunk. When we were well out I turned briefly to ask him, 'And who the hell are you?'

He *was* waving an arm, and on the end was a real bottle of rum. 'Me?' he asked. 'Me, I'm only a bloody Wop.' He was lying back against the side of the dinghy, Recamier-fashion, swigging from time to time. 'Only a bloody Wop Lieutenant-Commander who was educated at one of your better public schools. Cheltenham. You know it? Eh? Pissed. That's what I am. Pissed as an owl.'

My *vis-avis* was leaning forward once more towards me. 'Compli*ment*, *Capitaine*, compli*ment*,' he intoned, doing his best I suspected to discount the old Cheltonian performance. The sooner I got this lot on board the PT boat, the better. I wondered how Bates was getting on with his passengers.

The American sailors were adept in hauling the passengers up from the dinghies; once on board they picked themselves up to crowd together round the bridge while the rubber boats were brought inboard and stowed. Lieutenant Boebel, the Captain, asked me, courteously, if that was all. I replied that I hoped so, and he then gave the order for slow ahead on both engines to allow us, for the next hour, to creep discreetly away into the darkness...

The passengers were sent below, and given a generous supply of steaming hot coffee while Bates was provided with dry clothes by the American sailors. After a quarter of an hour on the open bridge I realized I too was soaking wet and getting cold. At the same moment the Captain also saw my plight.

'Gee, Commander,' he said, 'you really are wet.' It was too cold to laugh at the colloquial meaning. 'Tell you what. If you go down to my cabin you'll find some pants in a drawer under the bunk. Should be some shirts there, too. You're welcome to help yourself. On the back of the door you'll find a spare bridge-coat. That belongs to Commander Barnes. And ask the boys to give you some coffee.'

No second invitation was necessary, and five minutes later I was feeling dry and warm in the Captain's trousers (a bit tight, but dry) and the Commander's bridge-coat, a splendid garment of very pliable oilskin, fleece-lined and with a beaver collar big enough to cover ears and the back of the head. The shirts really were too small. One of the sailors then came in with a cup of coffee and a message. 'One of the passengers is asking for you, Commander.'

I knew which one I hoped it was not. 'Where are they?'

'Right next door, in the next space.'

'Right. Thanks for the coffee. I'll go and see them.'

There they were, all six of 'em, sitting in a row, and all smiling — even the drunken Lieutenant-Commander, his bottle of rum now empty on the table in front of him. In the middle was a large red-faced man of about fifty. He had to be '*Compliment, Capitaine*' ' he couldn't be anyone else. To confirm it he rose and held out his hand.

'Compli*ment*, *Capitaine*, compli*ment*,' he beamed as we shook hands, and then he gestured for me to sit beside him. Excitement at the success of the operation, combined with relief at being out of danger needed some sort of safety valve for him to let off steam; he started, with accompanying dramatic hand movements to tell me about the work of his group. At the risk of appearing unappreciative, even rude, he had to be stopped. When I did so he was immediately crestfallen at such incuriosity, and after a brief pause for reassessment, he told me he was a General — a *Major*-General, he hastened to add, *not* a full General.

An interesting piece of information but it didn't get us far. I asked him if he had experienced much difficulty during the previous week whilst waiting to be taken off. Yes, he said, indeed he had. Here was something he really could talk about, no details of personalities were needed. He and his group had been under suspicion by the security authorities for some time: eventually things had got so bad that they decided that those known to be under the greatest suspicion should leave the country. This decision had been signalled to OSS, and had reached Colonel Livermore in Bastia a matter of hours later. Then their real difficulties had started: firstly, to reach the region of Orbitello from their base in Rome, a distance of about 100 miles, meant travelling through security zones on which checks were being made tighter every day. The group had moved in three separate pairs: if one pair got caught it was better than all of them being scooped up. On the way they had all been forced to take refuge several times with known sympathisers. It had taken a week for them all to be assembled in a farmhouse near the proposed pinpoint. At that moment communications with the Rome radio operator had been cut: it looked like disaster. One of the group had to return to Rome, somehow he would have to get an explanatory telegram off to OSS stressing the urgency of a boat to pick them all off. Meanwhile those waiting near the pinpoint could only wait: they could contact no-one to find out whether the courier had got through, whether a boat was coming, or whether the courier had been caught — to be tortured and give them all away. It was, as the General remarked with a hand outstretched as if about to catch a cricket-ball, a very tense situation.

To add to their burdens, the farmer in whose house they had hidden near the shore, had been the soul of hospitality and tact, but when night after night the group returned to his house after their vigil on the beach he began to express doubt about their organization, especially their ability to leave the area. He wanted them off his premises. As it was he was running a mortal risk which increased with every passing day. Our arrival was, therefore, cause for much greater relief than, at the time, any of them could express. Hence the lemming-like rush for the dinghies on the beach.

The explanation over, the General subjected me to another of his beaming smiles and a wave in the general direction of the other members of the group to show that they were included in what he had been saying. They beamed in chorus, although the Lieutenant-Commander, by this time, had his eyes closed.

'You know, General,' I said, 'you gave us quite a fright this evening when you didn't answer the challenge on the beach. I had to do it three times. My Petty Officer was all for shooting you.'

He laughed long and loud before putting his hand inside his coat and withdrawing a large and ancient automatic.

'And with this I nearly shot you, *Capitaine*.'

Oh? Why? What mistake did I make?'

'*Capitaine*, our courier had been gone a week, and there had been no boat. If the courier had been caught he would have given away our

125

whereabouts. The Germans might have said to themselves, 'Ho, ho, it is we who will send a boat to catch these gentlemen. All at once.' That would have been easy for them.'

'So you really weren't sure who I was?'

He nodded briskly. 'No, *Capitaine*, we were not sure.' He gave a small chuckle of embarrassment. 'We were very nervous. The first two times you challenged one of us thought you had a German accent, and we nearly fired. Only when you called loudly the third time did I know you were English. I said so to my group. You see my wife is English.'

And so she was, as I discovered years later. If he knew any English, himself, he never owned to it. We had quite a bit more to do with this group during the ensuing months, and what splendid people they were.

★ ★ ★

Through whose, or what influence we acquired our two ARBs has never been satisfactorily explained. All I know is that SOIS summoned me to his office one day, and that when I got there he was partly hidden behind a mound of signals on his desk. From the pile he extracted one to hold it aloft as though it smelt of fish which might have gone off.

'I don't know what you've been up to,' he said, 'but this thing here,' he waved the offending piece of paper about,' says that two ARBs are arriving to join your collection of funnies.'

'I haven't been up to anything, sir.'

'Well, that's not stopping the arrival of the ARBs. It says they should be here tomorrow.'

'Aye, aye, sir.' What the hell was an ARB? Let's try a feeler: 'We're a bit tight on accommodation at the moment, sir.'

He didn't even glance up. 'They'd better be put somewhere near their compatriots. Keep them happy.'

'Aye, aye, sir.'

By the way he spoke I knew bloody well that he knew that *I* didn't have a clue, and was waiting for me to ask him. I tried again. 'Any special orders for them, sir?'

This drew a look of laboured tolerance. 'Special orders? No. Why should there be? But you let me know what they're like when you've seen them.'

'Aye, aye, sir.'

He could be very ornery.

Back at the villa a little while later I sought out Prof thinking that he might know the answer to the riddle. If he didn't then, perhaps, I could pass on the problem as SOIS had done to me. A casual approach seemed best. 'By the way, Prof, we've got a couple of ARBs arriving sometime tomorrow. I shall be rather busy. D'you think you could look after them? See that they're properly accommodated and so on. SOIS suggests putting them somewhere near their compatriots. Seems a good idea.' I moved towards the door. 'Now I have to go out. An appointment with the Commandant du Port. See you later.'

But he was before me, his hand on the doorknob as though about to open it for me. He was also blocking my escape and became sickeningly deferential. 'Forgive my abysmal ignorance — sir — but what the hell is an ARB?'

'I haven't the slightest idea, Prof, but two of 'em will be here tomorrow morning, and I've got to see them and tell SOIS what they're like. Suppose you find out.' This time I made good my escape, but somehow the technique wasn't anything like as smooth and incisive as that meted out to me.

At dinner that evening we all tried — Prof, Tom, Ranald, the Colonel, and the others — but at the end of what became increasingly ribald guesses we were no nearer the answer. Next morning, just as I was about to get down to work the telephone rang on my desk, and I picked it up to hear just one word — 'Hello'. It was enough to know that the voice belonged to an American. After I said who I was, the caller, like all his countrymen, announced exactly who *he* was.

'Good morning, sir. This is *ARB 403* reporting arrival, sir. Lieutenant Pratt, American Air Corps.'

'Oh, good.' In spite of the details they didn't tell one much, but I tried to sound welcoming. 'We had a signal about you yesterday. Where are you now?'

'Down in the port, sir. Would you like me to report in person?'
'A very good idea, Lieutenant. If you tell me where you are I'll send a car to fetch you.'

As I put back the receiver Prof walked in and I asked him if he would go down in one of the PUs to collect this new guest. At first he thought I was pulling his leg, but I reassured him.

'Are you confident,' he ventured, 'that SOIS isn't pulling yours?'

'No, not absolutely, but we'd better fall for it if he is. We can't risk being rude to the Americans.'

Half an hour later the door of the office opened and Prof put his head round the edge. '*ARB 403*, sir,' he announced, as he ushered in a smartly dressed American Air Corps Lieutenant who came to a heel-clicking halt in front of the desk with one of those curious little salutes much in vogue amongst gangsters of the pre-war cinema. With a broad friendly smile he introduced himself once again.

'*ARB 403*, sir. Lieutenant Pratt, American Army Air Corps, reporting for duty.'

My hand was wrung in a vice-like grip.

'Welcome, Lieutenant. Do sit down. Have a cigarette.'

In the background Prof was ostentatiously preoccupied, avoiding
my quick glances of pleas for guidance. Time enough to settle with
him afterwards.

'I hope you had a good trip,' I continued.

'Oh, yes, sir. Fine thank you. No trouble at all.'

'And what about the other ARB? There are two of you, aren't
there?'

'Yes, indeed, sir. We arrived together.'

'Good. Tell me Lieutenant,' to illustrate what I meant I made a
small sweep with my arm, 'd'you know what we do in this outfit? Has
anyone told you?'

'Why, yes sir, I think I've a fair idea, but I sure would like to know
more.'

'And how d'you visualize fitting in with us?'

'Well, sir, I guess we can find some way to help.'

Across the room I looked hard at Prof who assumed one of his most
vacuous stares before changing his mind all at once and becoming the
efficient First Lieutenant. 'As a matter of fact, he said briskly, 'I think
these two Air Rescue Boats which Lieutenant Pratt has brought up
here from Casablanca *can* be of considerable help to us.'

Air Rescue Boats with the Air Corps in command — exactly com-
parable to our own Air Sea Rescue craft being run by the RAF. How
silly not to have spotted it. The Lieutenant was speaking, '.. I would
very much welcome if you would visit with us, sir, to inspect both
boats.' He hesitated fractionally before adding, 'We're proud of them.'

Now that we knew where we were — 'Of course Lieutenant,
nothing would please me more. How about some coffee? (thank God
to have remembered the American passion for coffee just in time) and
then we'll go straight down to the boats.'

They took some finding in the most unsalubrious part of the new
harbour; we would have to have them moved to a more comfortable
and convenient berth. Neither Lieutenant Pratt nor his fellow skipper,
Lieutenant Moritz, seemed in the least put out by their surroundings.
They were so obviously delighted to find that they now 'belonged' to
someone — someone, moreover, who looked like having a real job for
them to do.

The boats themselves made a strange impression. At first glance
they looked rather like unarmed MTBs which, having failed somehow to grow up had been converted into a stoutly built yacht — a

Right The author at the end of the war.

Below The author's identity card at the beginning of the war.

Page 2.

Page 3.

Navy Form S.1511

Surname WHINNEY

NAVAL
IDENTITY CARD No. 00418

Other Names PATRICK

Rank (at time of issue) LIEUTENANT R.N.V.R.

Ship (at time of issue) N.I.D.2. ADMIRALTY

Place of Birth BOLTON, LANCS.

Year of Birth 1912

Issued by

Signature of Beaver

Visible distinguishing marks

8.7.40

Left The real thing — Professor Peter Sylvester-Bradley of Leicester University not long before he died.

Bottom Left Lieutenant Knox Eldridge, USN, at the wheel of his boat.

Bottom Right Lieutenant Gene Clifford, USN (L) with his executive officer Lieutenant Mac Kennedy.

Above left Lieutenant Boebel, USN, and his 'exec', Lieutenant Wes Gallagher.

Above right Lieutenant Frank Pressley, USN (L) with 'exec' Lieutenant Lowell Palmer, USN.

Below Seated (L to R) Lieutenant Steele, Doug Maitland, Boebel, Knox Eldridge (full face) and Jack Torrance (sitting reversed in chair) with one unknown British officer.

Above Bastia Old Port, 1944.

Below Another view of Bastia Old Port in 1944.
Bottom Gene Clifford's *PT 204* after a collision off Bastia with German NR boats laying mines.

very nice sort of craft to own in peacetime, except for the fuel bill. In order to perform their designed function of picking up air crews who had had the misfortune to 'ditch' in the sea, the accommodation below decks consisted of a single saloon-cum-sickbay which occupied more than half the ship's length, and for comfort's sake, was sited amidships. It was a big space; it needed to be to receive the increasing size of the big bomber crews. At that moment it was not easy to see how these boats could be of much use to us, but the least we could do was to show appreciation of the fact that they had been offered in the first place.

Next, the crew had to be introduced rather than inspected: two engineers, two deckhands, and a Coxswain, plus the Captain. Although they could not have expected an immediate inspection of the boat, they were all dressed in immaculately clean clothes, and they seemed cheerful. Moving on to go round the craft itself, we started in the engine-room where again, all was the neatness of constant good maintenance, and it was plain that she was a happy ship; a pleasure to walk round. In the combined wheel-/charthouse the same conditions prevailed. It was also simple.

'What navigational aids do you have, Lieutenant?' There seemed to be precious few.

'Oh, just the usual, Commander. A compass and —' he looked a trifle embarrassed as he pointed to a wooden box stowed away in a corner behind some books, ' — we do have a sextant.' He smiled before adding, 'But I'm not too happy with that. Then there's the radio which you can see over there.'

'And you've come up all the way from Casablanca?'

'That's where we were.'

'With nothing more than the compass?'

'Sure, Commander, we just stayed in sight of land all the way.' He laughed. 'Except for the last bit, I guess, and we didn't think we could miss hitting either Sardinia or Corsica, coming from Bone.'

A practical optimist, and none the worse for that.

'You don't carry radar?'

'Well —' he gave me a searching look, as if weighing up his chances. 'Well, sort of, you could say.'

'What sort of?'

'Want to see?'

'Yes, certainly.'

'If you'll just step out through this doorway, I'll show you.'

Out on deck he put two fingers into his mouth and gave a piercing whistle. Almost immediately the hatch on the quarterdeck flew open and a small coffee-coloured head crowned with a GI forage cap shot up and looked towards us.

'You whistle, Cap'n?'

'Sure, Pete. Come on out and meet the Commander.'

From the hatch emerged a boy of about twelve years old, dressed in full GI's uniform. He was clearly an Arab.

With a proud flourish of his hand towards the boy the Lieutenant announced, 'This is our radar, Commander. A little unofficial, you might say — but Pete can see *and smell* things on the ocean long before any of us has any idea of what's coming up.'

'Good God,' was all I could say in astonishment. Hardly a sign of approval as far as the Lieutenant was concerned.

He continued to explain. 'He really has kept us out of trouble many times, Commander. We picked him up in Casablanca about three months ago. Since then we've clubbed together in the ship to provide enough money to give him a college education as soon as the war's over. He's that good.'

'Do your authorities know about him being on board?'

'Well — I guess I have to admit that officially they probably don't, but Pete is known to most of our fellows.' (In other words his group of ARBs.)

'Suppose the boy's killed in action, what then?'

'Oh, we've been into that. He has no family. That's how we took him on. He was all alone living on the waterfront. But we wouldn't let him come with us on any mission where there'd be any danger.'

There was nothing else to be said, temporarily at least; the Lieutenant and his crew seemed to have thought of everything, and the situation looked stable.

The next-door ARB commanded by Lieutenant Moritz was able to put on every bit as good a performance as the first one, bar, of course, the radar. While we were walking round the boat he confirmed all that Lieutenant Pratt had claimed about Pete the Radar. It was a conundrum.

A little later in the office I pondered. Here we were dealing with another nationality, two different nationalities, in fact. To consult the patient Barnes might provide additional complications in that the ARBs belonged to the Army Air Corps: interference by the US Navy might well create more problems than it solved. Leave well alone?

For once, Prof had no bright ideas, so the whole matter became pigeon-holed in the hope that inspiration might come to the rescue. Next morning it, or something like it, did.

Presenting myself at SOIS's office I asked Charles Buist, the young Staff Officer Operations (SOO), what sort of mood 'master' was in.

'Not too bad,' he replied. 'Why d'you ask? Have you got some hideous request?'

'Oh, no. On the contrary. He wanted to know about the ARBs. Now I can tell him.'

Charles smirked with amusement. 'So you've found out about them?'

I nodded. 'Now be a good chap, and tell him I'm here.'

Obligingly he went off, to return minutes later to say that SOIS was ready to see me. As usual at that time of day he was hunched, frowning, over the morning's crop of signals.

Without looking up he asked, 'And how are the ARBs?'

'Fine, sir. Good little boats for their purpose but a bit small and slow for our type of work: 28 knots maximum, and no proper silencing.'

He tilted his head up about 25 degrees to look at me. 'The trouble with you is you're never bloody well satisfied. I get you fast craft from the Italians, you borrow from the Americans, and now some simpleton in the Admiralty produces more for you and you're complaining. You're bloody well insatiable.'

I could only protest. 'I didn't ask for them, sir, as I said yesterday.'

'Ah, but yesterday you didn't even know what an ARB was, so how could you know that you hadn't asked for them? They might have been anything as far as you knew — Air Raid Boots, anything. You had no idea.'

'No, I hadn't, sir. But now I have.'

Having had his fun he flashed a smile; the leg-pulling was over.

'All right, now that you've seen 'em, what work d'you think you can give them since they're here?'

'I'm not quite sure, yet. As I said just now, they are a bit underweight, so to speak, for our sort of work. Except for one thing.'

'Oh? What's that?'

'The type of radar they carry.'

'Radar? But what the hell are they doing with radar? You said they are so small.'

The wise thing was to halt there and explain the joke. I don't know why I didn't.

'It must be useful for their ordinary work. Personally I think you ought to see it, sir.'

He gave me a searching stare. 'I'll send one of the staffies down. Tell Charles to go and have a look.'

'Would you mind, sir — ' here we go, off the deep end '— if I suggest that as these are American boats coming under your command they would appreciate a visit from you, personally?''

He hesitated, uncertain. Then he nodded.

'All right. I'll come. Call for me at 11.30 and you can drive me down.'

'Thanks very much, sir. I'll nip down and warn them.'

On my way I stopped at the villa to warn Prof of what was in the wind. I had to tell someone. He produced one of his most gigantic guffaws.

'Buckets of blood! I wouldn't miss this for anything. What time does the balloon go up?'

'Eleven-thirty.'

'Some balloon. I'll be there for the bang.'

That was rather what I was beginning to think, but it was too late now.

'Nonsense, Prof. Dicko can stand a leg-pull as well as anyone.'

'Well,' replied Prof smugly, 'you're certainly putting the theory to the test.'

I sent him off to warn the ARBs of the impending visit, and then, at 11.30 sharp I picked up SOIS from his office. On the journey down to the port he said nothing but when he saw where the boats were lying he looked round the area in disapproval. 'We must get them out of here. This is a dreadful spot. See if the PT boys can help. There should be room to fit them in somewhere with their fellow Americans.'

'I'll see Barnes about it, sir.'

When we drew up alongside both lieutenants were there to welcome SOIS with the smartest of their gangster salutes. Stepping out of the car SOIS was at his most charming, shaking hands with both young Captains before standing a moment or two to examine the boats from the jetty.

'Very smart,' he said.

In unison the Americans smiled and said, 'Thank you, sir.'

'Right,' said SOIS becoming businesslike, 'now let's have a look round.' With that he advanced towards Pratt's boat.

If anything, she was smarter and cleaner than the day before. SOIS was visibly impressed but I could see his eyes searching round the vessel for some signs of the radar. We fetched up in the wheelhouse with his curiosity still unsatisfied. The compass and the sextant were given only token attention before he turned to the Captain.

'I'm told you have a new type of radar. I'd like to see it. That is,' he added hastily, 'if it's not on the American secret list.'

Pratt's jaw dropped in surprise.

'New type of radar —? Secret, sir? — ' his face creased into a broad embarrassed smile. 'You *really* want to see it, sir?'

'Yes,' replied SOIS, his voice crisp, his previous doubts returning with a rush.

'Sir,' Pratt gestured with his hand towards the door, 'would you mind stepping outside a moment?'

Momentarily SOIS hesitated, and then we were out on deck. Pratt repeated his performance of the previous day. Almost before the whistle had died away Pete the Radar's head shot up through the hatch.

'God Almighty! What's that?' SOIS was staring in disbelief.

The Lieutenant was beaming with pleasure at what he interpreted as such a gratifying success, and then launched forth into the explanation about Pete the Radar that he had given me the day before. While he was talking SOIS turned round slowly to favour me with a long and baleful stare. When the Captain finally ran out of superlatives in his panegyric of Pete the Radar it seemed more than likely that SOIS would end his inspection without further ado. Not so, at all. With a courteous show of interest he asked to meet the boy. Pete the Radar's face was the picture of liveliness as he chatted away to the tall spare Englishman who wore so much gold lace. It was a big moment for him and he was going to make the most of it.

He was an engaging youngster; speaking with a strong American accent in better than pidgin English, he confirmed all that Pratt had said about him, often referring to his own happiness in being in the boat. His enthusiasm was infectious and I could see (with welcome relief) that, under this influence SOIS was cooling off. Matters seemed to be improving still further when I heard SOIS say that, much as he had enjoyed inspecting this boat, he would also like to see over Lieutenant Moritz's boat, lying alongside. However, such optimism was short-lived. As he turned to say good-bye to Pratt he pointed an accusing finger in my direction and said, 'Do you know what this loathsome toad told me before I came down here today? He said you had a unique type of radar. Well, you have, and I'm very glad to have been introduced to it.' He paused to stress his next point. 'But it is *not* to be used on operations. Please remember that.'

Pratt's eyebrows jumped at the 'loathsome toad' and he glanced anxiously at me.

'We never would, Captain, sir.'

Inspection of Lieutenant Moritz's boat did not take so long, being a repetition of what we had just seen. Again, as we were leaving SOIS shook the Captain's hand.

'Very smart,' he said. 'Congratulations. But tell me, how d'you manage without radar?' 'Well, sir, I guess we just follow the other boat.'

'Very wise.'

As we went ashore I caught sight of Prof half concealed behind a big lorry some twenty yards away on the jetty. Cautious not to be seen by

SOIS he held up an enquiring thumb. In reply, behind SOIS's back, I could only extend both hands, one thumb up and the other down. He wagged his head to and fro, raising his hands in mock prayer.

Silence reigned for the first two minutes of our drive up the hill from the harbour, each of us waiting for the other to speak. We must have been a little more than halfway home before he said,

'Well?' in a very flat tone of voice.

'Well, sir,' seemed the only appropriate reply.

'I ought to run you in.'

'On what charge, sir? What have I done wrong?'

'You know bloody well.'

'Yes, sir.'

A further minute's silence. Then he laughed.

'All right,' he said, 'but don't try it again. Now I'll give you a gin if you'll stop trying to break my neck. You drive too bloody fast.'

* * *

Paddy Davies's office staff consisted of two invaluable helpers: Alice, the generously built ATS girl, and Sergeant Arnold, who proved himself so capable as a constructor of silhouettes of land- and seascapes.

The first step in preparing any operation was to visit Paddy's office to obtain details of enemy coastal defences and patrols likely to be met in the area. Presentation of this information depended to some extent on how well Paddy knew you. To the newcomer he was always polite and precise — well, he was precise to everyone no matter how well he knew them — but to those of us who were used to him he would turn on the lighter side of briefing. As will be remembered when he was dealing with the rather pompous Commander and the 88 mm gun emplacements, the essential difference between the Commander and ourselves was that we knew he was being funny.

Sergeant Arnold, of serious, conscientious character, worked in an architect's office in peacetime, so I believe. It was marvellous training for the job he did in Paddy's office; from the technical point of view, that is. In all other ways he must have been a pretty puzzled man for some time after his arrival. It is hard to imagine that levity has much room in the architect's office, hilarity none. In Paddy's office neither were ever far away. The Sergeant must have wondered often during those early days just what sort of an office he had landed in; but for all his flippant exterior Paddy demanded the highest standard of technical work — the benefit of which discipline we, in the operational field, all enjoyed.

Working long hours the Sergeant patiently translated General Ordnance maps of French and Italian coastlines into such silhouettes as one would see on a clear dark night on approaching a beach. By memorizing these drawings it was possible to feel 'at home' when nearing the pinpoint. It is not possible to overvalue the work that he did towards making recognition of our whereabouts easier.

Years after the war, when my wife and I were going through yet another of our seemingly endless housemoves, I came across an ancient tin box with my father-in-law's name inscribed on the lid. Even in the midst of the general upheaval curiosity prompted me to have a look. Inside was a number of folios of varying sizes containing some exquisitely executed watercolours of ships, seascapes, harbours, and landscapes, all dating from the early nineteenth century, during the Napoleonic war, done by my wife's great-great-grandfather as a Captain in the Royal Navy whose duties included the patrolling of foreign coasts. His voyages took him far afield, even to America. Rummaging further, some simpler sketches came to light, drawings of coastlines only. When they were spread out on the floor there was an immediate feeling of familiarity — that same sensation of being 'at home' with the Sergeant's painfully built up silhouettes. I turned one over, and there, on the back in fine writing was the name of the place (bay, or cape, or district) and the date of each work. Many of them were of parts of coastline where we had operated during the war; so detailed and fine were they that it was easy to recognize pinpoints which we had used in several operations. The main difference between these silhouettes and those produced by the admirable Sergeant lay in the Sergeant's use of mathematical calculation and black and white architectural hatching against the Captain's sheer accuracy of vision shown in delicate colours.

What an astonishing and coincidental duplication of effort!

* * *

There came a day when, going in to gather such operational intelligence as he might have to offer, I found Paddy not to be quite his usual ebullient self: he seemed preoccupied, and communicative only to the point of providing the information needed; the customary quips and humour were noticeable only by their absence. Some problem — something out of the ordinary — would have been needed to bring on this mood of distraction. He said nothing about it until I was at the door, leaving, then he muttered, 'I wonder if you've got a moment to spare?'

Whatever it was he seemed deadly serious about it.

'Of course. What's wrong?'

'Oh nothing's actually wrong.' He fidgeted about with pencils and rulers on the desk. 'It's just so awkward. Frankly, I've never come across it before.'

'Can I help?'

'My dear chap, how kind of you to offer.' Picking up a packet of cigarettes he took one out and lit it, to inhale the smoke gravely, as if the future depended on it. 'You see Alice has been to me this morning in a high old state I can tell you.'

'Oh? Someone been making unwelcome advances?'

'Nothing so simple, I'm afraid. When you hear the trouble you may think it a pity that they haven't.'

By now he was getting into his stride.

'Suppose,' I suggested, 'you tell me what's wrong.'

'Can you bear it if I do?' He didn't wait. 'Well, about an hour ago Alice came bursting in here, looking pretty flustered she was, too. What she said was, "There aren't any. There really aren't. I mean I've been everywhere and I can't find any. None in the shops, or other places. Mr Davies there simply aren't any, and what am I going to do?" You can imagine how much all this conveyed to me, and the poor girl was almost in tears with frustration. Quite ghastly, my dear fellow.'

'Well, what was it all about? Did you discover?'

'Oh, in the end I did, but not before I told her to go and brew some tea, and then we could talk about what she couldn't find. Off she went. She was gone so long I thought she'd left the building. When she did come back she was still in a hell of a state, telling me all the places she'd tried, but I still didn't know what she was looking for. She went on to complain that the people here must be extraordinary as she couldn't even make them understand. She kept on with, "But there just aren't any." I got no more sense when I asked her, "Any what things aren't there any of?" Eventually — after a long time, mark you — I did manage to get a word in to say that if she didn't tell me what she was looking for I really couldn't help her to find whatever it was that was missing.' He took another deep draw on his cigarette. 'This seemed to hit some hitherto unstruck chord of reason, and she stopped talking altogether. For about a whole minute. Before that there seemed no end at all. Then she appeared to come to a pretty serious decision. Very slowly she said, "You know about women, don't you?" That surprised me, I can tell you. I mean if there's one thing I do know a bit about — in fact, quite a lot about — but I'll never know enough about — it's women. Nobody can know enough about those things. So I said to her, "Alice, the one thing I know about women is that you can never have

136

enough of them." I mean I was doing my best to put her at her ease, poor girl, but somehow that seemed to put her off, and we started all over again. When she got to the "things" bit I said, quite sharply really, "what things" — just like that — and she came out with it. "You said just now, Mr Davies, that you know about women." So I said, yes, and then she said, "Well women — you know — they're different from men — " So I said, "And a very good thing, too. Otherwise we'd all be in a terrible muddle." Then she said, "I mean every month, Mr Davies." My God, I got it then, but it was a damned close shave. Near as a toucher she'd have gone off again and she might still be at it. Think of that, my dear chap.'

'And what,' I asked, 'have you done about it?'

'Oh, that's all under control now. I've made an Immediate Operational signal to the queen AT in Algiers. D'you know there's an aircraft coming up here tomorrow morning which can bring tons of the "things". Isn't that lucky?' He stubbed out his cigarette and looked up with a smile. 'Wonderful girl, Alice.'

Chapter 7

CHANGES OF LUCK

Christmas and the New Year of 1944 saw a sharp increase in the demands of the cloak-and-dagger experts on our operational resources. Nothing succeeds like success, and once we had shown that our taxi service actually worked there was sometimes a scramble to hire our odd assortment of vehicles. Gratifying as this may have been to the operational personnel — at least they felt they were doing a useful job — the increased physical strain was a factor we had to treat seriously. Prof and I tried to work out a roster system in which no officer was on ops more than two nights consecutively. Shuffle around as we might, there were many occasions when we had to break the rule. (At one point I found myself doing five nights in a row as well as having to plan the next day's ops. It was a sure way of making what could be an expensive mistake. But God takes care of drunkards and fools so that in the event all was well although I slept for more than 24 hours after the final night.)

Experience also taught us that, as in gambling, any one of us could experience runs of good or bad luck. The latter could have a devastating effect on the morale of the individual, so much so that it took a deal of patience and care to restore real confidence and rekindle enthusiasm.

The new year wasn't very old when one of our number ran into this very trouble. Let us call him 'X' for he was a first-rate officer with a solid history of success behind him. One day he came into my office, and after some humming and ha-ing, suggested that he should apply for some other appointment. I knew that ops hadn't been going too well for him in the immediate past but hadn't realized he had clocked up so many recent failures. He was, he said, thoroughly depressed, and he looked it. We discussed the situation in detail when I tried to comfort him by assuring him that no blame attached to him. On the contrary, he could justifiably claim to have saved several debacles. He remained unimpressed: his morale, temporarily at least, had gone clean out of the window, a clear warning that he could not be sent off on another operation until and unless we could effect some sort of running repairs to his general mental state. Another appointment, by itself, was not the answer; the reverse, in fact, for his personal good. Whatever we decided no chances must be taken.

Prof was most upset when I told him what had happened. 'X' was a popular as well as able young officer. As a temporary restorative Prof suggested that a short spell in the comparatively lotus-eating atmosphere of Algiers might provide an answer; there would be plenty of office work for 'X' while he was there and after a month, perhaps, he would return renewed, and ready to go again. The decision was rendered the more difficult because we were so hard-pressed, demands growing all the time, and I did not wish to let our customers down just when they had come to rely on us. In the end we decided that the two of us should call in 'X' for another talk when we would try to convince him of the truth that we all experienced runs of misfortune, and that these were bound to come to an end if one persevered.

When he arrived in the office and saw that Prof was there, too, he gave a wry smile. 'This looks ominous,' he said.

'What looks ominous?' I asked.

'The two of you being here.'

'Nonsense. We just want to see how we can get over this present difficulty of yours.'

His whole attitude was one of deep dejection. 'Well,' he said, 'I think there's only one way left, and that is for another appointment. I feel now that everything I touch is bound to go wrong.'

Prof produced just the right note. He gave a gentle laugh. 'My dear "X", we *all* go through these patches. Why d'you think you should be the exception and different from anyone else? You can climb back — as I say, like anyone else.'

But 'X' wasn't to be moved as easily as that. 'I don't know,' he said, 'but on the last two ops I've *known before* sailing that something was going to go wrong and that we'd have a failure, and we did.'

'Can you,' I asked, 'point out one single mistake on your part which either caused, or might have caused the failure?'

At least he considered the question carefully before answering, 'No, not really. There have been minor errors in hitting the pinpoint dead centre, but that's about all.'

'Then don't blame yourself. It's the run of the game.'

'Oh, I don't particularly, but there seems to be a gremlin in the works each time. Either we're chased off by patrols or the chaps don't turn up on the beach, or the weather turns sour. There's always bloody well something. Even one of the resisters, when we arrived at the right place at the right time, just wouldn't land.'

'Can't say,' commented Prof, 'that I altogether blame him. But seriously, 'X', don't you think that you could work your way out of it?'

'Perhaps,' admitted 'X', 'but meanwhile I really believe I should let someone else take over. At the moment I simply cannot get it right.'

'You're sure you want a change?' I asked. 'I'm quite prepared to recommend it if you insist, because you've had as long a stint as anyone else — longer than most, in fact. And you've done damn well, as I think you know.'

No one said anything for several moments while we reflected. With another wintry smile 'X' broke the silence. 'I think I should pack it in, you know...'

I held up a hand. 'Just a second before you decide finally. I have a suggestion to make. Supposing I asked you to help me over the next op — the one tomorrow night — how would you feel?'

'Help in what way?'

'We're carrying out the first composite operation, landing two sets of men belonging to two separate organizations, about seven hundred yards apart. I want to be sure nothing goes wrong, and I'd like you to come with me as assistant-cum-dinghyman.'

Prof's eyes opened wide in protest. 'But what about his own op —?'

'We can re-arrange that.' A way would have to be found. 'Will you come?'

'X' didn't like it, shifting about in his chair. 'You're just trying to be kind,' he said.

'Not at all,' I insisted. 'Tomorrow night will be complicated — I don't say difficult, but with two sets of chaps to be landed there can easily be a mistake and I want your experience there.'

'Of course I'll go if that's what you really want.'

'That's what I do want. If, after tomorrow, you find you'd like to resume the discussion we certainly will, but right now Prof and I must make up the order of batting for both tonight and tomorrow.'

When 'X' had gone Prof extracted the operational schedule from one of the trays on the desk, spread it out, and pointed to one of the sections. 'If,' he said, 'you take "X" with you on this combination op who is going to do the little joker that he is now booked for?' His finger indicated a pick-up operation from one of the nearer islands.

'Good question, Prof. How about you?'

His mouth opened, he said nothing, he swallowed. 'What d'you mean,' he asked, 'how about me?' He was very alert.

'I mean, would you like to have a cut at it, yourself?'

'But —'

'Oh, I know you're not supposed to, Prof, but we don't want to lose "X", and this seems the only way we're likely to avoid that. If we let him have another go on his own tomorrow, and he fails — for no matter what reason — we've lost him. It's a question of priorities. You could help us out. See?'

He was trying dispassionately to weigh his eargerness to try his luck against the possible consequences of his going on operations.

'If you think it'd be all right —' he said, hesitantly.

'I wouldn't be suggesting it otherwise. I'll tell you now, quite frankly, I don't think your customers will turn up for embarkation — even their sponsors are sceptical, but because they have given their word they wish us to send a boat.'

'Of course, I'll go, but I'm damned if I know whether I wish to succeed or fail: if I fail it may be good for "X"'s morale, but bad for the customers — and vice versa if I succeed. Gawd!'

'Let's leave it to the event, Prof.'

'By all means.' He was smiling like a small boy unexpectedly offered an ice-cream. Leading Seaman Downes should go with him: they would make a good team.

There came a time when certain of the sponsoring authorities sought to be allowed to send their own escorting officers on operations to look after their resisters on passage to the pinpoint of landing: some of these escorters had experience of the sea, others had none. When the question was raised officially I made the cardinal error of agreeing to the arrangement, unwittingly putting an uncomfortable rod in pickle for the flotilla. Arguments began developing between the ops officers of the ACF as to whether the boat was at the correct pinpoint immediately before landing. This was not the moment for dispute, being bad for the morale of all concerned, not least the resisters themselves — the very people we were trying to serve. We tried to back-track, pointing out the folly of the principle, but alas, the precedent had been established. An appeal to SOIS produced an even worse result. Having listened to both sides he ruled that in the event of a disagreement the escorting officer's opinion was to be accepted, right or wrong.

To us, the ops officers, this was a most unwelcome setback. On the other hand it was difficult to argue with the analogy used by SOIS who based his reasoning on the relationship between taxi-driver and fare. The fare is always right. There was one small loop-hole in that the Captain of the boat concerned could overrule the escorting officer if he thought his boat was being put at risk.

The operation 'X' and I were about to attempt had two sponsors, one for each set of resisters. One sponsor was quite happy to let us handle the operation from the time the resisters embarked to the time we landed them, the other asked if they might send not only an escorting officer but also their own dinghymen. Compounding my original mistake I said yes to both requests for the good reason that the escorting/dinghymen were our good friends Andrew Croft, and his silhouette-drawing Sergeant, both skilled boatmen, and Andrew with a good knowledge of the sea. There was little likelihood of awkward differences of opinion.

For security reasons we were asked to use a PT boat. Lieutenant-Commander Barnes, helpful as ever, detailed Lieutenant Boebel, captain of *PT 214* whom we already knew. All, therefore, was set fair — even, on this occasion, the weather. Much more than usual was at stake in this operation — the result would also decide 'X's future.

We were quite a party. For SOE Andrew had two men and two women to land, while 'X' and I had two men. On board both parties were separated, one being put down for'ard, and the other aft. You could do that in a PT boat, but a MAS was too small, having only the tiny wardroom for accommodation.

Punctually at 20.00 we cast off, and once clear of the harbour proceeded at an easy 25 knots northwards for the next four hours; everyone, including 'X' I was glad to notice, was in calm optimistic mood. Around midnight we eased to 15 knots, a speed which we held over the next hour when it was time to make our run-in to the pinpoint. As we approached the shore we began to make use of our memorized silhouette of the hinterland as it materialized. The Sergeant's draughtsmanship proved faultless as the various cliff faces and mountains became easily recognizable. About a mile from the pinpoint we adjusted course to go straight in, and some fifteen minutes later we stopped the ship 400 yards from the beach.

From this moment things began to go wrong. Andrew stated that we were not at the correct pinpoint. 'X' and I maintained firmly that we were. By every argument we knew we tried to persuade him that he was wrong, all to no avail. Fortunately there was no ill-feeling, simply a difference of conviction, Andrew claiming that we had come too far north by some two or three miles. Twenty minutes of discussion proved nothing more than the need to use SOIS's ruling in such events; we had to bow to the wishes of the fare (in this case, Andrew). Turning south we eased slowly down the coast, a manoeuvre which we always tried to avoid for fear of being seen by enemy land patrols, or, worse still, shore batteries. We had little fear of inshore sea patrols — we were already too close in to the coast for them to be inshore of us.

Forty-five minutes later when we were about 800 yards from the beach, Andrew announced that we were off the pinpoint. 'X' and I once more, and for the final time, disagreed.

At this point I realized I had made yet another mistake. 'X' and I were responsible for landing our two men; I should have insisted on doing so at the correct pinpoint where we had first stopped. Too late to worry about that now; all we could do was to warn our charges and ask them if they would like to have a shot at setting foot ashore where we then were.

Both dinghies were lowered into the water, Andrew and his party climbing into one while 'X' and I waited for them to get clear of the ship before bringing our two men on deck. When we stood, all four of us, looking at the shore I told our resisters exactly what happened — that we were two to three miles too far south of where they should have landed — and asked them if they still wished to land, providing we could find a suitable place. Should they decline I promised to bring them back again at the first opportunity to put them down where we had originally agreed. They conferred for several minutes before opting to have a go at an immediate landing, providing I could tell them exactly where they were, and that it was not too far from the small town for which they were making. We took them below into the wardroom where we showed them on both charts and maps where we were. Again there was a short consultation before they repeated their wish to make the attempt. They were very brave men.

Time was beginning to run short as 'X' and I pulled briskly towards the shore, our two passengers seated in the stern sheets, clutching their few belongings. By casting an eye over our shoulders from time to time we inspected the line of the shore: the nearer we got the less seemed the chances of finding anywhere to land with the rock face rising sheer out of the water all along the coast as far as we could see. We turned north-west to paddle parallel to the beach, as close to the rocks as we dared, searching for a break in the solid wall of cliff, when suddenly 'X' spotted some lights flashing straight ahead of us. We stopped and studied the pattern of activity until we were sure that what we were watching was Andrew and his party trying to land. Quickly we turned round and retraced our course, south-east, continuing until we had passed where we had tried earlier. Inevitably, time was running short when we came round a rocky bluff and saw a stretch of shingle between what appeared to be a massive stone construction sitting some fifty or sixty yards inland from the water's edge. We had no idea what we were looking at even when we got close enough to identify what we took to be two large arched 'doorways' in the 50 ft high structure. It was a possible landing place and we pulled for it, only to have our attention claimed by two unexpected lines of surf breaking on the rock-strewn beach. For a moment or two we swirled helplessly before grounding. We leaped out quickly to drag the dinghy clear of the water to let the passengers step out dry-shod. Much importance was quite properly attached to avoiding such tell-tale give-aways as wet clothes or even wet shoes on a perfectly dry night. The security forces weren't all that stupid.

For half a minute we stood, the four of us, staring at the great mass of stone wall towering upwards into the night so that we could not see the top of it. Leaving the two men standing by the dinghy 'X' and I made a rapid recce in the hope of locating a path or road leading out of these sombre surroundings. Only when we were within feet of the structure did we realize what it was — a railway embankment, bridging the bay in which we were standing. The two 'doorways' were, in fact, arches running underneath and right through the embankment, a much more promising prospect, and we pushed on close up to the stone face, the crunching noise of our seaboots on the shingle being drowned by the hissing of the surf. Entering one of the archways, which was large enough to house a London bus, we began exploring inwards. Although the place was pitch black we could just discern the outline of the far end. With no warning there was a sudden frantic scrambling noise directly at our feet; this was followed by a muffled shout. While I was jumping about three vertical feet I heard 'X's phlegmatic, 'Christ. What's that?'

'Tommy-gun ready?' I whispered, ready for another jump.

'Yes. All ready,' replied 'X'.

'I'm going to switch on my torch.'

'Right.'

The beam of light revealed a very ancient, wizened crone crouching among an untidy assortment of faggots. We both burst out laughing.

'Eh, Mama,' I managed, still a bit confused, 'what are you doing here at this late hour?'

'Nothing, *signore*, nothing. I do no harm. I collect wood.'

If she imagined we were German there seemed no reason to disabuse her. 'Is there,' I asked, 'a path leading up to the road from here?'

'*Ma si, signore* — straight up. I am going up now.'

'Good. We'll escort you.'

'No, no, signore, that will not be necessary. I know my way.'

She rose to her feet — she was tiny — picked up a bundle of faggots a good deal bigger than herself, and made off by the light of the torch towards the other end of the archway while 'X' and I followed close behind. Before we reached the end I switched out the torch.

There was a stream flowing down through the rocks to the foot of the embankment, and beside it ran a rough path, just visible in the gloom. The crone picked her steps with care, avoiding many little pools, slowly to disappear up the steep incline into the night.

'Good-night, Mama.'

'Good-night, *signore*.' she called over her shoulder.

'X' and I made a hasty return to the two waiting men and told them what we had discovered; they were pleased but wanted, once more, to be reassured as to their exact location, and this we did for them. If the old crone could pass up and down the cliffs in the middle of the night there seemed good reason to believe that they could, too. Pulling the dinghy up well clear of the water, the four of us then marched quickly up the beach and into the archway, 'X' and I leading the way past the faggots. When they saw the path the two men studied it a bit doubtfully. 'It's very rough,' said one.

'I agree,' I replied, 'but the old woman managed to carry a heavy bundle of faggots up it.'

'But it's not that that we mind. The path is so rough we could cut our shoes on the way up. If we're stopped by a patrol they will notice.'

'It's up to you, then. If you'd rather turn back, now is the moment.'

The pair of them went into another huddle. At the end they announced, 'We'll go. But please give us a hand over the first few yards which seem so muddy. We must keep our shoes clean.'

'X' and I carried them bodily over the worst patches and then they were off, picking their way carefully over the rocky path while we turned with a whispered, *'Adio'*. We just caught their reply, *'Adio. Grazie, signore'* as they disappeared upwards.

On the way back through the archway we had a quiet chuckle about the fright the old crone had given us. It was noticeable that 'X's spirits had risen and he was much more his old self. Perhaps she had helped towards this.

Walking at ease down the beach still talking quietly we remarked on the increase in wind and sea; it looked as if we might have a tough pull back to the PT boat. Just before reaching the dinghy we turned to have another look at the embankment when, to our surprise, a bright light flashed out from the southern end, to be answered immediately by a similar flash from the northern end. For a full minute we stood beside the dinghy to see if we were the cause of the exchange of signals. Had the old woman, perhaps, been stopped and questioned? Had the men we had just landed been arrested? Nothing.

'One sentry seeing that his oppo is still awake, I should guess,' said 'X'.

'Extraordinary that they haven't seen us,' I replied.

'Perhaps they have. Perhaps they think we're local fishermen.'

'Either way, this is no time for dawdling. We'll keep an eye open as we pull out to the PT boat.'

Launching the dinghy back into the water wasn't easy with the increase in the surf, and 'X' lost one of his seaboots which became jammed between two rocks. Once clear of the breakers we had our work cut out to make good headway out to the PT boat which we estimated would be lying about 800 yards from the beach. The rubber dinghies were light, and with almost no draught they were always at the mercy of wind and wave; the weather at that moment was from right ahead. We had been away from the ship for 45 minutes, and it was now a quarter to five, barely an hour before the first streaks of dawn when air and sea patrols were liable to be encountered. The spray slopped over our backs and we were making little headway, perhaps 200 yards in ten minutes; at that rate we should be another half hour before reaching the mother ship. As we learned later, much the same thoughts had been going through the mind of Lieutenant Boebel, the PT boat Captain, and he decided to come and have a look for us. 'X' and I were beginning to have doubts about ever finding the ship when she loomed, hugely, out of the dark to bear down on us. A very welcome sight. In no time we were on board, and sucking down the sustenance of 'self-heaters' in a warm, dry wardroom.

While we were changing into fresh clothes Andrew joined us. His first words were to apologise for having insisted that 'X' and I were wrong over the location of the pinpoint. This was generous — and typical of Andrew. He could easily, as others did on other occasions, have maintained his claim to save his *amour propre*: whenever this happened the atmosphere of the whole op became soured. Now he asked how we had got on and when we told him he was both amused and pleased. He had had no luck at all, meeting nothing but sheer rock face wherever they looked, until finally they had had to give up and return to the PT boat. The two women in the party — assumed, possibly to impose an extra burden in finding an easy place to land — had shown an admirable calm throughout, wet and uncomfortable though they were after an hour in the dinghy.

On the return trip there were two minor alarms, one just after leaving the pinpoint when we observed flashes coming in our direction from the shore, away down to the south-east. We waited for the fall of shot round us. Nothing happened. Five minutes later a target was observed on our radar screen. The Captain altered course to avoid contact and increased speed from 15 to 25 knots, but the target continued to close on us. We guessed that we were probably dealing with a German coastal patrol: with two women and two men civilians on board and being far from home with no possibility of calling up support, the

146

last thing we sought was an action. We increased speed so that the target gradually dropped astern. At 08.30 we were back in Bastia.

While enjoying one of Maria's magnificent breakfasts I asked the 'Colonel' if Prof had returned safely.

'Aye, I think so,' he replied cautiously, 'I heard the noise of what the Prof calls singing, coming from the bathroom, not half an hour since. I reckon he must be back.'

Almost simultaneously Prof walked in.

'How did you get on Prof?' I enquired.

'Oh, very enjoyable. Haven't had such fun for years.'

'Any luck?'

'Well, I've got nothing to show for the night's work if that's what you mean but, oh, my! What a lot of goings on. The place seemed alive with people but we couldn't tempt any of 'em on board.'

'What actually happened?'

'There really isn't much to tell, you know. We arrived at the right place at the right time — there could be no mistake about that, the island's too small — and then there was an eruption of activity, with torches being flashed hither and yon and what seemed like a lot of running about but no shots or anything unpleasant like that. We really couldn't make head or tail of it; but one thing was quite certain and that was that we didn't get any signal from the shore. A pure waste of time, except for the amusement of wondering what was going to happen next. Things quietened down after a time and we hung about hopefully for a further hour and then packed it in. Can't imagine what was going on. How did you get on?'

I saw him examining 'X' out of the corner of his eye, and I explained briefly what had happened.

Looking amiably at 'X' Prof said 'Well, I'm very glad you got your lot away.'

After breakfast I buttonholed 'X'. There was no need to ask him about the effect of the previous night; he was already a different person. But I did ask him if he would like to have a cut at a short operation that same night — one which, on the face of it, should be easy, but which might also complete the business of restoring his confidence.

'Certainly,' he agreed. 'Looks a piece of cake.'

He wouldn't have said that yesterday.

'Maybe,' I said, 'but please don't treat it as such.'

In the event, the operation was a lot more difficult than either of us had expected, the shore party being discovered by the enemy just as they were about to go down to the beach to start signalling the boat to come in. Things immediately became hectic as the resisters bolted for their lives along the cliff tops, the enemy patrol in hot pursuit. 'X' wat-

147

ched proceedings anxiously, manoeuvring the MAS boat so as to keep the hunt in sight without himself being observed. Several times he thought he saw his chance to dart in, and lowered the dinghy into the water; each time he was frustrated, the patrol being too quick, and the chase continued. For three hours the battle of wits and stamina went on, and 'X' was beginning to believe he would never succeed, when, almost as dawn was breaking he received the correct light signal from a point some way up the coast. At the same time he could see where the enemy patrol was searching by the lights they were using freely in their haste to track down their quarry. Here, at last, was a chance, and 'X' moved quickly, taking the MAS as close as he dared to the beach in order to cut down dinghy time. Pulling at top speed for the beach he embarked two exhausted, frantic men and got back to the MAS just as the patrol reached the spot where the men had been taken off minutes before. When 'X' had finished his verbal report, he sat back, and said, 'And that's about all, I think.'

'A piece of cake, eh?'

He looked down to smile in embarrassment. 'I'm sorry. You were quite right. But I did treat it seriously on the night although it all looked so simple.'

'It often does. Now. Want to go on?'

He hesitated so long that I became anxious about what he might be going to say. Without warning he became very formal. 'That depends rather more on you than me — sir'.

'I'm asking you, though.'

'In that case I'd like to go on, please.'

'Good. No op tonight, but be ready to go again tomorrow night. I can't tell you where yet. Prof will let you know in the morning.'

'Thanks very much.'

When he got up to go out it was plain that the weight had been lifted, his parting smile was relaxed and easy. He did go on. He went on to get himself deservedly well decorated a few months later.

* * *

The telephone rang. The voice at the other end was unmistakable.

'Hullo. What beastliness are you up to this sparkling aforenoon?'

'Nothing special, sir. Writing up reports.'

'Well, if you come up here at about noon I *might* find some gin. There's something — not urgent — I want to discuss. I'll expect you at noon.'

'Aye, aye, sir. Thank you very much.'

' 'bye.'

On the stroke of midday I found him talking to Charles Buist, his Staff Officer (Operations).

'I don't know,' SOIS was saying, 'I'm not very keen. We've never done it before.' He looked round as I came in. 'But here's the chap who should know.' He pushed a packet of cigarettes in my direction. 'For God's sake, sit down. You're too bloody big standing up.' Obediently I sat.

'Now,' he resumed, giving me his full attention, 'Charles has had a request from the Senior Italian Officer, Commander Thingummy, to send one of the MAS boats down to Maddalena for some sort of repairs. As you know we never allow them to go to sea without one of your chaps on board. Have you got someone you can spare to go down with this boat?'

'When?'

SOIS looked at Charles who replied, 'In about three days' time.'

'Three days from now,' I said, 'we shall still be in the middle of the operational period. I know we can't spare anyone then; we're fully booked for the whole period. Is it so urgent that it can't wait? Say, another twelve days?'

SOIS raised an enquiring eyebrow, 'Can't he wait?'

Charles shook his head in doubt. 'The Commander claims it's urgent.'

For a moment or two nobody spoke. Then SOIS turned to me again. 'What's your view about letting the boat go without a British officer on board. D'you think we could risk it?'

'Which boat is it?' I didn't know them all as well as each other. Having selected the best three or four we tended to stick to them, leaving the remainder comparatively untried. Charles gave me a MAS number the crew of which I scarcely knew beyond the Captain's name. We had used the boat, but rarely, although the Captain was known to, and well considered by one or two of the ops officers.

Now I said, 'Don't know the boat at all well personally, but there's nothing against any of them. Did the Commander give you any idea of what repairs are required?'

Charles shrugged. 'Not really. He just said that he likes to keep all the boats up to the mark on their maintenance schedules in case there's a breakdown amongst those we are using for the current ops. This boat is apparently overdue.'

SOIS nodded. 'Perfectly reasonable I should have thought.' He turned to me. 'What's your view?'

'Frankly, sir, I'm not keen. We've never done it before, but then —' one could argue all day about it; SOIS didn't like it any more than I did '— there seems no alternative. Perhaps we should risk it.'

149

'You really haven't got anyone to send? No-one spare?'

'No-one, sir. I'm sorry.'

'Right.' He turned to Charles, and became very precise, ticking off the points on his fingers. 'Tell Commander Thing he may send the boat down without a British officer on board. Next, I want to know the time of sailing, the ETA (estimated time of arrival), and lastly I want to be told when she actually reaches Maddalena. Understood?'

'Aye, aye, sir.'

'Now,' he scowled, stabbing a clenched fist into the palm of his other hand, 'I'll give you both something to drink. Just one each, no more — my supply is extremely short.'

His supplies were short, but he lied about 'one each'.

★ ★ ★

In the middle of January the Major-General's group came to life again with a rush. They had been busy since their arrival in Corsica re-grouping to send back to Italy the strongest party of intelligence experts they could muster, and — so we were now told — they were six in number, and were anxious to take in a 'quantity' (we never had a group prepared to specify *exactly* how much) of radio equipment.

This was the sort of news which we, the 'taxi-drivers', liked to hear as a reward for the nights we spent at sea in often abortive attempts at landing or picking up these courageous people.

Such a large party, plus their equipment, could not comfortably be accommodated in an MAS boat, and moreover, since they were working for OSS, *PT 215* with Lieutenant Steele in command, was allocated for the operation. He was the same chap with whom I had made the second unsuccessful try at picking up the two French resisters. We both hoped we would have better luck on this occasion. As dinghyman I chose Leading Seaman Downes.

In this work the unusual soon became the commonplace, so that the operation without a surprise was something of a novelty. This one, with all the signs of being a straightforward affair turned out to be the standard commonplace unusual. (I could never make out just why the many surprises visited on us were seldom pleasant ones.)

All parties had agreed to assemble on board *PT 215*, Lieutenant Steele's boat, at 17.00: privately, however, I had arranged to arrive half an hour early so that the Captain and I could go over the plan quietly in his charthouse. Downes and I turned up punctually with two rubber dinghies which we hoisted on board before I went below to the charthouse where I found everything laid out and being studied by the

Captain. But he was not alone. With him was the Captain of *PT 203*.
What went on that 'my' Captain should be discussing 'my' operation
with a third party? Even stranger was the news that *both* Captains were
taking part in the operation, each in his own boat, one acting as escort
to the other. Why had escorts suddenly become necessary? Steele explained, not without minor embarrassment, that in recent weeks the
boats of his flotilla had suffered numerous mechanical breakdowns,
probably, he thought, due to lack of full maintenance facilities at
Bastia. This had obliged Lieutenant-Commander Barnes to insist that
his boats should never leave harbour unaccompanied.

Well, we couldn't object. The waste of duplicating manpower had
to be weighed against the risk of a PT boat becoming stranded off the
enemy coast — perhaps with our precious passengers on board. To the
Americans PT boats commanded a known and very high value as offensive weapons; our resisters were just unknown quantities in terms
of war value. They could be worth comparatively little as, perhaps,
simple couriers or they could be of incalculable importance as major
political figures. All that was part of the clandestine world, and of no
interest to the PT flotilla Commander.

The three of us, then, the two American Captains and I, ran through
the programme of the night's activity; by the time we had finished the
main party of passengers — in three groups of two each — had arrived
on board, and were immediately escorted below. We were about to
cast off when one of the escorting officers approached to suggest that
he should introduce me to the leader of the party to be landed. For
security reasons this was something I tried always to avoid. Was there,
I asked, some particular purpose in my meeting the leader? Before the
escorting officer could answer a large good-looking man stepped from
the charthouse and came up to me.

'My name is Giuseppe, and I am the leader. The General has
spoken to me about you. Please, at what time do we land?'

While speaking he had managed the usual handshake.

'You are scheduled to be put ashore at eleven o'clock. That is, if we
get the correct signal at the other end.'

Vigorously he bobbed his head and smiled. 'You will, *Capitaine*,
you will.' (He must have caught the '*Capitaine*' from the General.)
'But before we go I would like to mention that we have one lady
among our group.'

'A lady? Oh, fine,' I replied, perhaps a bit offhand. 'Brave girl. Any
special instructions about her?'

'No, none, thank you, *Capitaine*, but I thought you should know.'

'Thanks for telling me.' Indeed, it was considerate of him to let me
know although it was difficult to see what difference it could make to

the op. To us they were all just so many 'bods' — to be treated with equal care, no matter who they were.

The OSS officers went ashore, and at 18.00 we cast off, leading the escort boat, *PT 203*, towards the harbour entrance. We had barely left the jetty before Barnes' decision about using two boats for the operation was vindicated: one of our engines refused to start. Lieutenant Steele looked both glum and embarrassed at the same time, and who could blame him? He said he would like to try 'trailing in' the non-starter once we were clear of the harbour. On one engine, at slow speed, a shallow draft high-speed boat is difficult to steer, making our course to the entrance pretty erratic. In compensation when we did reach open water the recalcitrant engine started without a murmur of complaint, and we were off.

An hour out, as if to emphasize still further the wisdom of sending two boats, the escorting *PT 203* developed engine trouble and was obliged to stop. We waited for a quarter of an hour before the engineers could get her going again; when they did we had to increase speed to try to make up for lost time. We couldn't afford more break-downs. Meanwhile the weather, so often the main hazard, was deteriorating, not seriously, but enough to introduce a further complication if it continued to worsen from the same south-westerly direction, to blow straight on to the pinpoint. We pushed on for another three hours and were about to alter course for the final run-in at reduced speed when the escorting boat reported further engine trouble. Wind and sea were now about force 3–4, enough to make dinghy work difficult but for a small veer to the north-west. Lieutenant Steele, torn by his orders from his Squadron commander that the two boats should at all times remain together, and the very real wish to go ahead with the operation, sought my advice. It was a question of weighing up the undesirables: sticking to Barnes' edict and cancelling the op, or, sending the 'lame duck' home while we got on with the op, with the possibility at the end, of invoking Barnes' wrath at having his orders over-ruled by a foreign naval officer.

'D'you think, Commander,' asked Steele, 'we should continue with the operation?'

'Yes, Captain, I do,' I replied firmly.

Steele laughed. 'OK, Commander, you said it. I'll tell the other boat to return to harbour.'

Alone, at slow speed to reduce the underwater exhaust noise to a tolerable 'rumble-bubble' as the exhausts became exposed to the air with the rolling of the boat, we proceeded in towards the pinpoint. A quarter of an hour later we picked up a target on the radar, guesswork defining it as an F-lighter and E-boat escort. They were on a course which would take them close across our bows. It took twenty minutes of valuable time to shake them off, at the end of which we were already ten minutes late.

A further ten minutes and we saw the signal from the beach. A very welcome sight. Simultaneously I noticed that what wind there was now came from the north, straight off the beach which would now provide a lee to give us a flat calm approach inshore. When the radar operator reported that we were 400 yards from the shoreline we stopped the ship to lower the dinghies into the water. Downes and I climbed down and began embarking stores: there seemed to be no end to them as we stowed them evenly round the bottom of the boats. Then came the passengers. My head, as I stood up in the dinghy, was about level with the deck of the PT boat so that I looked up to see the first passenger silhouetted against the sky, a figure dressed in knickerbockers and a sweater. To show I was ready I held my arms up meaning that the figure should sit down on the deck from where it was easy to guide the legs towards the middle of the dinghy; dinghyman and passenger usually grasped arms for the final slide down. Nothing happened; the figure didn't move.

'Take my hands,' I said.

With a sort of awkward movement which made me think the passenger was about to topple over sideways, a pair of hands found mine; they were soft and small. It was the girl about whom the leader had spoken before we left.

'All right. Now sit down.'

'I cannot. I cannot manage —'

I tried coaxing. 'Come on, it's only a little way.'

Without warning she launched herself bodily at me and we fell in a heap at the bottom of the boat. That, I supposed, was one way of doing it as we disentangled ourselves.

The dinghy with four people and a large quantity of stores was, indeed, heavily laden, and cause for profound thanks for the flat calm water, as we paddled inshore. Never having been much of an admirer of radar, my confidence in it was not enhanced when it became apparent that we were actually a good 700 yards from the beach. Downes kept his dinghy abreast of mine until we were within twenty yards when we both grounded. As usual the passengers all moved to jump out immediately until they were told to sit tight while we got out and pushed the boats over the false beach into 4 ft of water. I had only just remembered it in time, myself.

Willing hands were waiting to help us as we reached the shore, but we were still in a foot of water owing to the weight we were carrying. I ferried one of the men ashore, pick-a-back, then the second, but when I came to the girl she remained seated. Standing beside the dinghy I said, 'Up' rather as to a child.

She made no move save to extend both arms towards me. 'Please,' she said, 'your hands' as if she were that child.

She was very light in my arms. Putting her down on the dry sand I was surprised when, for a couple of seconds, perhaps more, she held on to me as if to get her balance. Then, with a brief 'thank you' she was off up the beach — and I was able to understand the reason for the earlier awkwardness. The knee-breeches and stockings she was wearing revealed that one of her legs was withered away to almost nothing, and nearly useless, from polio. Now hopping and hobbling away into the night she was off to fight the war.

* * *

Whatever may have been the success of the Major-General's group they were certainly active, for only three nights later we were off to the same pinpoint for the same group on the most ambitious operation we had yet tried: to land six, and embark eight other group members. In addition there might be up to fifteen escaping prisoners of war. As if these numbers weren't enough OSS was sending no less than five of their officers to accompany the expedition. Quite a party. One could only shudder at the thought of what would happen to OSS security should we have the misfortune to run into a trap at the other end, or encounter enemy patrol craft *en route*. Although it certainly wasn't our direct worry it increased the onus of our responsibility.

This time, however, no PT boats could be spared. With no alternative, OSS agreed that we should use two MAS boats, Ginger in *541*, and her sister ship *543* (still carrying her torpedo tubes, and therefore with less speed) under the command of Lieutenant the Marchese Centurione. These two were among the best, if not *the* best, of the Captains of the flotilla. With us we took three rubber dinghies, each capable of carrying five men. Our youngest officer Ranald Boyle was to act as assistant ops officer and ride in *543* while Bates and Downes were to come with me in *541*.

Observing what had become standard security measures the OSS party arrived on board *541* in dribs and drabs over about half an hour. A casual bystander could not but have been impressed if not astonished at the number of American uniforms on board but that was a hazard to be accepted.*

---

* In spite of genuine efforts Port security, as far as I know, never succeeded in stopping all civilians roaming round the jetties. Some, yes, but not all; it only required one ill-intentioned onlooker to create a lot of mischief.

Then, when all were safely 'stowed' out of sight below decks, came a hitch in the form of an unexpected message from the Italian end of the General's organization. No-one knew what the message said, but its very arrival at the eleventh hour meant that we had to wait to find out. Rather than waste time Ranald and his Marchese Captain were instructed to take *543* out of harbour, and lie off until we joined them. A quarter of an hour went by — one became so accustomed to these last minute hold-ups that we almost came to expect them — and then confirmation arrived that we could proceed.

The trip to the pinpoint was uneventful, the boats maintaining close company in line ahead at 30 knots. They may not have been as comfortable as the PT boats, being smaller, but they were faster, and over the months of fairly intensive operations they proved themselves less susceptible to breakdown. In fairness be it said maintenance of an MAS was a good deal less complicated than dealing with the highly sophisticated American boats.

A little before 21.00, after three hours on mains we switched down to auxiliaries for the fifteen-mile run in to the pinpoint where we were due at 23.30. We had left a good margin of time on the 'silent' auxiliaries to cut the noise factor to the minimum for the shore party waiting for us. Visibility was, as on our first sortie into the area, patchy and unpredictable so that we sighted land but a scant quarter of an hour before we picked up a good bright torch signal from the beach.

By prearrangement Ranald and *543* lay about a quarter of a mile off the beach while Ginger edged *541* to within 200 yards of the shore: there we stopped while all three dinghies were lowered into the water. Bates, Downes and I climbed down into them to wait for the passengers now coming out on deck and being shuffled round by their respective keepers who were dishing out final instructions and exhortations.

As I watched a figure detached itself from the throng to stand immediately above me on the deck of the MAS boat. The 4-in heels of the black patent leather court shoes shone even in that dim light, the legs (what I could see of them) in their silk stockings were finely shaped, and there was the faint but unmistakable aroma of expensive scent. I could have stood there for ages. As it was I said, 'You can jump.' And she did. Close-to she seemed very beautiful; it seemed a shame that there was no time to do it all over again.

Taking one more passenger I observed Bates and Downes were ready to pull inshore, each with his pair of resisters seated in the stern. Together we sculled in.

This time the false beach presented no problem, the dinghies not being so heavily laden. With an extra sharp pull on the paddles we slid over the top of the bar into deeper water, and thence on to ground on good firm sand. The girl wasn't heavy as I picked her up to carry her up the beach. At that close range it was an effort to put her down. When I did, like her predecessor, she gave me a very pretty thank you before disappearing into the night. It was time to re-focus on what I was supposed to be doing.

The group to be embarked was standing in a small knot a little to my right, and appeared to be engaged in an animated discussion. Joining them I heard a strange but somehow familiar brand of English from a big man in the centre.

'And who are you?' His back was turned to me as I put the question. He whipped round in surprise.

'Chrissman! And who are *you*?'

'I've come to fetch you off.'

'Well, my name is Bombardier Snyman, and I'm South African.'

'So I gather. Any more of you?'

'Why, yiss, there is, but they're all afraid to come to the beach, man. There's so many traps. Bad men about.'

There were, it seemed, some fifteen or twenty fellow escapers hiding a couple of hundred yards away in among some trees: they knew he was with the Italian group and thought him a bloody fool for trusting himself to them. They weren't going to budge, fearing yet another betrayal into the hands of German security forces. Many escapers had put their faith in those Italians only too anxious to scoop the German reward for recaptured Allied PoWs.

It was not possible to give Private Snyman more than five minutes to persuade his apprehensive friends that we were genuine and with that he disappeared at a brisk trot into the darkness of the hinterland. Meanwhile we got on with the embarkation of the eight members of the Italian group, each dinghy making one trip. Having got my lot on board I returned to the beach to find a breathless Bombardier waiting.

'No good, man,' he puffed, 'they won't come. Chrissman! I say to them I tell you it's the Royal Navy, but they don't believe me, see?'

'All right, Bombardier, you scribble a note to 'em in Afrikaans, and one of these Italians will get it delivered, so that in future they will not be so shy.'

It was a poor substitute for rescuing a number of Allied soldiers, but it was all we could do. I wondered afterwards whether the note got through and, if it did, was it believed? The return passage was smooth and uneventful: I enjoyed it in the belief that all on board were happy with the conclusion of a successful operation. But I was quite wrong.

Later that same morning Ginger asked to see me and from his angry expression I knew that something serious was amiss. He started off by extracting from me an undertaking that whatever he might then tell me should go no further. We had, from time to time, experienced trouble of one sort or another with escorting officers; there were a lot of them and, inevitably, some were better than others. We knew them all. Some criticized the comfort on board, others complained that they were often hungry, or that we were sometimes short with them when they didn't understand the dinghy drill — all minor points dealt with easily enough. But there was one man, a Commander in the Italian Navy, and then on the work books of OSS in Naples, who had caused so much friction among the MAS boat crews that I had convinced SOIS into banning him from accompanying, or being in any way concerned with our operations. To ensure that it stuck where it applied SOIS had issued the injunction in person to OSS, so that there could be no room for misunderstanding.

Ginger told me that not only had the offending Commander been on board on the previous night but that he spent the entire time on passage back to Bastia, in stirring up trouble among the crew, picking holes in their behaviour, criticizing the discipline and the appearance of the ship. He had not hesitated either to repeat all his cavilling to Ginger, himself. Here it should be noted that Ginger and his boat had been out on operations for the three previous nights.

I was so angry at this news that I told him I could no longer stick to my undertaking not to take the matter further, and that I had to inform SOIS immediately of what had happened. His distress was painful to watch; he pleaded so hard that I relented to the extent of agreeing to delay further action until we had had time to cool down. In no circumstances, however, could the matter be left there for the whole unsavoury process to be repeated. In return Ginger promised to let me know straight away should the seditious Commander ever appear near any of the MAS boats.

After he had gone I sought the advice and opinion of Prof and Tom when we discussed the matter at length. Possibly because I was tired at that particular moment I was still for making an issue of the business, going the whole hog by reporting in detail to SOIS. Tom, who had on a previous occasion been on the receiving end of the Commander's subversive efforts with another crew, was inclined to agree that enough was enough. Neither of us wished to find ourselves plagued by this bastard again. In his customary professorial way, Prof was able to stand back from the problem. He hadn't been personally involved up to that moment. Bearing in the forefront of his mind the effect on good relations between ourselves and the customers he considered that action at some less exalted level might prove less disturbing and just as effective in the long run. But at what level? His good sense prevailed.

I rang Colonel Livermore and asked him if I might call on him shortly to discuss a serious matter. Maybe something in the way I spoke, maybe he had been forewarned, I don't know — all he said was, 'OK, Commander. I have a meeting with the boys right now. But you come on over, and I'll break off when you arrive.'

When I met him half an hour later no time was wasted in letting him know what we all thought and what we intended to do to prevent a repetition, ending up by asking him if he could think of a single good reason why the matter should not be reported to SOIS. Whilst letting this lot fly I could see a look of growing incomprehension on his face, so when I stopped his first words were not surprising; his mouth and eyes were both wide open. 'But,' he pleaded, 'I had no *idea* the Commander was on board. Sure, I know he's been banned by SOIS, and for that reason alone we'd never let him go. If you hold on one minute, I'll have our officer from Naples talk to you — he's in the meeting I just quit.' With that, he was gone to reappear accompanied by another American Colonel to whom he introduced me. We went through the whole thing again, if anything in even blunter terms. Not only were we angry about last night but also about previous occasions. To do him justice, this new Colonel was immediately horror-struck and full of apologies, explaining that he had no knowledge of the offender's history of what amounted to straight sedition — an uncomfortable admission to have to make about one of his own staff — and gave me a solemn undertaking that the Commander would never be allowed anywhere near us again. I then told him that SOIS had already issued such a ban: for all the good that that had done did he, the Colonel, see any reason why I should not now report the whole affair to SOIS, himself?

The Colonel swallowed hard at the idea. 'None that I can see,' he replied evenly, 'but I very much hope you won't.'

'All right, Colonel, I won't, but I'll be much obliged, if you'll tell that bloody Commander of yours that the *only* reason I'm not doing so is because a Lieutenant in *his* navy had the sense of decency and loyalty to ask me not to. The Commander should learn from his junior's example.'

'Rest assured I'll tell him that very thing.'

Thank God and the OSS, none of us ever saw the Commander again. Anglo-American relations returned once more to that 'serene and happy sea of cordiality'.

Chapter 8

CALAMITY AND A NARROW ESCAPE

Scarcely had I returned from the meeting with the OSS Colonels when Charles Buist, the Staff Officer (Operations) rang and 'invited' me to see Captain Dickinson.

SOIS was standing at the window staring out to sea as Charles announced my arrival. Coming back to his desk he picked up his cigarette-case and offered me one.

'Go all right last night?' he asked. He was unusually quiet.

'Yes, thank you, sir.'

'Good.' Drawing on his cigarette he exhaled slowly. 'Has Charles told you the news?'

'What news? I don't think so.'

'About the MAS boat we sent down to Maddalena.'

'No, sir. What happened?'

'It never arrived.'

'Why, was it sunk on the way?'

'No. It went to la Spezia, instead.'

'Good God. Was the Italian flotilla Commander on board?'

'No, fortunately. Just the normal crew.'

'A straightforward defection, then?'

'No. The crew butchered the officers and took the boat over.'

'Bloody hell.'

'Apparently, they hadn't got far when they did it. They simply cut the officers' throats and bolted for la Spezia.' So, after all, those earlier '*Heil Hitlers*' weren't just bravado.

'Can you tell me how we know all this, sir?'

'Yes, the Italian broadcasting system gave out some of it; the remainder came in the form of some intelligence reports.'

'Do the other Italian boats know?'

He nodded. 'Their Commander told them what they hadn't already heard on the news broadcast. Better for them to know the whole truth than to use their imaginations to cook up some appalling nonsense.'

'I'm very sorry about it, sir.'

'Well,' he shrugged, 'that's war. We both, you and I, made a mistake. Now what we have to worry about are the ones who are still here. What's your opinion of them?'

'Oh, the ones we know best we've come to trust. Ginger, the Marquese, Iapelli — and others — I find them first class.'

'Good. I'm glad to hear it. But you'll have to warn your young officers to keep their ears and eyes open for any further sign of trouble. We can't afford to lose any of *them*.'

'I'll have a yarn with them, sir.'

'Do that. Now get off and get some sleep.'

'Aye, aye, sir.'

'And good luck for tonight's ops.'

'Thank you, sir.'

Tom was particularly shocked by the news: he had known the murdered Captain well, and liked him. For his part, Ginger was simply aghast that such a shaming thing could happen in his service; in some curious way he seemed to think some blame attached to him, personally, although his reasoning was obscure.

The Italian commanding officer of the flotilla preferred not to discuss the subject at all. He had had ideas at one time of taking passage, himself, to Maddalena in the boat, and now he was dumb with horror. We heard that he took stringent measures to prevent any repetition, but we, the ops officers, never had any doubts about the boats we knew well. Unwise, perhaps, but we were vindicated in the end.

★   ★   ★

Some of the resistance groups we had to land seemed dogged by ill-luck. Night after night we would try either to put them ashore or pull them off the beach; each time something would happen to ruin our efforts. Whether such failures were as frustrating to the resisters as to us I can't say, but one such group endured no less than five shots at being landed not far from Sestri Levante, between Genoa and la Spezia. The group consisted of two men and two women. Very soon they became known among the young ops officers simply as 'the Girls' (or something like that). Whatever their profession they certainly lacked neither courage nor tenacity of purpose, and proved themselves at all times unrufflable.

Above Lieutenant Steele at another sort of wheel, in Bizerte.

Below RON (Squadron) 15 in Bastia Old Port.
Bottom German F-lighter, the objective of many attacks by Allied coastal forces on the west coast of Italy.

Above An artist's impression of PT boats at sea.

Below British and American Coastal Forces officers.
Bottom Lieutenant-Commander Stan Barnes, and Douglas Fairbanks, Jr, before the invasion of Elba.

Above (L to R) Lieutenant-Commander Barnes, Admiral Hewitt, USN, Rear-Admiral Morse, and Captain N. V. Dickinson, DSO, DSC, RN (SOIS).

Below Palermo. Lieutenant Eldridge, USN (standing) and his crew.

Bottom MTB RON (Squadron) 15 alongside at Palermo in 1943.

Left Lieutenant Gene Clifford in the cabin of *PT 204*

Below left Crash boat PTs, Maddalena, 1944.

Below right Lieutenant J.B. Mutty, USN, Exec Officer Lieutenant R. O'Brian, USN, Divisional Leader Lieutenant-Commander S.M. Barnes, USN, Commanding Officer Maddalena, October 1943.

'Who's going to have a go at the Girls tonight?' was the ambiguous cry when the operational non-moon period came round each month. The first two attempts were made, I think, by Tom. For what reason they failed I cannot now recall. The third attempt I have already described: during our first composite op an attempt was made to land them at what turned out to be the wrong pinpoint. One might have imagined they would have had enough after three flops, but no, they were game to continue.

The fourth attempt should have worked, there was no doubt about that. It would have done but for the escorting officer (an RNR I'm sorry to say) who, having embarked his charges in Bastia then disappeared below (with a bottle of some sort of liquor as we discovered later) and did not re-appear on deck until informed that we were at the pinpoint and waiting for him to ferry the group ashore. There was no question of not being at the correct place; we were in Ginger's boat, and he and I had been there twice before, and knew it well enough. When our escorting officer arrived on deck he peered round for a few minutes in the dark before launching the dinghy. Having embarked his passengers he and his other dinghyman set off towards the beach. Less than a quarter of an hour later he was back again claiming that he had been taken to the wrong spot and that there was nowhere to land. According to the SOIS ruling the customer was always right. We turned for home.

Next morning the escorting officer complained that he had been taken to the wrong place. He never came on another operation with us. There are limits.

The fifth attempt was undertaken more or less on the spur of the moment. We had been putting the finishing touches to preparations for an operation to the south of France when a signal arrived informing us that the pinpoint was 'blown' and occupied that morning by the Germans. Disappointing though this was there were compensations. *MAS 541* had been allocated for the task but Ginger, himself, was ill; nothing was known of his coxswain's ability when in command of the boat. And we were in need of a night's sleep. So it was an ill wind... Then conscience bobbed up. What about 'having a go with the Girls?', as the young officers were fond of saying. They deserved our best endeavours if anyone did. Moreover the weather looked good and we wouldn't have so far to go as on the French op.

Once the sponsors had been found and informed they were delighted. Unfortunately, they said, they could not provide either escorting officer or dinghyman. We agreed to undertake both tasks, but we would have to work fast if we were not to be too late.

Ranald went off to warn Ginger's coxswain of the change of plan,

161

Petty Officer Bates completed preparation of the dinghy, while I worked out the navigation. An hour later, at 18.30 we slipped from the jetty with 'the Girls' and their two male companions settled below in the tiny wardroom. Ginger's coxswain, Captain of the boat in his master's absence, proved a taciturn individual, speaking little, resigned to Heaven knew what — certainly nothing good. I had never had to deal directly with him before. Once outside I gave him a course to steer at 30 knots. All seemed set fair enough for me to take the three steps down from the bridge, and two strides more across the wheelhouse and into the wardroom, to have a chat with the passengers about procedure when we reached the pinpoint. Girls and boys had arranged themselves comfortably, seated on the two bunks, all reading what looked like comics. They listened while I explained that we hoped to land them at about midnight, showing them on the chart where they would be in relation to the nearest village. They smiled, expressed their thanks and said they hoped we would have better luck this time.

When I returned to the bridge the first thing I noticed was that we had altered course. When I asked the Cox'n why he replied that he was 'adjusting to the mean course', an unimpressive bit of news, particularly at that speed. Ranald told me that the ship had made several alterations in the few minutes I had been below. There was little to be done about it except to give the Cox'n a sharp warning not to order any further alterations without permission either from Ranald or me. What had been in the back of his mind is difficult to understand. A glorious spirit of Italian independence? Now there could be no knowing what error to expect in our landfall. At 30 knots you travel a long way in a short time. We could only wait and see. Fortunately the weather was calm and there was no reason to hurry.

Three hours further on found us switching over from main engines to auxiliaries for the final six knot approach to the coast: not long afterwards we had our first warning of the deceptive visibility lying ahead. Up to that time I cannot remember ever encountering fog in those waters. Now, without previous indication we ran into our first patch of thick sea mist. Some little while later we emerged to find land in sight. It didn't take long to realise that we were five or six miles too far east. So much for the Cox'n's 'adjusting to the mean'.

Altering course westward we ran parallel to the coast at a distance of about two miles. We were thereby cruising in waters frequented by the enemy inshore patrols, instead of crossing the strip at right angles, cutting the time of vulnerability to the minimum. To go right inshore at that point would have been to invite being seen from the land.

Large patches of feathery mist drifted slowly about the whole area, obscuring the land from view — and also giving us a measure of protection — as we made our way west. There wasn't a breath of wind. Ranald nudged me as I was peering through the binoculars trying to follow the line of the beach. 'Can you see anything out there on the port beam? I think I can spot something.'

I looked, and sure enough, there was an E-boat lying stopped about 300 yards from us. We altered away from her, presenting, if she saw us at all, only a stern silhouette. But there was no challenge. If they saw us they must have taken us for one of them. We hadn't increased speed or done anything suspicious. We were operating in a MAS boat, flotillas of which were still operating on the Axis side, manned by either Italian or German crews.

The time was 23.00 with still another four miles to run to arrive within the pinpoint area. Allowing twenty minutes for the final run in our passengers should be landed pretty well on the stroke of midnight. The mist was, however, thickening and, therefore, we decided to move in closer, to about one mile from the beach.

As we emerged from one particularly dense patch of mist the whole place was suddenly illuminated by a set of flares fired from the shore. By their light we could see in detail a complete village in its sea level setting between high rock formations on either side. The whole scene had an unreal air of the operatic, lacking only the thunder of Wagnerian music and a male voice choir.

As the flares died away we were back once more groping our way in the dark mists; there was no noise other than the faint whine of the auxiliaries and the swish of the bow wave, so small as to be barely audible. An uneasy feeling persuaded me to go up on to the foc's'le in an attempt to get a better view of our position. There, in the absolute silence I suddenly recognized the sound of breakers ahead. We really were too close. Easing away from the coast the next event was the firing of three red flares from patrol vessels lying about two miles further out than us. We were, therefore, in a good position well inshore of danger, but to make safe even safer we edged in a bit more to the point where we could make out the shaded lights of the occasional car moving along the coast road.

Occasionally the look-outs would report seeing these lights until they understood what they were looking at: then they kept quiet.

Punctually at 23.40 we made our final turn in to the beach and the pinpoint which now lay about one mile ahead. We were nearly there. We hadn't been going more than a minute or two on the new course when one of the look-outs announced, '*Luce* (light) *Commandante*.'

Not taking my eyes from the binoculars I was using I replied, '*Va bene. Grazie.*' Another car on the road.

Twenty seconds later the look-out repeated his '*Luce, Commandante*,' but rather more urgently.

I still didn't move, we were going in well.

'A car going along the coast,' I said, almost mechanically.

When, however, two look-outs and the Cox'n all whispered feverishly, '*Eh Commandante, luce, luce, LUCE*,' I did look up.

There, about forty yards away on our port bow was another MAS boat.

Almost immediately afterwards out of the mist, appeared two more, one to starboard and the other to port. In seconds we were in the middle of a triangle of enemy boats all of whom were issuing light challenges. We had to gain time, seconds counted. I gave our signal torch to Ranald.

'Make any reply letter you like, but fumble it and let them see that the torch has dropped to the deck.'

Calmly he took the lamp and started some admirable conjuring. Meanwhile dropping from the bridge into the wheelhouse I strode across to the wardroom door and pulled it open. Even in that tense moment I was surprised: there were the two girls one stretched out on each bunk face down, propped up on their elbows still leafing through their magazines while the men sat at the foot of the bunks smoking peacefully. I remember that one of the girls was waving her legs slowly back and forth as she read. The sort of scene you might expect to encounter on a hot summer's day by the Thames.

'Sorry, you people, but we may be in difficulty. Please whatever you do, don't move out of here,' I said quickly and slammed the door shut.

The helmsman's steering position in the wheelhouse was immediately beside the wardroom door.

'*Mortori principali. Vitessa massima*,' I ordered, and shot up the bridge ladder. Main motors. Full speed. I had no time to wonder how long they'd take to get going. As my head came out on deck they roared into life, the clutches were let in with a bang and we lunged ahead into high acceleration. The jolt threw me flat on my face on the hatch combing, and when I tried to get up I found that the Cox'n's legs were round my neck. He had been standing astride the hatch. His grip tightened as I pushed on up and he felt himself hoisted into the air: when he was all but upside down he fell off sideways. The first thing visible was one of the enemy boats fine on the port bow about thirty yards away. For a moment it looked as if we must hit her. They were still challenging with their light, presumably unable to believe we were not one of them in spite of our eccentric behaviour. We passed within about eight yards of her so that we could see the staring incredulous faces watching us go by. They weren't inactive for long, but we had the element of surprise to give us a small but welcome start; we were beginning to move quite fast.

Tracer shell began coming from two boats in a matter of seconds, the direction being good but the elevation poor — some eight or ten foot above our heads. We did the unexpected by jinking inshore: for several seconds the tracers followed before they lost us. For about three minutes we were at emergency maximum speed (in which time we covered over two miles) before coming down to 40 knots and heading out to the safety of open water. Five minutes later we reduced again to fast cruising at 35 knots, the danger past.

A figure in overalls joined Ranald, Bates and me on the bridge. Capo Pulchri, the ebullient Chief Engineer produced an excited music-hall salute with some heavy shading of the eyes, accompanied by a grin from ear to ear. '*Io, Capo Pulchri,*' he shouted above the roar of his engines, '*il primo motorista della Marina Italiana.*' His other arm flew up from behind his back to flourish a big bottle of Chianti in the air, before extending it in my direction. There could be no denying him. As I took a swig I reckoned he *was* probably the finest mechanic in the Italian Navy. Certainly at that moment he was.

When we were well clear I went below to see the passengers.

'I'm terribly sorry about tonight.'

The men shrugged nonchalantly, the girls spread their hands; all gave smiles of commiseration.

'It couldn't be helped,' said one of them.

'True,' I replied, 'but I would like to thank you all for remaining here so quietly during that bit of fuss.'

'But you warned us, *Commandante*. There was nothing that we could have done to help. Only to stay here.'

'Well, thank you all the same. Want to have another try?'

They all smiled. 'Any time, *Commandante*.'

They were a gallant bunch, the 'Girls' and their escorts: I hope they survived.

* * *

As, no doubt, the reader will have gathered, composite operations were never our favourite task. There are any number of old saws applicable to them — 'a chain being only as strong as the weakest link' — 'too many cooks'... — and so on, but the plain fact was that for any or all of such wiseacre reasons this type of operation started as an odds-on failure.

My heart sank, therefore, when we were called upon to carry out a

165

quite nauseating plan concocted by I-know-who-but-prefer-not-to-say, to land four men, and embark eight escaping prisoners-of-war, all for SOE. Additionally we were to land two men for OSS. A single pinpoint was to be used, one which, in our view, was already over-used and, therefore, likely to be closely patrolled. That might not have been too bad if it hadn't been complicated by the addition of a reception committee which was scheduled to meet those landing. If, for some reason, the committee didn't turn up then only three of the SOE men were to be landed; however, if they landed successfully, then the OSS men were to follow in and land, too. Only if the reception functioned properly was the fourth SOE man to be put ashore. Simple as child's play as everyone must agree.

From previous experience most of us had learnt what was practical and what wasn't, especially when there was mention of escaping prisoners-of-war. These latter had a first-class organization of their own, separate from any other of the clandestine services, and this they operated with efficiency and fierce courage, but it was also true that when they became involved in such ops as the one proposed, things had a strong tendency to go awry. The escapers themselves had no training in such affairs, they spoke nothing but English (exceptions being very rare), and the thought of a quick return to England made them over-exuberant. Who could blame them? But they didn't make the omens look very attractive.

Mercifully we were to be spared having to do any dinghy work, each sponsor electing to provide his own dinghymen. Our role, therefore, was confined to the donkeywork of finding the craft and the dinghies, obtaining the latest intelligence on the area from Paddy Davies, working out the navigational aspect with the Captain of the craft, and lastly, being responsible for all liaison between the Captain and the sponsors. Quite enough in a composite op of this complexity.

The ever-patient, ever-obliging Barnes agreed to lend two of his PT boats, *PT 209* (Lieutenant Eldridge) as the operational craft, and *PT 217* (Lieutenant Pressly) as the supporting escort. As mentioned earlier, increasing difficulties in obtaining spare engine parts for the PT boats created an acute problem in proper maintenance, a factor which made the American Commander even more insistent on never allowing any of his valuable craft to operate alone.

The 'Colonel' (our Scottish Lieutenant Dow, RNVR) had never taken part in a composite op, and this seemed a good opportunity to initiate him: he came as my assistant. When he heard what we were about to try he whistled through his teeth. 'They're wantin' a lot for their money, aren't they?' I could only agree. When we totted up the number who would be embarking at Bastia to execute this amazing triple act we arrived at a total of sixteen, of whom we hoped to land six, before embarking the eight PoWs at the one pinpoint. Sixteen extra on the way out, eighteen on the way home — if all went according to plan.

We took the usual security precautions of embarking a few at a time: by 19.00 they were all tucked away in various parts of the ship. Earlier we had put on board and stowed on the upper deck two normal size rubber dinghies and one much larger one. Nothing remained but to get under way. Ten minutes later we slipped and proceeded, our *PT 209* leading, with *217* taking station close astern. The weather was flat calm and the visibility good.

The 'Colonel's' eyes were agog. In his practical Glaswegian mind he had, I think, written off the whole project as 'plain daft'. On the bridge he turned to me. 'D'ye think we'll ever, *ever* get this lo' sorted out? It's a hell of a lo' o' people we have on board.' He was plumb right. I replied that much would depend on what we found at the other end.

Andrew Croft, cheerful as ever, and one of the principal actors in the drama, came up on the bridge for a gossip. He was personally taking his party ashore when we arrived, his arctic explorations having given him much skill in dinghy work. The meticulousness of his planning was based on avoiding at all costs that dirtiest of words 'failure'. 'Everything under control?' he asked.

'As far as it ever will be with this crowd on board,' I replied.

'Well, my chaps know what to do. Their task is quite straightforward, providing the reception committee is there.'

'D'you know how many escorting officers — non-participants that is — there are on board?'

'We're just four, to handle the three dinghies.'

'Exactly. And the others are *six*, to handle *two* chaps.'

'H'm — in terms of chaps that seems a lot.'

'It does.'

Andrew always talked 'in terms of'.

Further conversation petered out as the hiss of the main engines dwindled to nothing and the ship came to a sluggish halt. Heads popped out of hatches inquisitively. Were we there already? Meanwhile there was an animated conversation on the 'intercom' between the Captain and the chief engineer culminating in the arrival of the chief engineer in person on the bridge to report that one of the engines had burst a water-jacket. The Captain looked enquiringly in my direction. 'Well, Commander, you heard?'

'Indeed I did.'

'What would you like to do? Transfer the personnel and equipment to the other boat?'

'Why, yes please. That's all we can do.'

Lieutenant Eldridge slid his escorting *PT 217* alongside in flat calm water — we might just as well have been secured to the jetty in Bastia so little was the movement — and everything and everybody was transferred safely from one boat to the other with no hitches, and (as far as one could tell in the dark) nothing forgotten. As the senior Captain of the two boats Eldridge also transferred himself into the escorting craft, leaving his own boat in command of the First Lieutenant to limp back to base on the remaining engine.

Thinking of future good relations with Commander Barnes I raised the matter of his strict but sensible edict prohibiting unescorted boats operating on their own. In doing so I was careful to explain that on a previous occasion when a boat had broken down we had continued alone and Barnes had raised no subsequent complaint. This seemed to satisfy Lieutenant Eldridge and he agreed to continue. Meanwhile half an hour had quietly slipped by since we stopped, and I heard the 'Colonel' as he hunched himself into a corner of the bridge grizzling away darkly to himself about, 'Wha' a skylark this is turnin' out to be.' I was only surprised that the op had gone so far, so smoothly.

Under way once more, leaving the other boat to its own devices, we increased speed slightly to make up for lost time.

For two more hours we trundled along comfortably 'with nothing to mar our joy of a night full of stars and a glassy sea'. Then came the moment to ease back the throttles to a modest 9 knots preparatory to the final run-in to the pinpoint. This was also the moment for the unexpected to start happening. Nothing sensational, but having its effect nonetheless.

'Target, bearing Red-two-O,' came from the radar operator.

'What is it?' demanded the Captain.

'Can't say for sure, sir, right now. Looks a fair size but could be two boats. About two miles distant, speed 10 knots. If they hold their present course they should pass one mile ahead of us.'

'OK. Keep reporting.'

Whatever the target was the Captain altered course to give it a wide berth. Three minutes later, before we had had time to resume our course for the pinpoint, there was another report of a further target coming in fast on the port beam. Judged by its speed the operator though it was probably an E-boat. Once again we altered course, and went on dodging about until the Captain considered it safe to aim for the pinpoint, by which time it was clear that he didn't much care for this kind of slow speed nonsense: he was used to manoeuvring at high speed where actions, offensive or defensive, were quick and decisive, and where, given the smallest chance you became aggressive. Here, aggression was the last thing we sought.

When a whole convoy of F-fighters and their E-boat escorts came up on the screen he stopped the boat altogether for a whole ten minutes, cursing and swearing under his breath. He had my sympathy. Targets kept being sighted — we were in, or certainly near the coastal shipping channel — until all at once the radar operator also started swearing. He sounded as if he was sweating, too.

'Cap'n,' he called, 'the screen's gone out,' by which he meant his equipment had failed, but his expression was rather more apt.

The Captain darted down to have a look for himself; when he returned some thirty seconds later, he said in a crisp fed-up voice, 'We're in trouble with the auxiliary generator.'

'So?'

'Without the auxiliary generator the radar can't function at low speed, and without radar I guess we'll have a hard time finding our way in.'

'But we're already in sight of land.'

'Sure. But I want to get a good fix.'

'We can do that visually as soon as we get a bit closer to the beach.'

'Yeah, I know, but I'd still like to get a reliable position from here.'

'Any chance of mending the radar?'

'Well, we can try a 180 degree turn, but I'll have to have some speed on the engines to start the main generator.' He was peering about in the dark, unhappy at being unable to 'see' the lurking dangers. 'If that doesn't work, Commander, I'm wondering if you'd like to continue with the operation?'

'Let's try your quick turn trick first. If that doesn't work we'll think about it then.'

'OK — We'll try. Here we go.'

So saying he opened both throttles, the boat surged ahead rapidly to 20 knots, and the wheel was put hard over to produce the requisite tight turn.

The reaction throughout the rest of the boat was instant and eruptive. Strangely hatted heads shot up from hatches, excited voices demanded in several languages to know what was happening, and one agitated Italian made a dash out on deck only to be pulled back by his coat-tails by unseen hands reaching up from below. Even some of the many escorting officers were heard expressing their anxiety at this unscheduled tactic: quite loudly, too.

Andrew stirred beside me. 'Would it help if I were to go and have a word with the boys?' he asked.

'Please do, by all means,' I replied. 'Just tell them, if you would, that what we're doing is all for their own good, and that there's no danger.

But, in any case, for God's sake, to pipe down.'

He disappeared while we completed our turn at speed, and by the time we were round he seemed to have restored both order and confidence; there was no further noise from below, and everyone stayed where they should be. The radar operator's voice came over the intercom. 'I got a picture, Cap'n. Not good, but improving.'

'OK.' breathed Eldridge in relief. 'Now I'll get that fix, quick.'

Reducing speed to our previous 9 knots he had the boat pointed in the general direction of our destination and then went below to study the radar screen to get his fix. Surprisingly quickly he came back to announce success. Would I like to see where we were? Yes, please, I would. After all the manoeuvrings, stopping and starting and turning, we were almost exactly on the line of a direct course between Bastia and the pinpoint. The Lord takes care of...

But we weren't to be left without further distractions to keep our interest alive. A large fire was seen to break out — perhaps as a result of an air-raid — on land still some way off but directly ahead. Simultaneously some spectacular fireworks shot into the air some five miles to the east along the coast. Happily the more volatile of our passengers were ignorant of these entertainments as we droned on inshore.

Just before 01.00 the radar finally gave up the ghost, by which time we were barely five miles from the pinpoint. Very properly the Captain queried the wisdom of continuing the run-in without the use of his 'night-eyes' in what was such a busy area. Although he didn't say so I think the passenger reaction to his earlier tight turn had caused him to wonder what might happen if we were unfortunate enough to run into trouble. I had wondered, too. I understood his position: here he was trying to land and embark a crowd of extraordinary people, his boat full of them, while he was obliged to creep around on their behalf as if frightened of his own shadow — instead of performing his orthodox role of being beastly to the enemy.

'Oh, I think we should go on, Captain,' I replied, 'we're so near the pinpoint, and we're well placed for a straight run in.'

'OK, Commander, here we go.' There was cooperation for you.

To reduce speed yet again he had to cut out one engine. PT boats being made for high speed disliked running on a light load for any length of time; 7 knots provided a reasonable load for one engine only. We continued on our way, maintaining our course — and a sharp look out.

A light flashed out from the shore, fine on our starboard bow, and was quickly answered by a vessel on our starboard quarter. Evidently we weren't alone but this was nothing to do with us. We were now close to our destination, and Andrew disappeared below to warn the escorting officers and passengers to collect their gear together ready to come on deck when given the order. Another twenty minutes should see us stopped and the dinghies lowered. It was best not to think what might happen after that.

The shore silhouette was now visible in sufficient detail for us to check that we were precisely where we should be; had we had any doubts these would have been dispelled a few minutes later when two flares fired to the east of us illuminated a good section of the coast — and a couple of E-boats lying stopped about two miles on our starboard hand. Lieutenant Eldridge studied them carefully, pursed his lips and expressed the hope that they would remain there. At 02.00 we arrived at the pinpoint. The time was at hand to let the dog see the rabbit...

Andrew was still down below, winding them up, so the 'Colonel' was despatched to tell all escorting officers the good news, and get them to bring their charges on deck ready for the 'off'.

'This,' I heard the 'Colonel' say as he stumped aft, 'should be very interesting.' And certainly there was every reason to agree as the crowds surfaced through the hatches on to the upper deck. Ship's officers and men, escorting officers, dinghymen, and resisters milled in every direction getting in each other's way, offering advice, asking questions in at least three languages. Going aft I found Andrew standing on the quarterdeck with his binoculars watching intently for any sign of the reception committee's light signal. Normally there was no fear of mistaking such signals, but that night there were already a number of lights to be seen round the village, some of them moving which made them seem to be flashing. It made the task very difficult. Once or twice Andrew thought he saw the signal only to find he was being misled by the profusion of movement ashore. The amount of time we could spend off the pinpoint was strictly limited; there was only one thing left to do — go and have a look. He would take Sergeant Arnold and paddle ashore in one rubber dinghy, and put his three men who were to be landed, with their own dinghyman, in a second dinghy. He would then lead while the second dinghy would follow at a distance, astern. Should Andrew run into trouble this would leave the following dinghy a better chance of regaining the safety of the PT boat. Meanwhile the OSS group were to remain on board and wait for Andrew to give them the all-clear to go ashore: this he would do by light signal.

The two dinghies were launched over the side, and disentangling his party from the throng on deck, Andrew got them safely down into their allotted little boats before himself casting off from the mother-ship. He and his Sergeant pulled briskly away towards the pinpoint — the village jetty. Then came the turn of the second dinghy to cast off. From the bridge I watched the oarsman bend vigorously to his paddles and the dinghy started to move. It had gone three yards when it stopped so abruptly that the dinghyman fell over backwards into the lap of the man sitting in the bows. Someone had failed to let go the painter. Shouts followed between dinghy and ship — very rude shouts, indeed, from the dinghyman when he recovered a sitting position. To a loud and confidant assurance of 'OK' from somewhere in the ship the dinghyman again drove his paddles into the water, went a further three yards and again went over backwards. Next time he was more cautious as he paddled a few extra yards before being brought up all standing. The 'Colonel' went aft to cope. At the fifth attempt the dinghy got away, and the 'Colonel' returned to report, 'D'ye know wha' they did? First it was the painter — that was the funny bit. Then — can ye believe it? — they had forgotten to let go the lines used for lashing the dinghy down to the deck on the way over here. Can you beat that? I wonder will they ever get ashore?'

It was, indeed, an interesting speculation. What else could go wrong in the next two hours, the time allowed for the dinghies to be away from the ship?

Presently one of the OSS escorting officers came on the bridge to enquire if we had any news from the beach; his party was becoming restive with the delay. Constant watch through binoculars gave no indication one way or the other of how things might be going in the village. True, there had been a small increase in the number of lights circulating round the central area, but there had certainly been no signal from anywhere along the waterfront. More as a matter of conversation than anything else I asked the escorting officer if either of his two waiting men knew the village. To my surprise he told me that one of them was a native of the place.

This might prove useful, and I suggested that he might bring the man up on deck to see if he could point out to us the exact location of the jetty from where we were expecting to receive the signal. Obligingly he went off to the after end of the ship to return, shortly, with a bizarre figure dressed in an ankle-length macintosh affair, and wearing on his head a very wide-brimmed Anthony Eden hat of the sort favoured by the more 'arty' of the pre-war dramatic critics, or, for those who remember him, by Popski, the spy, of Pip, Squeak, and Wilfred.

This strange phenomenon was presented to me quite simply as, 'This is the guy, Commander.'

'Good. Perhaps you could ask him if he can point out the exact location of the jetty we're looking for?'

The escorting officer went into a huddle with his charge, and there was a good deal of gesturing and pointing, ending with the phenomenon gazing long and intently at the shore but showing no sign of recognizing anything; to help him I offered my binoculars which he took, pushing his enormous hat on to the back of his head in order to peer through them. As he did so he swung his head in rapid sweeps from side to side. Abruptly, with a kind of grunt he handed them back to me and look round wildly.

'Well?' I enquired.

'This is not my village. Not the right place. It is all wrong,' he shouted and waved his arms.

'What village do you come from, then?'

He told me.

'This,' I said, pointing towards the shore, '*is* the village. This is where you come from.'

'*Ma*, no, no,' he shouted.

'Look,' I said to the escorting officer, 'we are at the village he *says* he comes from. I can show you on the chart if you like. Please get that into his head. Either he doesn't come from here at all or he doesn't recognize it from the sea. It is — whatever he says — the village he says he comes from.'

The escorting officer let fly a torrent of words, and there was a deal of arm waving on both sides, in the middle of which his charge suddenly bolted off down the deck, aft, his 'arty' hat coming off to disappear into the drink as he went. Eldridge, the 'Colonel' and I were taken aback by this performance and had had no time to recover before being astounded by the reappearance of the same man now wearing an American naval officer's cap with the peak aligned over one ear. He was still waving his arms and now gabbling incoherently.

'OK, Gino,' soothed the American officer, 'you'd better come below with me and lie down for a bit. That'll make you feel better.' So saying he attempted to take the man gently by the arm. The suggestion and, perhaps, the arm holding provoked a final outburst of protest; happily this didn't last long before he allowed himself to be led off, still muttering. Rather as though he was getting used to these odd events the 'Colonel' asked, 'Can anything else happen?'

'I wouldn't like to bet on it,' I replied. 'But meanwhile keep your eyes on those E-boats. We don't want them to become interested in us, too.'

Minutes later I heard the 'Colonel' making peculiar gasping noises in the background. 'Jest lo-o-ok at tha-a-at,' he wheezed, pointing to the stern of the ship. Unheard and unseen by us, a fishing boat with four men in it had crept in under our stern where one of them had quietly made the boat's painter fast to one of our bollards. The 'Colonel' almost throttled with indignation. 'Wull I cut their pain'er?' he demanded.

Lieutenant Eldridge, equally, viewed the situation with strong disfavour; he wanted to know if this might not be a form of camouflage to cover an attack by frogmen or some other unpleasant device. We all trooped aft to have a closer look.

'Good-evening,' I ventured to the visitors.

'Good-evening, *signore*,' came the polite reply.

'Stopping long?'

'Oh, excuse us, *signore*, but it saves us putting down our anchor if we tie ourselves to you.'

'But I'm afraid we're not anchored.'

'No? What a mistake we make! We apologise.'

'Never mind. But we'll be shoving off in a minute.'

'Thank you, *signore*, for telling us. Alberto, let go that rope, and we'll go, too.'

Suddenly I remembered the opportunism of Capo Pulchri. 'Got any fish?' I asked.

'Eh, *signore* — it's terrible, so few we have.'

'Better further up the coast, perhaps.'

'Perhaps, *signore*, perhaps. Goodnight, *signore*.'

'Good-night.'

The boat drifted off slowly into the night as two of the men pulled languidly on the long oars.

Lieutenant Eldridge was still a bit suspicious. 'What did they say?' he wanted to know.

'Just that they hadn't caught many fish.'

This reply seemed to increase his doubts still further. 'You really think they were fishing? You believed them?' He clearly didn't.

'I believed them. I think they really were fishing.'

'Well, of all the darned nerve...'

Further speculation was cut short by the noise of approaching paddles splashing, as the dinghies made their way towards the ship; their time was up after two hours away. As soon as both boats and men were inboard the Captain, now greatly relieved, gave the order to start up one engine, and we got under way to creep quietly out to sea on the homeward passage, with no fear of further alarms from that infernal radar screen.

Presently a somewhat puzzled Andrew joined us on the bridge. 'I don't know,' he ruminated, staring out into the dark, 'I really don't.'

'How did it go ashore?' I asked.

'Extraordinary,' he replied. 'I can't understand it. We found the address of the man who was supposed to be organizing things, and there was just no one there. We knocked on several doors, and some quite angry people answered — but not a sign of the reception committee. A great pity, because we then did a recce of most of the village and as far as I could see we could have landed an army and nobody would have stopped us. In terms of effort it was an awful waste. No sign either, of the PoWs although we did ask about them from one of the inhabitants. Most extraordinary, the whole thing.'

'It sounds it,' I replied. 'Things looked quite busy from where we were watching, but that was probably you and your boys.'

'Probably. Anything happen on board while we were ashore?'

'Oh, nothing much. One or two things, just enough to keep us awake.'

Metaphorically Andrew sucked his teeth. 'A damned disappointing operation,' he remarked, writing the whole thing off.

But not boring.

★ ★ ★

What did we do for amusement during the non-operational days of the month? There really wasn't much time for more than trivial diversions. Three days of preparation before ops, ten, or at a pinch, twelve days of actual operations, followed by three days or more of clearing up, sleeping, and writing reports, getting boats repaired, and so on, didn't leave much over before the whole business of preparation started again. Assembling equipment, working out the schedule of operations with the sponsoring authorities, selecting and briefing the ops officers for the next series to ensure that as soon as the non-moon period started we had a sensible programme to follow. Since frequent changes were inevitable for one reason or another, during the operational period we had to allow room for flexibility — just like any other taxi service. The customers couldn't always be ready on time and sometimes they needed to be fetched in a great hurry.

When a set of operations was completed it was pleasant to go down to Algiers to report, and be debriefed. It was a moment to meet old friends in the Club Interallié for a meal or a drink, to swap news, and relax a bit. There wasn't a great deal of free time, though. Briefing and programming the next set of operations required visits to a number of authorities and much discussion, so that the days whisked by all too quickly. But if there was a scarcity of public entertainment in Bastia this was compensated to some extent by the extraordinary mixture of nationalities from amongst which emerged a surprising number of amusing people only too happy to display a variety of talents.

One such was Dick Cooper, a British officer with, among other outlandish gifts, the power to hypnotize. His career had run an odd enough course from birth, a humorous but often rebellious nature landing him in some strange situations, not the least being a long spell in the French Foreign Legion. From there he emerged as, I believe a Sergeant, speaking rather better French than English, and covered from head to foot, literally, in tattoo mottos, initials, verses (all unprintable), designs, and pictures, most of them very rude indeed. Dick's favourite amusement was to lure some unsuspecting girl into expressing interest in the tattoo marks on the backs of his hands. A quiet casual glance from the girl was enough to set him off.

'Ah, I see you looking at my hands, dear girl. Good tattooing, isn't it? That was done by an Arab in the desert. There's a better one up my forearm...'

Up would go his sleeve. Everyone knew what was coming next, except the girl. The graffiti got higher and higher. Off would come his battledress blouse, then his shirt, his shoes and socks. During this appalling strip-tease he added a lurid commentary of what was coming next. Depending on the girl's reaction he would gauge how far he could go — but he always went one stage further than she believed he would.

When no ladies were present he didn't bother, he just went the whole hog. An amazing standard of ingenuity had gone into the tattoo work on the more intimate bits of his anatomy: he and the artists must have enjoyed many a fascinating hour thinking up the finished work. How Dick, himself, stood up to what must often have been excruciating agony one shudders to imagine.

The hypnotizing act could be startling, so startling that there was frequent difficulty in finding a volunteer. Newcomers were the best bet: anyone who had witnessed a performance had more sense. Dick's favourite backdrop for demonstrating his skill was a bar which in former times had been a cabaret called the Moulin Rouge. What else could such an atrocious dive be called? It was the only one in the town. The proprietor, a wily man, encouraged impromptu turns by his patrons, even the strip-tease which he pretended not to see. The hypnosis act was more popular, however, because it attracted a bigger crowd, and called for a lot more drink. (The only drink served was a nauseating mixture known simply as 'l'apéritif'. It was anybody's guess as to what went into it, but the end result was red.)

Whether Dick really hypnotized his subjects or terrified them into a state of unconsciousness bordering on death was a matter of opinion. Just to watch the performance for the first time was quite unnerving enough. First he would tout the bar for a volunteer. Those who had seen the act before could be counted on to lend their support to Dick's claim that it was 'nothing to be afraid of, my friends. In fact it is a very pleasant experience'. There was a good deal of shouting and laughter until the victim came forward; then there were cheers. Two stout tables were arranged end to end and the volunteer would stretch himself out on top.

Dick's normal expression was a curious mixture, best described, perhaps, as one of pugnacious friendliness, something which they taught him in the Foreign Legion, possibly. All that changed when he was about to hypnotize someone. He assumed a grimace of diabolical ferocity as he advanced slowly on the now prone form. Black eyes flashing, bristly toothbrush moustache strained so tight across bared teeth that it seemed certain to come in half, tattooed hands with fingers wide spread, now held in front of him, he crept like a cat towards the table. For several seconds he would stand beside the subject's head, glaring down at him, his breath whistling through his teeth. What normally happened then was that he would drop his hands to his side, relax, and say in a very ordinary voice, 'I say, old man, I wonder if you'd budge up a bit on the table. Your head's too far from the end.'

Little did the poor chap realize the danger of what he was doing as he wriggled up until the back of his head was just over the edge. Dick left him no time to think better, before lunging at him with a hiss of in-drawn breath, seizing him with one hand under the chin and the other at the back of the neck. With eyes boring into eyes about six inches apart Dick would begin bending the chap's head back, down towards the floor, while whispering through clenched teeth.

'You're sleepy. You're very tired. You must go to sleep. You can't keep your eyes open. You're exhausted. That's all you can think of. Sleep...' Meanwhile his attitude said all too clearly, 'Go to sleep, you sod, or I'll bash you.'

By now the victim's head was almost upside down and his neck seemed in danger of breaking. Dick was once accused of stopping the blood supply to the brain; his reaction was an indignant denial and a claim that he was 'hardly touching the man' who was 'just naturally falling asleep'. Finally he would straighten up slowly and with a seraphic smile announce, 'Ladies and gentlemen, he's asleep.'

Asleep, strangled, or dead, the victim was, indeed, still.

'Now what shall we make him do?'

After the inevitable rush of bawdy suggestions the choice seldom varied. Make him swim. Once more Dick addressed the unconscious figure, coo-ing at him that he was at sea, that the ship had sunk under him, and that he was only a hundred yards from the shore. '...you're

177

doing well. Going through the water at a comfortable crawl. But look out, old man. What's that just behind you? It's a shark. You've got to go much faster. Quick, old man. Swim, swim, SWIM.'

He would step back from the table and clap his hands. 'Right, old man. Wake up!'

The unconscious form would then sit up, open his eyes, get off the table onto the floor and start swimming for dear life. A few seconds later the roar of laughter would bring him back to reality, and he would get to his feet with a sheepish grin, unaware of what all the laughter was about.

Dick had several other tricks, such as sticking pins through his arms, and holding his breath for longer than anyone else. He was always fun, and an invaluable entertainer.

Chapter 9

RAIDS AND MISTAKES

Just before one of the operational conferences in Algiers a report came
in that the French group whom we had tried twice, each time unsuc-
cessfully, to embark from the south coast of France, was now in
serious trouble being harassed unceasingly by the German counter-
espionage services. Several members of the group had already been arrested. The essential needs were now money and re-establishment of
communications between the survivors and London. It was likely,
therefore, that they would ask for a boat to take money in to a reception
committee, and to bring one member of the group back with us to
Bastia from where he would be despatched back to the UK.

All this had been agreed before I arrived for the conference, the only
questions remaining were where and when the operation should take
place. We could guess that the pinpoint would be somewhere to the
west of St Tropez — as on the two previous occasions — but the timing
was still vague owing to the numbers of the group being on the run
from the enemy and in no position to make reliable plans. As a mark of
its importance the operation was given first priority, a rare occurrence,
the normal rule being first come first served.

On return to Bastia I told Prof what was in the wind and we arranged the new programme with an eye to making such sudden changes as
to be ready for this particular operation when and if the moment came.
And come it did. Only a few days later.

An officer from the sponsoring organization turned up at the villa
just before lunch to tell us that his headquarters had received a rather
garbled message from France asking that a boat should stand by to
carry out *an* operation on that very same night. There was, however,
no clear indication of what they wanted to achieve. The only firm in-
juction was not to send any boat until and unless they confirmed that

they could carry out their part. Such confirmation would, we were assured, be with us by 16.00. A glance at the night's schedule showed that we could be ready provided the confirmation came through on time. We should have to sail by 16.00 at the latest in order to cover the distance involved — over 150 miles each way — and be well clear of the French coast before dawn next day. Air patrols were known to be active in the area.

Calculations showed that the minimum time between leaving Bastia, undertaking the operation, and being ten miles clear of the French coast on our way home could not be less, even in favourable circumstances, than twelve hours. This made no allowance for bad weather, navigational errors, enemy patrol evasion, or delays within the shore party to name only the principal hazards which so often influenced timings. (Some eyebrows may be raised at the mention of navigational errors. Let me say in our defence that MAS boats operated on dead reckoning alone: metaphorically, at least, you drew the course to steer on the chart, pointed the bows accordingly and then just went. Only the PT boats had radar, and that wasn't always to be relied on, as we have already seen.) The arithmetic was explained to the sponsoring officer and he assured us that he would keep us closely posted with any developments.

The rest of the day whisked by, everyone busy preparing for the night's ops. Meanwhile Prof and I shuffled the programme round so as to leave me spare and ready to go on the French op at a moment's notice: in that event the 'Colonel' would come as assistant, with Leading Seaman Johnstone as dinghyman. Original plans had provided for Ginger and me to carry out an operation on to the Italian coast that night; the only change we now made was for Tom to take this over while the 'Colonel' and I took the Marchese and his boat. The Marchese was an excellent officer and was (as described earlier) someone with whom I had already worked and understood. More often than not he and his boat were employed on more aggressive operational patrol work and for this reason their torpedo tubes had been retained on board. In consequence his boat had a top speed of only 36 knots against Ginger's 47 knots.

Once more, to ensure the increased operational range the dreaded floppy extra fuel tanks were shipped, this time into a deck space made smaller by the presence of torpedo-tubes. With the rubber dinghy lashed down on top we were ready to go. We waited. Zero hour of 16.00 came and went without a signal of any sort. The sponsors were upset and apologetic. There was only one thing to do — stand the operation down — and this was agreed. Word must be passed to the boat, but before that, attention was called for in the preparation of other operations.

At 16.40 the telephone rang again. A message had now been received from the French group confirming that the operation was 'on'; the sponsors were sending an officer round immediately with all details. Two minutes later he arrived, to give the exact pinpoint, which we checked straight away on the chart, the letter, the colour, and the frequency of the light signal we should expect from the beach, and a thick parcel containing a substantial sum of French francs (no doubt made in England by the ton). He also confirmed that we were required to bring back with us one member of the reception committee. We hurried down to the Base.

Not more than ten minutes later we cast off — a record getaway — but nearly an hour later than our estimated latest safe time of departure. We could only try. On our way up to the northern tip of the island, Cap Corse, we wondered what sort of weather we might find round the corner between Corsica and mainland France: so much now depended on speed. When, an hour later, we made our turn to the west to settle down to our top cruising speed of 30 knots, the weather wasn't ideal, about force 3, wind and sea, from the south-west, which gave a rather bumpy ride; at least we were able to maintain speed although constant pounding made steering an accurate course a test of skill and endurance for the helmsman.

This time the pinpoint was a little deeper into the long tapering sleeve of water contained between the mainland on the north side, and on the south by the long line of the Iles d'Hyères. This meant that for the trickiest part of the operation we could be observed from both north and south at the same time. Well, we hadn't been seen last time: with luck we wouldn't be seen this time.

Three and a half hour's checking on the helmsman steering through an uncomfortable head sea brought its reward in a landfall shortly after 21.00 which showed an error of about three miles too far north of Cap Camarat — a reasonable margin. Main engines were shut down and we went over to auxiliaries. Once in the lee of the Iles d'Hyères we were making good between 5 and 6 knots in smooth water.

The time for the reception committee to make their first signal from the beach was fixed at 01.45; they were to flash the letter 'C' once every five minutes with a blue-shaded torch. The visibility was good and we should see it from a long way.

At midnight we started up the narrow entry to the sleeve of water separating the Ile du Levant (that post-war notorious nudist colony) and the mainland. The noise of the auxiliaries in the still air seemed awful; so bad, in fact, that we felt obliged to cut to half speed at 01.00. That we were able to do so was due to kinder weather than had been foreseen: now within about five miles of the pinpoint we had a small but welcome margin of time in hand, four miles in the MAS and the last mile in the rubber dinghy would be easy going before the first signal from the shore was due. Fearing to arrive too early we stopped ship: if we had to wait anywhere, well offshore was the place. The auxiliary engines were kept running. We could take no chances about a possible backfire on restarting.

Meanwhile scanning the shoreline with binoculars in the direction of the pinpoint there was no sign of any activity. We started on the move again: at the end of twenty minutes the whole boat suddenly started to vibrate violently. At the same instant a faint white light could be seen coming from the pinpoint. Speed was reduced to slow on both engines and the Chief Engineer came up on the bridge to confirm what we had already guessed, that there was something heavy round one of the propellors. A fine time for one of the many imponderables to happen. But there could be no stopping now. Should the necessity arise to use main engines in emergency, we could only hope their sheer power should cut through whatever was fouling us.

At about one mile out we saw for the first time a very faint blue flashing from the shore: so faint was it that I wouldn't have trusted my own eyesight but for confirmation by Johnstone that he had seen it, too. We stopped ship and lowered the dinghy. As Johnstone and I climbed down into it I had a final word with the 'Colonel'.

'Don't move the ship unless you have to. Keep her just where she is. If we're not back by 04.30 you are to leave immediately, and return to Bastia. Meanwhile try to get the port prop cleared. Understood?'

Peering down at me from an outsize duffle-coat which threatened to gobble him up the 'Colonel' gave a craggy smile 'Aye.' he said.

'And don't let them alter the engine revs unless there's an emergency.'

'Aye. I got that.'

Look-outs and patrols were especially sensitive to noise and changes in noise, or, indeed, lack of noise. At night particularly, sound seems to travel amazing distances in still air. And the night was very still.

'Remember,' I emphasized, '04.30 is the limit. That should give you a bare 45 minutes to clear the coast before dawn. Is that understood?'

'Aye, that's fine. I'll get going all right. But good luck right now — and just you get back here before 04.30. I'd hate like hell to have to come back next month to get ye.'

'Thanks Colonel, we'll try. So long.'

The packet of money was almost 3 in thick, about 15 in long and 10 in wide. Hundreds, perhaps thousands of French banknotes freshly minted in England where they knew how to make the finest, toughest paper. With the package securely crammed into the front of my battle-dress I reckoned I was wearing a first-class bullet-proof vest. The only trouble was that I should have been wearing it on my back to be of any real use as we pulled ashore. Oh, well...

The sea was as flat as a mill pond as we paddled in. It was so smooth that by looking sideways you could see the reflection of the shoreline in the water. Even the quiet dipping of the paddles in and out seemed to be noisy, but we were glad of the exercise to warm us up for it had been cold on the bridge. Every so often we stopped to observe the blue flashes which seemed to be very weak. That they were there at all was a great spur on our way. Meanwhile the noise of the auxiliaries continued to whine loudly across the water. I wondered if they had managed to clear the prop.

The closer we approached now, the greater the frequency of the signals from the torch, but rarely could one distinguish the correct letter, 'C', from the flickering flurry of dots and dashes. When we were five or six hundred yards from the shore we saw a white light moving along the beach about 100 yards to the left of the pinpoint, while on the right two more white lights could be seen, one moving and the other stationary but flashing on and off. The reception committee signal was, then, coming from between two sets of activity.

As the topography of the shore became clearer, the pinpoint itself showed up as a very small promontory with the rather grandiose name of Cap Negre, rising sheer out of the water (with no beach) to a height of perhaps a hundred feet. On each side of the promontory, perched at varying heights on steeply sloping ground were a number of smallish buildings. One of these now revealed itself as an enemy patrol centre. As the door kept swinging to and fro with the coming and going of patrol members, so the interior light flashed out over the sea. A busy corner of the world, this, with the noise of the auxiliaries still plainly audible. (At least she was still there.)

When we were a mere hundred yards from the shore, the previously blue signal from the reception committee turned white and increased considerably in strength. Either they had deliberately removed the blue filter, or it had fallen off, or they were trying to tell us they were in trouble. For a few seconds we stopped paddling and watched; the light continued to signal in an irregular pattern. It was so bright that the more it flashed the more likely we, and they, were to be observed. We had to go in quick. 'Come on, pull' I said to Johnstone. His only reply was to bend to his work with an 'Aye, aye, sir. Got the tommy-gun 'andy, sir?' I had it right beside me.

Moving fast towards our objective we didn't make much noise. Not until we were within ten yards or so could I see the two figures standing on a ledge of rock on the promontory; at five yards I whispered the password, and got back an agitated but correct reply. While Johnstone backed the stern of the dinghy towards the men I fished out the money ready to hand it over, but when we were right in under the ledge one of the men jumped straight into the boat.

'Here's the money,' I whispered, handing the package up to the man still crouching above me.

He waved it away, excitedly. 'No, no,' he spoke in a rush 'I cannot stay.'

'What's wrong?'

'The Germans know we are here. They are chasing us.'

True, the place did seem active with quite a lot of movement about, especially round the patrol hut.

'But your people need the money. They said it was urgent in their last message.'

'We know that. We know, but we have only just escaped the Boche patrol who are,' he pointed upwards, 'only just above us. They are still searching for us.'

'What d'you want to do, then?'

'We must both go with you. There is no other way.'

'And the money?'

'We will take it back with us.'

'Couldn't we land you again a few hundred yards away from here?'

'No, the whole area is alerted. We fell over the cliff to get here. I have no arse to my trousers and he', (indicating his companion) 'has only one shoe which is badly torn. We cannot go back or we'll be caught.'

Under my breath I said a very rude four letter word. But Johnstone picked it up. 'Good idea, sir. Told it's pretty good round 'ere...'

He certainly was a dedicated man.

'All right,' I said to the man on the ledge, 'come on into the boat.' Reaching up I gave him a hand to slide quickly over the edge until his feet touched the rubber tubing of the dinghy; then he collapsed into the bottom of the boat and I saw that he spoke the truth about his trousers.

As we pushed off I looked at my watch. We had 35 minutes to find the MAS boat.

To steer accurately by field compass while pulling a rubber dinghy is not easy, especially at night.

'We could see you at 400 metres,' whispered the nearest Frenchman.

'If you could see us, why didn't the Germans also see us?'

'Because they were busy looking for us,' he replied.

The curious fact was that we never *expected* to be seen by the enemy in our rubber dinghies, and, so far as I know, we never were.

Pulling on into the dark we tried to maintain a steady back bearing to keep us moving in a straight line but this became more difficult as the landmarks receded. After twenty minutes we stopped pulling and I called for silence. At an indeterminate distance, in a direction impossible to define with any accuracy, we could hear the monotonous whine of the MAS auxiliaries: but that was all. Ten minutes more of hard pulling provided no better clue, and I decided that we must now risk a quick signal with the torch in the general direction of where the ship should be. Only five minutes remained before the 'Colonel's' orders required him to leave the area for Bastia, and he would obey — no matter how reluctantly: of that I felt confident.

Three times I flashed one plain dash at slightly differing angles in the general direction where I hoped the MAS would be, and then Johnstone and I resumed pulling. We reckoned that the noise of the auxiliaries was, if anything, growing fainter, until, all at once, there was the Marchese in his MAS boat bearing down on us, looking enormous against our puny size. The fact that she was under way meant that they must have seen our signal. At 04.28 all four of us climbed aboard, hoisting the dinghy after us.

'Well done,' said the 'Colonel', 'ye had me worried — almost.'

'Did you see my signal?'

'Aye. I saw *a* signal, and guessed it might be you.'

'Thanks, "Colonel". Tell me, what would you have done if 04.30 had come and we hadn't turned up?'

He turned towards me, and even in the dark I could see his wry Glaswegian smile. 'The question doesna arise,' he said.

'And the port prop? All right now?'

'Cleared while ye were away. A great bundle of wadding, looked like someone had thrown his mattress overboard.'

Meanwhile the Marchese had already turned the ship's head to an easterly course and was beginning to open up the auxiliary throttles to half ahead — about 3 to 4 knots; it was as much as he dared without altering the noise pitch too abruptly. There was no time, at that moment, to think of the needs of our passengers, and through the 'Colonel' I excused my apparent discourtesy, saying that I would come below as soon as I could. What the 'Colonel' used for language I could only leave to his ingenuity, but I needn't have worried — Johnstone had already taken over the job of finding warm clothing and other comforts.

Half an hour later the Captain and I agreed we must push on if we were not to be caught by the dawn, now only fifteen minutes away. We were still within two or three miles of land as we steamed east between the mainland and the Iles d'Hỳeres. At 05.30, an hour since we had brought our passengers on board, when the sky was already light we switched over to main engines at 30 knots until they were warm enough to take the full speed of 36 knots. We were still in the clutches of the mainland and the Iles d'Hỳeres which we could now see in some detail: if we could see them, they could see us. We were lucky, perhaps, to be in a MAS, which was used by Allies and Axis alike, as against the PT boat with its distinctive American lines.

Soon we were back in the ruffled waters outside the lee of the coast. With an offshore wind, noise no longer mattered. Below, Johnstone was acting as nursemaid to our guests, one of whom was just beginning to show signs of seasickness, poor chap. We took them both up into the fresh air and fed them with 'selfheaters' while they revived enough to give a brief account of their previous three days trying to locate a suitable pinpoint. Time and again they had come close to capture when inspecting coves, beaches, promontories, and other likely places. The Germans hadn't ruled out an Allied landing in the south of France, and were very alert. Perhaps they were, but it was a long coastline, and the main concentration of German troops was in the north against a much more serious threat of the Channel invasion.

Then the young Frenchmen had experienced frightening difficulty in maintaining contact with their wireless operator whose task was to relay their findings back to London. He was on the move while they were on the run. Finally they had become convinced that the Germans knew of their presence at Cap Negre a few hours earlier, because, at the last minute, when they were nearing the pinpoint earlier in the evening they had been seen and chased by a patrol, only succeeding in escaping by jumping over the edge of the cliff to fall some 20 ft in amongst some scrub from where they slithered the rest of the way down to the point where we picked them off. They said they knew we were coming when they heard the whine of the auxiliaries at 01.00 — the very moment when we had reduced speed to minimise noise. They had also seen the rubber dinghy approaching when it was still 400 metres from them. Fearing that we might miss them they had removed the blue filter from the torch and increased the frequency of the signal to attract our attention, and to guide us to them. Some signal it was, too. The fact that they weren't spotted by the patrol was their one piece of vital good luck.

Now they looked exhausted. They were both young, in their early twenties, neither wearing more than a shirt and between them most of two pairs of trousers and three shoes. One of them had red hair, something which had a bearing on much later — and happier-events.

They sat at the back of the bridge, blankets round their shoulders, looking straight ahead as if willing Corsica to appear miraculously over the horizon. Not long afterwards he of the red hair was pretty seasick, but both of them were curled up fast asleep when we came alongside in Bastia at 10.15.

* * *

In every theatre of war there were sad accidents from time to time, and we were not immune from that most frequent cause of needless loss of life — failure to recognize a friend or to respond correctly to a challenge.

I recall, during my time in Corsica, one Allied MGB blowing another MGB almost clean out of the water in four minutes through just this fault. The challenger challenged, and challenged with no response from the other boat. The challenger then did what he had to in the circumstances: he opened fire. In the subsequent enquiry it was revealed that the other boat had been concentrating all its attention on some distant enemy target to the total neglect of keeping an all-round look-out. Such is war. Tom had almost as narrow a squeak later on when carrying out an operational investigation in our one and only 'B' class ML. But that comes a little later.

Shortly after the Allied liberation of Corsica the Americans conceived the wholly laudable plan of installing a small section of communicators on Capraia, an island lying some 25 miles north-east of Bastia, and about the same distance north-west of the enemy-occupied Elba. It was, therefore, a useful vantage point for observing enemy shipping plying along the Italian west coast. This operation was, in fact, the precursor of the establishment of the American Observation Post on Gorgona, described in an earlier chapter. Either island, Capraia or Gorgona, could warn us of any impending seaborne attack on Corsica (not at all likely at that stage of the war) or of E-boat mine-laying operations, some of which caused both damage and inconvenience.

It was hardly to be wondered that the Germans didn't much care for these island Peeping Toms sitting on their doorstep reporting on their maritime affairs, and one night in February they sent a raiding party to hot things up for the inhabitants of Capraia.

As soon as the locals understood that this was a German raid and not those kind Americans arriving with more goodies, they wasted no time at all in warning the resident Americans what was afoot. The latter took to the abundant *maquis* of the island without delay, with the request that they be told when all was over. Thorough, as always, the Germans made a good job of wrecking the wireless installation before taking themselves off again. That was all that was apparent when, some hours later the Americans emerged from hiding to set to work quickly cannibalising enough bits and pieces of the wrecked equipment to get some sort of message through to their HQ in Bastia.

But the Germans had also laid mines round the one jetty in the diminutive harbour, a fact duly reported to the Americans who did their level best to make this clear in their message. Most unfortunately — tragically, as things turned out — the report was so garbled as to make poor sense, although repeats were demanded until well into the night.

At the time this was happening we were right in the middle of our twelve-day operational stint, all pretty busy. The first I knew of events was an urgent summons to SOIS's office just before I was due out. There, in addition to Captain Dickinson I found Lieutenant Peter Karlow USN, then seconded to OSS.

I didn't know Karlow well, but he had a reputation for being sensible and able. He and SOIS were poring over and expressing serious concern about the message from which the only clear deduction was that there had been a raid by the Germans; after that no amount of 'snagging' (guesswork in decoding) could produce more than the one intelligible word 'mines'. But whether the sender was trying to say that there were, or there were not, mines, was anyone's guess. SOIS assumed the worst, thereby making it out of the question to attempt to reach the island during the dark hours. Perhaps, he reasoned, there might be some clearer information in the morning. He then gave Pete Karlow *carte blanche* to ring me at any time — in daylight hours — to provide a boat to take him up to the island.

Next morning he was on the line, first thing. Could I let him have a boat immediately to go to Capraia? He would be ready in 30 minutes. I said I would call him back when I had made the necessary arrangements. Here was a chance for the ARBs. They had been straining to be allowed to do something useful, and this was straight up their street.

Not knowing what to expect at the other end it was essential to send experienced officers capable of dealing with the unusual. Tom, with Ranald as assistant was about the strongest combination we could wish for: they could go in *ARB 403* (now in command of Lieutenant Flack, of the US Army Air Corps).

Discussing the situation with Tom we decided that, with the strong probability of a minefield having been laid in, or around the tiny harbour on Capraia, the ARB should also leave the island well before dark on the return trip; this would give the crew the opportunity of mine-spotting in the shallower waters both going in and coming back. By

18.00 he was to be back in Bastia.

He, and Ranald, went off to warn the ARB, while I rang through to the OSS office to let them know that the boat would be ready in not more than half an hour. Would they please inform Lieutenant Karlow and ask him to embark as soon as possible. The time was a few minutes before noon. Three quarters of an hour later Tom rang from the Base to say that there was no sign of the American Lieutenant. The boat had been ready for some time and they were standing by.

A thought suddenly crossed my mind.

'Tom, would you make sure the special radar in that boat is put ashore without fail before you leave?'

It took him a moment or two to fathom what I was driving at, his mind was on more important things than young Arabs gifted with superlative eyesight. When he got there he promised to attend to it.

Ringing the OSS office yet again I was told to my astonishment that Lieutenant Karlow had gone to Borgo aerodrome, some sixteen miles away. Cross, as well as surprised, I could only say that either the orders to the ARB should be cancelled, or that an OSS officer should replace Karlow so that the boat might sail without further delay. Time was of the essence since all our operations officers were due out later that evening. With commendable speed OSS made up its mind to send a Lieutenant Scarignani down immediately to embark in the ARB: he was, they said, fully briefed. At 14.00 the ARB sailed.

A quarter of an hour later the Marchese and I sailed in *MAS 543* up to Cap Corse to do nothing more exciting than have a look at the weather on the western side of the island. From experience we had learned that this was really the only safe way of assessing what to expect during the night. Weather was, after all, one of the most important influences on the timing of our ops. In wartime no one broadcasts a weather forecast.

On our return at 16.45 surprise awaited us in the form of Pete Karlow standing on the jetty. He said he had to go to Capraia immediately. Restraining a temptation to remind him about keeping boats waiting I did ask him where on earth he had been, adding that I had already sent one of his officers up to Capraia with Tom in the ARB. Then he apologised; there had been a mistake, a misunderstanding in his office. He, himself, was the only officer who should have gone. As if to trump any aces lurking in unexpected places he told me that while I had been at sea he had been to SOIS, explained the whole situation, and obtained his blessing for another boat to be made available to him. He was a resourceful operator.

All that remained was to detail *MAS 546* (Tenente di Vascello Iapelli, a first-rate Captain of the same calibre as Ginger, and the Marchese) for the job. With all ACF officers already committed, I would go with Pete Karlow. Should we manage to get back in time, then the Marchese and I would carry out a minor operation already planned to one of the neighbouring islands that night. It would be a bonus. Capraia was the priority problem.

As Peter and I hurried along to where *MAS 546* was lying, who should pop up as if from nowhere but Charles Buist, SOIS's Operations Officer. How he knew where we were I never discovered. Now he clamoured to be allowed to go with us; he was for ever seeking out ways and means of getting back to sea, and here he was at it again. But he was SOIS's right-hand man, and the whole idea was unthinkable — unless, of course, he got his master's personal go-ahead. That was quite enough for him as we stood on the deck of *546* about to sail. Full of hope, he was away up the jetty to a telephone while I watched him, returning in about three minutes, a grin all over his face. SOIS had given permission for him to go; eagerly he climbed up over the side. Only then did it strike me to wonder why both of us need go. I asked him, would he like to take my place? He'd like nothing better; he was aware that I had an operation that night and it made sense.

While this discussion was taking place the crew of *546* were being rounded up from their barracks and brought down to the boat. Preparation for going to sea was quickly accomplished, no fuelling being required for such a short trip. The Captain stood by as I ran through a rapid brief with Charles. *ARB 403*, with Tom and Ranald on board, should be leaving Capraia shortly, if they had not already left. *546* should meet them coming back round about the halfway mark. *546* was to contact the ARB and either Tom or Ranald was to transfer at sea to *546* for pilotage purposes before the MAS went on her way up north. Finally, *546* was to be back, alongside in Bastia by 20.00. This time limit would allow them an hour each way on passage and 45 minutes ashore to investigate.

At 17.15 the MAS sailed for Capraia. As she slid by where I was standing on the jetty, Iapelli gave me a little friendly salute.

An hour and a half later, at 18.45, *ARB 403* returned to Bastia. Tom reported that the damage in Capraia harbour was slight, and that the enemy appeared to have achieved little for the size of the raiding party they had used — two landing-craft escorted by three E-boats. Asked whether he had spoken to *MAS 546* he said no. This was odd, and even more disturbing when he added that he had seen the other boat, but had mistaken her for a Vosper of which there were a few in the area: they had crossed at what he estimated to be about two miles apart. The other boat had made no effort to call him up or contact him in any way.

With no possibility of being any further use to OSS in their Capraian difficulties, at least until the return of *MAS 546*, the Marchese and I were free to go off on a short operation, already planned, to Pianosa, an island close to the celebrated Monte Christo. Soon after midnight we were back in harbour again. An early night for a change.

When I arrived at the villa there was a message from SOIS; he wanted to see me as soon as I returned. Sensing some sort of trouble I went straight up to his office without waiting to ring first. He was poring over a chart of Capraia as I walked in. After asking me where I had been, and whether it had been successful, he seemed to hesitate quite a time before he asked me if I had any news of *546*. I could only repeat what Tom had told me some hours ago and explained my instructions to Charles. Gently he was rubbing his fingers together in thought. 'Unlike Charles to ignore an order. What time did you tell him to be back here?'

'20.00, sir.'

'Odd. And I don't like it. The Americans say they've heard their boys on Capraia trying to get through with some message or other, but they can't make out what it is. It's too garbled. My guess is that Charles will stop in Capraia for the night, but I wanted to hear what you — '

The telephone rang on his desk and he grabbed it. He said almost nothing as the voice went on at the other end: only his expression changed. 'You're sure? ...When did you hear?... They said nothing else?...' When he put the receiver back he looked up, his face blank, and said quietly, 'That was the American Air Corps. They say they've had a message from Capraia. *546* has been mined in the mouth of the harbour.'

'Any news of casualties?' 'No, none.' 'Are they positive they got it right?' 'Yes, absolutely,' 'The boat has been mined, definitely.' 'No other news?' 'No, none, just the mining.'

The next step was obvious. A boat would have to go up to find out more. SOIS said he would organise a doctor and Sick Bay Attendant to be ready at the Base immediately. All the ACF dinghymen were still at sea on operations. SOE very kindly agreed to lend their Petty Officer Smalley; if he could be picked up he would be ready in five minutes. First, though, *ARB 402* (Lieutenant Moritz, American Air Corps) was warned to prepare to go to sea. By the time Smalley and I arrived alongside the American boat the doctor, Surgeon-Lieutenant Pridhoe, and the Sick Bay Attendant were waiting, and we boarded together. Lieutenant Moritz was delighted to find that he was, at last, off to do what he had been trained to do — help out those in trouble. At 01.20 we cast off and made for the harbour entrance.

About half way to the island there was an engine breakdown. The Captain, poor chap, was mortified that on the very first occasion when he was called upon to deal with an emergency he should find himself wallowing with no engines. The engine room staff worked hard, so that we lost little more than half an hour. It certainly gave time for thought.

If there were mines round the entrance to the harbour there might well be more sown round the south and south-eastern corner of the island in the channel through which boats would normally pass on passage between Corsica and Capraia. When once more under way we struck out to the west in a wide arc to pass round the north side of the island, and then come down the east side to about a mile off the harbour mouth at 03.50. Here the boat was stopped while the dinghy was put in the water for the doctor and the SBA with their medical equipment to settle themselves before Smalley and I lowered ourselves down. Before leaving I told Moritz to do his best to remain where he was with his boat. Fortunately the weather was kind which made it easy for him to do so, and for us to pull inshore. The ARB was to keep a sharp look out for any light signals we might make from the beach.

It was still dark while we pulled in, but we could see lights moving ashore: people were awake. On arrival alongside the small jetty we were greeted by an American Army Sergeant who wasted no time in conducting all four of us up the main 'street' to the hamlet, where he said the women of the island were caring for the wounded. Through narrow alleys we threaded our way, eventually to enter a courtyard through a massive stone arch over which, even in the dim torchlight, I could see but not read some sort of inscription. In the courtyard we were guided through a doorway into a pitch dark hall where another door was opened to reveal a nun framed against the light coming from a room beyond. She greeted us quietly, and I introduced Dr Pridhoe to whom she made a small bow and stepped aside for him to enter. We followed.

The room was illuminated by a few candles grouped round a large continental bed on which Pete Karlow lay, his head and shoulders propped up on a pile of pillows. Above his head hung an impressive silver and wood crucifix, but it was at his face I was looking. Of naturally pale complexion he now seemed ghostly with dark eyes staring out from heavy bandaging round his head. He lay very still. At his side, near the bed, another nun was busy tidying up dressings and bandages, and basins which she had been using, meanwhile watching her patient with an expression of infinite compassion.

'Thanks for coming.' He spoke so softly that it wasn't easy to distinguish the words.

Right Lieutenants Pressly, Oswald, DuBose, Eldridge, and Grundy.

Below Bastia, January, 1944.

Left PT base office, Bastia Port.

Below left Tenente di Vascello Marchese Giulio Centurione, March 1944.

Below right Off Bizerte, June 1943.

Right Tenente di Vascello Paolo Iappelli, September 1943.

Below left Ranald Boyle on board Tom Maxted's yacht *Galatea* off the Turkish coast in 1987.

Below right Ranald Boyle (left) with Tenete di Vascello Iappelli, Tenente di Vascello Guido Cosulich at back (full face).

Above left Tenente de Vascello Marchese Giulio Centurione with some members of his crew.

Above right Giulio Centurione, looking tidy, in 1943.

Below Group of MAS boat sailors. Domenico Meleca in white coat in centre.

'I've brought a doctor — Surgeon-Lieutenant Pridhoe. This is Lieutenant Karlow. The doctor will take care of you.'

The doctor was already unpacking his kit.

'Thanks a lot.'

'Is it just your head?' I asked.

'And my leg. There's something wrong with it, but it doesn't hurt. In fact I can't feel anything with it.'

'Let the doctor deal with it. I'll leave you while he does so. Are there any other wounded?'

His eyes turned towards the nuns. 'I guess so. These ladies know where they are.'

Petty Officer Smalley and I were then escorted by one of the nuns down a stone-flagged passage in which there were a number of doors on either side. I remember being impressed by the way she moved so swiftly, and gracefully, the only sound coming from the swishing of her heavy robes. Stopping outside one of the doors she held up her hand for silence while she listened intently before gently easing the door open. The room was smaller than the one we had just left, the illumination coming from a single candle on a table between two narrow iron cots each with an Italian sailor lying motionless. Not until we were right in the room did one of them turn his head in my direction. 'Eh, *Commandante*,' he whispered.

'I've brought a doctor, and we're going to take you back to Bastia.' Under the bedclothes on each of the cots cages had been placed so that no weight should bear on the wounded men's legs. 'Is it both legs, or only one?'

'My foot, *Commandante*.'

'Is it very painful?'

'Not too bad. The Americans had some first-aid medicine for us.'

The other sailor was stirring slightly, but when I went across to speak to him he could only mumble indistinctly in reply that his leg hurt him before relapsing into semi-consciousness.

'We'll come and fetch both of you,' I said, 'when the doctor has had a look at you.'

'*Va bene, Commandante. Grazie.*'

On our way back to Pete Karlow's room I asked our escorting nun how badly she thought the two sailors were wounded. She gave a little shrug and spread her hands. 'The one who was awake, his foot is badly crushed. But the other one, he is worse. His leg looks like that of the American officer.'

I hadn't seen Pete's leg injury, his head wound seemed bad enough. When we returned his voice sounded a bit firmer, there was a marginal improvement in his strength. The doctor was repacking his bag as I gave him a brief report on the two Italian sailors. He said he would go and have a look at them if, in the meantime, I could set about trying to organize some form of transport by stretcher from where we were down to the jetty. When he had gone I was able to ask Pete, 'How does it feel now?'

'Oh, since the doc fixed me up I feel a bit better. I just hope it lasts. But my leg has no feeling. It is completely numb. Would you take a look and tell me what you think. The doctor wouldn't say anything when I asked him.'

With a flick he whipped back the covering blanket.

For a long moment it was difficult to know what to say. One of his legs was perfectly normal, nothing wrong with it. The only description I could find to fit the other one was that it was 'dead'. There were no bruise marks, no wounds, no visible difference in shape from the good one, nothing in fact, except that it was without life.

'Well,' he asked, 'what do you think?'

From his tone it was not difficult to discern that he had already guessed something near the truth. He had only put the question in the hope of some reassurance.

'It looks damn painful to me,' was all I could think of saying. 'You mean you really can't feel anything in the whole leg?'

'Not a thing.' He twitched the blanket back into place before his next questions. 'But I probably will later. And that may not be so hot. But how about those other guys? Did they have leg injuries, too?'

'Yes. One of them almost exactly the same as yours.'

During the silence which followed I gathered some steam for the question which had been uppermost in my mind ever since we had arrived, and which I had funked asking.

'Do you have any news of the others — the other members of the ship's company — and Charles?'

'Oh, yea. Didn't they tell you? Charles went with the boat, I'm afraid, and so did the Captain, Iapelli. I don't know for sure if anyone else was saved except the two men you've already seen. I did hear that there might be two more, but nothing certain.'

Words meant almost nothing. 'Poor Charles. I must go and organize the stretcher party.'

'You'll find the Sergeant very helpful.'

'Thanks. He has been already. See you in a little while.'

Petty Officer Smalley and I went out and found the Sergeant waiting in the hall. When we explained what was required he went straight into action: he would organize three stretchers, the same improvised ones that had brought the wounded this far, and a number of bearers. When Smalley and I saw the stretchers we knew at once that they would be far too big and heavy to ship in the rubber dinghy. They consisted of two sets of planks covered with rough blankets, and a ladder with some straw as a crude shock-absorber. All we could do was to return to the jetty and have a look round for a pulling-boat large enough to take the wounded while Smalley and I took the rubber dinghy out to the ARB.

Dawn was close upon us as we reached the harbour to find a knot of fishermen gossiping, hard at work going over the excitement of the last two days. Also among the crowd were two members of the MAS boat's crew, alive and unharmed: so Pete Karlow's information was correct. When I spoke to them, however, they did not make much sense, only being able to mumble, still suffering from the force of the explosion. I told them we would take them off with the wounded, and they could only nod in reply. To the fishermen I explained what we needed, and, willingly enough after a short sharp argument amongst themselves, they collected two awkward-looking boats from the untidy tangle of craft at the inner end of the wall, and brought them to the only steps. No sooner had the boats been manoeuvred into position to embark the passengers than the first of the stretchers appeared in the distance, coming slowly down the hill. In the eerie half light before dawn the scene was a singular one, made funereal by the ten or twenty hangers-on who, in their curiosity, crowded round the wounded men like mourners following a bier.

To get the three stretchers placed down the centre of the boats, two men in one boat, and one in the other, so that they were secured from movement but allowed room for the oarsmen to pull, was no easy matter and took a good ten minutes, with much advice and counter-advice being given by numerous volunteer oarsmen who would have resented any naval interference. In the bigger of the two boats there were four oars, and in the smaller only three, one large oarsman being balanced by smaller men pulling on the other side. The doctor and the SBA were each in separate boats while Smalley and I took the rubber dinghy. We were, indeed, a strange convoy as we left the jetty.

Meanwhile the nuns stood waving a shy, sad goodbye from the quayside. Without their devotion and care of the wounded, matters would have been infinitely worse. Pulling ahead of the other boats Smalley and I had an interesting view of the procession. The wounded men lying perched up on their stretchers resembled for all the world three ancient Roman dignitaries being ferried by slaves, each with an attendant at his head to protect him against discomfort. It was a weird spectacle.

In the improving light we saw wreckage floating by, black-painted pieces of wood, none bigger than about two foot square. Inshore, all along the pebbly beach there was a lot more, none of it of any size. Small wonder, really; if the MAS had been well-fuelled and the mine had been up to a minimum of 500 lb (we didn't then know what type of mines the Germans had laid) one could only marvel that anyone in the boat at the time could have survived at all. Those who didn't could never have known anything between full consciousness and oblivion.

We were in for an unpleasant surprise once we cleared the end of the breakwater. Instead of the flat calm we had enjoyed on arrival an easterly wind had now sprung up with the dawn to create small waves. Ordinarily these conditions would have presented no problem, although the dinghymen would have had to work harder than usual. Smalley and I now had to put our backs into it. A quarter of an hour in these conditions and it was easy to see that the oarsmen were getting tired, pulling raggedly so the boats advanced but slowly, and were getting slower all the time.

We could see the ARB bobbing gently up and down almost exactly where we had left her. Lieutenant Moritz had obeyed his instructions very well, but now the boat seemed a long way off. We pulled over towards the bigger of the two boats and I shouted across to the doctor to ask after his two charges. He replied that they were all right but asked in return how much longer we were likely to take, they were beginning to be tossed about by the sea. More shouting, this time to the flagging oarsmen, to encourage further effort, and to their credit they did their best, but this only increased the amount of spray being thrown over the wounded.

We were still only half a mile out, and being taken by the wind to the north, I hoped away from the danger of any mines. We, in our wooden or rubber craft, with no motors, had no fear of exploding anything but we weren't making any headway. It was a matter of Mahomed and the mountain. I flashed up the ARB with a handtorch. She must have been expecting the signal for she started to turn immediately before moving in towards us. Sensibly he came in on a wide arc, rather than straight in, circling away from land to the north before bearing down on us on a south-westerly course.

Then came the trickiest moment of the whole operation — the transfer of the wounded from the pulling boats into the ARB. It was a problem which had been nagging all the way. But I had overlooked the fact that this was the very manoeuvre at sea for which the ARB crews had been trained. Now Lieutenant Moritz and his men showed their real skill. There was no shouting. With no common language to help him Moritz laid his boat up to windward of the convoy, creating a lee, and then by signs indicated that he was going to let his craft drift down broadside to the bigger of the boats, the one carrying Pete Karlow and one of the Italian sailors. Moritz even managed to hold his craft off for a few vital seconds to allow the oarsmen to bring their boats parallel with his to cushion the impact.

The minute they touched, things really started to happen. The wounded were jolted a bit as the actual transfer took place but it was all done so quickly, and there was never a second's doubt that the ARB specialists had the situation under perfect control. Once the first two men were inboard and safely installed in the big cabin space, the oarsmen in the second boat seemed to gain confidence; one boat helped the other in getting the third man across into the American boat. It was a fine exhibition of seamanship — by any standards.

By 06.30 the rubber dinghy was hoisted inboard and we could wave farewell and unbounded thanks to the fishermen as they 'freewheeled downhill with the wind behind them' back to their diminutive harbour. Taking it easy so as to avoid throwing the wounded about in the seaway we were alongside in Bastia at 09.10. Of the thirteen crew of the MAS, there were but five survivors. The two sailors who were physically unharmed were, I discovered later, standing in the extreme bows of the MAS when she was mined. There was no heavy metal under them; the blast catapulted them into the water and that was all. A very remarkable escape.

* * *

But the crisis was not yet over.

The following morning SOIS received a signal from the Americans in Capraia in which they opined that the loss of the MAS was caused by sabotage, and not mining. Where this notion came from remained a mystery as far as I know but it had to be followed up, lunatic though it sounded. And Tom was the chap to do it, in the ML (Lieutenant Durston, RNVR). SOIS gave his approval. The ML hadn't had much opportunity for some time, and here was the occasion for her to get to work.

Arrangements were made for her to sail the following morning and, since the sabotage allegation had been made by OSS personnel occupying the island, some members of OSS Bastia should accompany the expedition of enquiry. Accordingly the ML sailed at 10.25 next day for Capraia. There was a big difference between an ML and a fast craft such as a MAS, or an MTB, or MGB, or PT boat. The ML was 120 ft long — double the length of a MAS — with a cruising speed of 15 knots against the 25 to 35 knots of the fast craft which, incidentally, by virtue of their speed, enjoyed much greater manoeuvrability. The ML however, had a greater range and could keep the sea in worse weather than her nippier relations.

On board the ML Tom was in charge of the operation overall. Leading Seaman Johnstone and Able Seaman Downes went as dinghymen. The whole thing was rated as unlikely to give rise to complications. A routine job. Weather conditions were excellent as the ML steamed sedately up the east coast of Corsica for the following three quarters of an hour at her cruising speed of 15 knots. Everything seemed set fair.

Coming out from the lee of the island, however, shortly after 11.00, she altered course to pass, as we had done earlier, north round Capraia, and immediately encountered such foul weather from the north-west — and as already indicated the MLs were fine seaboats — as to call for a reduced speed. One hour later an extraordinary event took place. When they were only three quarters of a mile off the north-west coast of Capraia they were suddenly attacked by two Mitchell B.25 bombers and a Spitfire escort from about 1,000 ft.

Tom said he saw them well before they attacked, and realising they were friendly craft he may well have felt a moment of comfort that friends were so close at hand. Such thoughts were rudely destroyed when the aircraft came swooping down from 1,000 ft to as low as 200 ft, bomb-bays opening, cannon and machine-guns firing. The bombs straddled the boat and the first B.25 then opened up with its rear gun but scored no hits. The second B.25 was a better shot as he came in, scoring two direct hits with his 75mm cannon, one on the hull six inches above the waterline, and the other just below the bridge, covering the boat with columns of spray, while smoke poured from the exploding shells.

The ship's engines were put out of action and she drifted to a stop while flares were fired to persuade the attackers that she was friendly. The aircraft had already started their second run in when they saw the flares which came in the nick of time. The pilots who could not have failed to recognize the damage they had done, then sheered off to fly away, apparently without so much as a backward glance, metaphorical, or real.

The whole attack lasted not more than a minute, but for the next two hours the ML fought to save herself from sinking, firstly, as a result of the hole on the waterline, and secondly, from drifting, engineless, on to the lee shore of rocks, and precipitous cliffs, three quarters of a mile away. Pillows, mattresses and a collision mat were brought in to stem the inrush of water, while an anchor was let go on eighty fathoms of 'grass' (480 ft) to check her drift in the rough seaway. The anchor didn't touch bottom, and she continued to drift.

In the engineroom the motor mechanic and his staff worked frantically to repair the damage to machinery. On the bridge they continued to try to attract attention by firing flares over the island only to find that low cloud prevented any chance of them being seen. The starboard anchor was let go on its normal cable. Neither anchor had any effect until the ship was within two cables of the rocks, and then one of them held enough to bring the bow round into the wind while she continued to drag inshore.

Contact with help on shore was rendered impossible by wireless: this having been wrecked by the hail of .5 bullets: all in all there seemed no means of saving the vessel. As a last resort the Oerlikon was fired over the island in the hope that this might attract attention but the American Observation Post remained obstinately hidden in the thick scudding cloud.

Only when the ship was within a hundred yards of the shore and being heavily pounded by the short rough seas did Motor Mechanic Graham, to his great credit — and the amazement of all on board — bring the engines to life, in time to save both ship and ship's company.

The Captain immediately gave the order to slip both anchors, and steamed slowly out of danger. Five minutes later two Spitfires and a Walrus arrived on the scene to escort the ship back to Bastia. By the mercy of providence, and the poor marksmanship of the attackers, only one sailor was slightly wounded in the arm by a piece of shrapnel.

How the attacking aircraft failed to observe the ship's clear, indeed obvious identification marks of yellow-painted foc'sle', and red-painted quarterdeck is past comprehension. All one can say about this event — with profound gratitude, too — is that some mistakes have happier endings than others.

★ ★ ★

No matter how agreeable they may be, all interludes come to an end sometime; this one did so in the spring of 1944 when I returned to the United Kingdom to a new appointment.

A week or so before departure my replacement arrived in the person of Lieutenant-Commander. Donald McCallum RNR, (need I add, always known as Mac) whom I had known and worked with in the previous year on the North African coast. In peacetime a Fishery Protection Officer, operating in the northernmost waters of his native Scotland, there was also little he didn't know about the sea in the Mediterranean. Curiously, this was the first time he had been separated from HMS *Minna*, the ship he commanded in peacetime, which had been engaged, earlier on, in long-range operations of the kind we were now carrying out at short range. He was, therefore, no stranger to the work.

Mac had the traditional, dry, earthy humour associated with north of the border, he was accustomed to the unusual, and he knew his own mind, all valuable assets in coping with the oddly assorted international clientele employing our taxi service. He inspired confidence.

Our first couple of days together were spent in visiting the various authorities, and introducing him to the Captains and boats' crews. Over the months the numbers had grown; we now dealt, on a regular basis, with American, as well as British clandestine organizations, and, depending on the type of operation to be carried out, we now used British, Italian, or American craft. Such were our relations with our 'cousins', and with the Italians that both had come to accept the principle of flexibility; it was often complicated to apply but seldom difficult in the event.

Mac asked all the right questions, although he offered little comment while sizing up the situation. When we came to Piccolo, however, interest turned to amusement. How, he was curious to know, had we acquired and managed to administer such an anomaly? The first question was easy, even if the answer bordered on the ridiculous; on the second, however, neither Prof nor I were able to be precise, the continued presence of the small Italian and his means of support being a personal matter between the three of us. We couldn't explain it rationally. He was part of the household and his affairs were handled on a basis of expediency. From time to time we would ask him if he had enough money — there was never any bother about food, we all knew that Maria spoilt him outrageously — on which occasion his standard answer was a shy smirk of acknowledgement of our solicitude, and an assurance that all was well. If any proof were needed he would rummage round under unspeakable overalls to produce a worn leather case containing a set of high quality very small precision spanners, in the back of which he kept his worldly wealth, a mixture of French, Italian, and Allied Forces' money. The amount he got from the Italian army, officially, was boy's pocket money. *How* it reached him was never revealed, although it was inscribed in some sort of pay book. We employed various unorthodox methods to make up his pay to what we thought appropriate, in other words what we could afford. To have paid him his real worth would have been beyond price — our price, anyway.

By happy chance his finest achievement reserved itself for Mac's especial benefit: up to that time, although he may have appreciated some of the Italian's value, I don't think he really believed what we had told him about his ingenuity.

On the third night of the hand-over, with no warning, just after dinner the lights went out, an almost routine occurrence which brought the routine response of loud shouts of 'PICCOLO!' from all present. From distant regions came a lugubrious answering shout of '*Va bene. Va bene. Subito*' followed by noises of an opening and slamming door, and some muffled Italian curses receding down the cellar steps. I explained to Mac that he would now witness Piccolo's highly-unorthodox arrangement for stealing electricity from the house of the collaborator living in the neighbouring sector. This was to be the moment for demonstrating the resourcefulness of the mechanic. Going over to the french windows I drew back one half of the blackout curtains, and turned to Mac. 'Come and watch,' I invited.

With a half grin, tinged with scepticism, he stood beside me, peering out into the night. Only then, to my dismay, did I notice that there wasn't a chink of light to be seen anywhere in the town. It was a general power cut, the second one we'd ever had. I felt rather like the ventriloquist who suddenly loses his voice at the beginning of his act. Not the easiest thing to laugh off. Further embarrassment was eased when Maria came in bearing candles.

'Too bad. This is rather more than even Piccolo can cope with,' I tried boasting a way out. 'If it were a sector cut our lights would be on again by now.'

While we were standing there more Italian curses could be heard returning up the stairs from the cellar. Any second he would come in to blame the dastardly inefficiency of the local electricity company. But he didn't. Instead there was the noise of the unlocking of the door leading out from the top of the cellar steps into the garden. Presumably he was going out to inspect the functioning of his illegal electric leads. To save our mutual blushes I called out to him, 'It's no use, Piccolo, this time it's a general power cut. We'll have to wait.'

The reply was so faint as to be almost inaudible as his footsteps continued on their way. '*Va bene, Commandante. Momento, Commandante. Momento...*'

'Where's he off to?' asked Mac.

I shrugged. 'No idea. But there's nothing he can do.' I turned back from the window letting the blackout swing closed again. 'Let's have a drink and forget it.'

Filling the glasses with the local 'infuriator' I couldn't escape feeling a bit mortified after so much boasting. While brooding on this I thought I heard one of the cars starting up out in the drive. Probably one of the young officers going off down to the Moulin Rouge to try his luck at whatever might be on offer.

'A pity about the lights,' remarked Mac, sniffing a bit. His tone was genuinely sorry, although not devoid of amusement. I was about to say something defensive when my attention was drawn to the ceiling

201

lights; the bulbs were beginning to glow red, and were getting brighter every second. Quickly I went back to the window to look out. Total darkness reigned. I called Mac over.

'Like to have a look?'

He was a bit slow to react. He'd been had before. 'What at?'

'Come and see.'

He joined me to scan the landscape for any sign of light. There was still none. Meanwhile the lights behind us in the room had regained their normal strength, and it was time to close the curtains once more.

Mac's eyebrows were now quite high. 'What's happened, d'you think? Could he — ?'

A trifle rudely I cut him short, 'Let's go and see.' We put our glasses down and hurried out into the night.

Under the trees in a corner of the parking space one of the pick up trucks was having its engine revved unmercifully by an unseen driver. It had no lights, but there was a slither coming from the opening of the canvas cover covering the back of the vehicle. Advancing across the gravel we peeped in.

There, amidst a cat's cradle of wires, gauges, and meters, was Piccolo crouched over an 1100cc Fiat engine which had been bolted to the floor, and to which had been attached a sizeable generator. From the generator two heavy leads ran out through the side of the vehicle, thence to be seen disappearing into the darkness of the night in the direction of the cellars of the villa where lay the main electricity junction box. As I looked into the interior of the van Piccolo glanced up, his face expressionless in concentration. I grinned and he grinned back.

'OK, *Commandante*?' he shouted above the racket of the engine noise.

'*Molto OK*, Piccolo,' I bawled in return.

With a cheerful wave of a spanner in the air he made some rapid adjustments to the surrounding paraphernalia.

'Where did you get the engine?' In case he couldn't hear I pointed to it.

The brief shrug and wry smile implied that I ought to have known the answer. 'The one we took out of the *Commandante's* car when we changed the engine.' His hand described a sharp upward gradient in the air. 'No hills to climb.'

'And the generator?'

'Eh!' Abruptly he jerked his head backwards and, with renewed attention to his work, adjusted one of the instruments by his knee, while Mac and I looked on in wonder and admiration.

After what appeared to be some weighty consideration he crawled towards us through the entanglement of wires, still clutching a pair of pliers and several screwdrivers. These he put down in a neat row, wiped his hands on a rag, and fixed me with a defiant eye.

'The generator, *Commandante*, — is good — no?'

'Excellent. But where did you get it?'

Slowly he began to gather the tools together again while he pondered an answer. He was already starting to move back into his electrical labyrinth when he paused just long enough to look at me and close one eye in a long wink. 'Like your sailors say, *Commandante*, the generator is — liberated. Yes?' Turning away once more he gave me a final glance out of the corner of his eye. 'Like me, *Commandante*.' The snigger of contentment was barely discernible as he re-addressed himself to his masterpiece. We were clearly in the way. I turned to Mac. 'Come on, let's get back to the "infuriator".'

In the dark, on our way, he laughed. 'I'm beginning to understand what you mean about Piccolo. Quite a boy-o, isn't he?'

* * *

EPILOGUE

I

Only a short while after my return to London I was summoned, in the absence of DDOD(I), by another senior officer in the Admiralty Ops Division. Without preamble he handed me a signal from SOIS reporting that *MAS 541* had failed to return from an operation and must now be presumed to be lost.

On board were Lieutenant Dow, as the Ops Officer, Tenente di Vascello Cosulich, as Captain, and Capitaine de Frégate Vieux-Martin with a team of French commandos. Also lost, although not mentioned, was the redoubtable, the irrepressible Capo Pulchri, the chief mechanic. Four men — Ginger, the 'Colonel', the Capitaine de frégate, and the engineer — all had become friends over the preceding months, all had now disappeared for good. It was very sad, indeed.

To the best of my knowledge there was never any conclusive evidence as to what happened. The operation started out as a French raiding party destined for a pinpoint somewhere in the Genoa area. With them they carried a quantity of demolition material. That they had not reached their target is beyond doubt; had they done so, tangible proof would have been available in the form of reports of a raid, either then, or later in the Italian archives.

Theories are several, but probabilities really only two. Either there was some sort of accident on board while explosives were being handled on passage, or, — what, on balance, is more likely — they hit a floating mine. In support of this theory I had seen a couple during earlier operations in that vicinity. Whether it was an accident or a mine the end would have been instantaneous. Hundreds of gallons of high octane fuel, an unknown but certainly powerful quantity of plastic explosive, plus the force of the exploding mine itself, would have left nothing but a very large hole in the water. The only piece of significant evidence which came to light quite quickly after the event was a report on the Italian news broadcast of an unusually heavy explosion somewhere off Genoa at the relevant time, but no explanation was volunteered.

★   ★   ★

In the following year the war ended, and the time came for rejoicing, especially in the European countries so recently occupied by the enemy. The French planned a great Victory Parade. I had gone over to Paris on official business as the junior member of one of the dozens of missions created in Whitehall (some overnight) many of which disappeared before you could say Jack Robinson — or anything like it — to visit, or more ambitiously, tour one of the former occupied territories. This, the art of obtaining free travel and varying amounts of hospitality at the expense of a foreign government (or, at a sly pinch, HMG itself) was known as 'swanning'. I don't doubt that under a perhaps more cynical peacetime name it continues to this day.

Our visit was timed carefully to coincide with the Parade, my seniors having been invited officially not only to witness the momentous event from agreeable points of vantage, but, more importantly, to receive impressive decorations for their contribution to the French war effort. No such plans were in store for the small fry, like me, who could either stand in the throng, or seek some other more entertaining distraction. By chance, and it was an extraordinary chance, soon after my arrival I ran into a member of one of the British clandestine sponsoring authorities in Bastia — one of the 'unmentionables' — and we fell into discussing the past, in particular some of the operations to the south of France. Just before parting he asked me my plans for watching the parade. Was I officially invited? If so, by whom? When I told him I had no particular plans, for some reason which at the time I could not understand, he seemed oddly pleased. Adopting a mildly conspiratorial air he said he thought there was someone in Paris who might like to meet me, and who might also offer me a good view of the parade. Would I like that? There were a lot of 'mights' about the offer but I accepted readily enough. He then disappeared to telephone to find out how the land lay. When he came back he was smiling but giving nothing away except an address and a time at which I had to be there on the day. In the hope that he wasn't pulling my leg I thanked him warmly, and we parted.

The day came, and the crowds started to gather all along the route to ensure a good view of events. Confident in the knowledge that my seat was secure I was in no particular hurry to arrive too early. What I hadn't foreseen was the number of streets sealed off by the traffic police. To be allowed to cross the Champs Elysées — which I had to — needed a powerful amount of argument. That one was in uniform made almost no difference at all. Everyone was in uniform. Seldom can there have been such a variety assembled in one place. Fortunately, there was still an hour to go before the parade began. Battling a way through the jostling, cheerful crowd, eventually I found myself on a corner formed by the Champs Elysées and the street I was looking for. I had arrived, and what a perfect spot from which to see the show — always assuming the apartment wasn't on the ground floor. It was on the second floor, and the door was opened by a uniformed maid, an unusual sight in those days.

Once inside what turned out to be a very large flat, the noise of forty or fifty very excited people, mostly on the young side with all the exuberance of that age, became almost deafening. I was grateful to find myself being escorted away from the brawl, through a salon which was quite empty, and thence on to a balcony looking directly over the Champs Elysées, where another crowd of prospective onlookers had gathered. I was the only foreigner present. Almost at once a tall, attractive, very well dressed Titian-haired lady detached herself from a group she had been talking to and came towards me, smiling in welcome. She extended an elegant hand. 'I'm so glad you were able to come. My name is Marie-M— and I've heard quite a lot about you.'

Her name was immediately familiar: I had heard more than a lot about her, as one of the foremost figures in the French resistance world. I had even heard the story of the time she was captured by the German counter-espionage service, and found that the only possible way of escape lay through some very narrow prison bars. To get through them she had had to strip off completely. Grazed, cut, and bruised she had struggled through to freedom. The following morning a message arrived in London, beginning, 'Suis nue dans le maquis ...' an appeal which, I was assured, had met with immediate response.

Now as she stood fully clothed, looking very chic, I expressed sincere admiration for the little I knew of her work. In reply she waved deprecating hands. 'Come and see the parade,' she said making way for me among her other guests. 'There's someone else you should meet — someone you've met already, but in rather different circumstances.'

Standing on tiptoe she peered over the heads in front of her until she spotted whom she was seeking, then she called out two names. In response there was a sudden backward movement in the front row of spectators, and two figures separated themselves to come towards us.

One of them had bright red hair.

'Do you remember each other?' she asked, looking from one to another of us.

It was the red hair that did it. Cap Negre, and the two young men falling down the cliff to escape hot pursuit by the German patrol. The anxious moments which followed after they dropped into the dinghy, the long pull back against the time limit, and then the moment when the Marchese came to find us in his *MAS 543* — and the 'Colonel's' dry humour as he brushed off the question as to how much longer he would have waited beyond the limit. Now, in the secure and comfortable surroundings in the middle of a peaceful Paris it was the occasion for all of us to relax, and laugh at the memory. Standing between the two young men, holding each by the elbow, our hostess looked at me. 'This is the reason why I am so glad you were able to join us today.'

Oddly, perhaps, the unexpected meeting created an atmosphere of temporary restraint among the four of us until Marie-M—, a perceptive lady, called for champagne. We were celebrating not only the grand victory: as we sat waiting for the parade to begin we lived the operation again, detail by detail, at ease to appreciate the humorous side of what had been such near disaster for the young men.

And what a parade. There would never be another like it. This was the day when every element of the French Forces had a right to representation; white men, black men, yellow men, in uniforms of khaki, dark blue, light blue, red, mixtures of colours, Spahis in their long flowing cloaks, Goums, Zouaves, they were all there, marching to a multiplicity of bands down the Champs Elysées. And the Allies, the British and the Americans had sent their contingents of sailors, soldiers, and airmen. Applause was catholic, for everybody regardless of race, creed, or colour, from a happy crowd waving and shouting encouragement as each unit went by.

In the middle of all the noise of music, cheering, and marching feet, there came from higher up the Champs Elysées the beginning of an unmistakable ripple of laughter, and an increasing number of '*Oh, la-la's*, as a large and important-looking unit of the American Army plus its own individual band, came thumping down the broad avenue. Someone was being funny, or there had been an amusing incident of some sort? Not at all. As the band came abreast our balcony the reason was clear for everyone to see. The big drum — and it was of giant, economy, gift-wrapped size — was not, as in other bands, slung on the shoulders of a brawny drummer, but was mounted on what, for all the world, looked like the chassis of a baby's pram; behind it, pushing hard, was a very ordinary size of bandsman only just tall enough to be able to see where he was going. It was, of course, a wholly practical, indeed sensible method of carrying a heavy weight over several miles of tiring march, but the crowd was agog with good-natured giggles. The French do not always show a proper sense of respect.

The moment everyone had been waiting for was heralded by a tremendous swelling roar from the densely packed mass of spectators as the open car containing the British and French leaders swept at medium pace down the Champs Elysées. The old Briton, dressed as an Air Commodore, sat back in the seat, relaxed, and enjoying to the full this hard-won demonstration of triumph to which he had contributed so much. Smiling and happy he waved, giving the occasional V-sign to draw an extra loud round of cheering. At his side, the austere figure of the French General sat bolt upright, one arm every so often being raised in a small mechanical gesture of acknowledgement. Not a word was seen to be exchanged between the two men who might well have been in separate cars for all the notice they took of one another. Even in that moment of international happiness it was a sad reflection on the solidarity of the wartime alliance — as my companions on that occasion were quick to observe.

* * *

In the spring of 1946 I found myself scheduled to make a brief visit to Italy — Rome, Trieste, and Milan. It was an opportunity I could not miss; I wrote to the president of the Cosulich shipping line telling him of my intended visit and asking him if he would be kind enough to arrange for me to see Ginger's parents on my way through. From Milan, a little while later I telephoned him when he informed me he had arranged for me to meet Captain Cosulich and his wife two mornings later in Trieste.

When I presented myself at the substantial offices of the line I quite understood why Ginger had always been discreetly proud of his family. The president, Ginger's uncle, was a charming man who asked me many questions about his nephew. Was he a good officer? Was he a good seaman? Had he got courage? What had been his duties? He wasn't just filling in time while waiting for Ginger's parents: he was delighted with the entirely truthful answers I was happy to give him. As soon as the parents were announced, however, he broke off. It was only then that I learned that Ginger's father had been, until recently, Captain of one of the ships belonging to the line.

The president led me out of his office, down a passage to a comfortable waiting room, explaining as we went that he thought the Captain and his wife would probably prefer to see me alone. We entered the room and there they were.

I don't know why I should have been so taken aback, but I was. I should have expected it. Father and son were absurdly alike, the one difference being age which had given the Captain a little more weight. Then he was on his feet, coming towards me a hand shyly extended in welcome as the president introduced us. The Captain wasn't listening, he was looking at me, holding my hand, a small smile round his eyes and mouth. It might have been Ginger.

The president withdrew from the scene so unobtrusively that I never saw him go, and the Captain, still holding my hand, took me across to introduce me to his wife seated on the far side of the room. Hardly a word had been said as I sat down on a chair opposite them seated on a high-back sofa.

Facing him, the extra plumpness and the slightly thinning hair (still very ginger) were more apparent, although the eyes were the same steady rather pale blue, and he spoke with exactly the same soft tones as his son, slower than most Italians. Perhaps the slowness was a characteristic of the Triestine, I'm not sure; it was certainly pleasant to hear. The *signora* was not unlike her husband: she was not as tall, and her build was almost dumpy, but she had what was evidently the family gentleness of manner, and the composure, as she sat up very straight in her chair, waiting anxiously for me to begin speaking of her son.

For a few seconds there was silence as we sat looking at one another: then the Captain thanked me for coming to see him and his wife. I must, he said, have gone far out of my way, the journey must have been inconvenient, and I could not possibly know how touched they were at my coming. There were no flowery phrases, he was very straightforward, very simple. He made things much easier than I had feared.

In return I told them first of how Ginger and I had met in Bastia, of the inspection of the flotilla, of the green helmet which he always wore at sea, of some of the more amusing incidents which we had shared, working round gradually to what they both wanted most to hear — how their son had done, and how he had died. Here was no difficulty, as I told them of his unfailing conscientiousness, and of his loyalty which could, in those early days of August immediately following the Italian armistice, have been very difficult for him to give. I explained, without going into detail, the sort of work on which he had been engaged, and that this had never required him to fight against his own countrymen. Lastly, on a personal plane, came the high regard, and very real liking which he had earned and enjoyed from all those of us who had worked and sailed with him.

They sat still, and silent, listening intently as I talked, while tears rolled, unheeded, down their cheeks. No sobs, none of the Latin lamentations which might have been expected. No gestures, even, for the son who, so clearly, they had adored. It was far more moving, so. When I had finished, they sat silent for a short while before he got to his feet, and held out his hand — he really was just an older Ginger. With my hand clasped between both of his, he thanked me again, impressing on me to understand how much the meeting had meant to both of them. They had never expected to hear another word, and this account of their son's last few months was as comforting as it was unlooked for. In her turn Ginger's mother made the same motions of pressing one of my hands between her two, and then the meeting was over. I was very glad to have seen them.

*　*　*

A year or two later on another visit to Italy on what was to be a strictly 'non-swanning' tour, I could not resist one bit of truancy to try to find, and if possible see, that attractive, and voluble Italian General who had been so lavish with his thanks on being picked off the beach at Orbitello. It wasn't as difficult as I had thought. I soon discovered his identity, and also that he lived not too far away from where I was going, in the area of Lake Como. A glance through the local telephone directory was enough to run him to earth. When I rang him up his initial reaction surprised me. He was extremely cautious. Who was speaking? Who? What British officer...? Boats...? Only when I mentioned 'Giuseppe' did he react, and then, I think, if he could have climbed down the telephone line to shake my hand he would have done so. Where was I? How long was I staying? Lunch, dinner, anywhere, any time. He arranged to pick me up the following day at noon at my hotel and from there we would drive out to his villa.

The meeting next morning was reminiscent of our original encounter, except that this time we knew one another's identity, and neither of us was armed, ready to shoot the other; but the '*Compliment, Capitaine*'s were still there, to be repeated time and again, until suddenly he changed it to '*Commandante*'. I never knew why; perhaps he thought I was due for promotion.

The General drove much as might be expected, with military verve, carrying on a non-stop commentary on the idiocies of other road-users, the political situation, the beauties of the countryside, and how splendid to be able to receive me in his own house. An exhausting experience, handsomely rewarded with some excellent champagne on arrival.

The villa was right on the lakeside with gardens running down to the water, but the strangest thing about the place was that the whole atmosphere exuded the best of an English country house. The furnishing, the garden, everywhere one looked it was English. A curious feeling until, suddenly, I recalled that the General's wife was English, although he feigned not to speak her language. He must have noticed my surprise for he chuckled.

'You find yourself back in England, *Commandante?*'

'No longer "*Commandante*", General, I'm a civilian now. Yes, I do, indeed, find myself back in England in your house, but then your wife is English, is she not?'

'Yes, she is.' When he told me who she was I was again surprised because her family was well-known. He volunteered no further information about her, however, and from then on the lady remained conspicuous only by her absence. In compensation, after about twenty minutes, the drawing-room door opened and in walked one of the prettiest girls you could hope to see. Tall, fair, in her mid-twenties, very graceful and dressed in the height of fashion. What the Victorians used to call a 'belle' in polite terms, and a 'corker' not so politely. The General looked as pleased as Punch, as well he might, while he made the introduction, and for a moment (a very brief one) made pretence that the lady had been invited for my benefit. He was careful not to let this impression get out of hand. Her name appeared to be no more than Giulietta.

Lunch was quite excellent, with a noticeable tang of Fortnum and Mason about the more extravagant bits, while the wines were a fine selection of the best that France could produce. The General had really pushed the boat out, and was in exuberant form as he regaled us both with a recapitulation of events at Orbitello; nothing was lost in the telling, either, causing pretty Giulietta a rush of 'Oooohs' and 'Aaaaahs' between fits of giggles. It was a far cry ... and thoroughly enjoyable.

Then followed a string of questions about England. (These tended to confirm the indifferent communications between husband and wife). Was everything still rationed? The prices of cars, houses, men's clothes? What did we lack most? An odd topic at such a time; on the other hand there was one thing I really did want to buy while in Italy — some silk for my wife — and here was the opportunity to say so. The General's face lit up, and Giulietta seemed to take an interest, too.

'Silk, did you say, *Commandante?*' He became agitated, shifting his considerable bulk around in his chair and waving his arms in what turned out to be enthusiasm. 'But I own a silk factory not twenty kilometres from here. We shall go there this afternoon, and Giulietta shall help you to choose something very special for your wife.'

He was as good as his word. He was also at pains to see that I sat in the front seat of the car with the chauffeur — 'your long legs, *Com-*

mandante' — while he sat very close to Giulietta in the back. I didn't blame him; what's the use of having a chauffeur if you can't do that? I have never, before or since, seen so many gorgeous silks; it was a veritable feast of colour and texture, making decision a time-consuming business. The one I eventually chose (with Giulietta's help, of course) was worn, admired, and enjoyed for many years. If the General thought he was in my debt for having collected him off the beach — and there was no reason why he should, we were both doing a job — then he more than repaid it on that day which I am unlikely to forget.

Alas, we were not to meet again, for he died not long after, as I was to learn by a remarkable coincidence after a gap of many years at a time when I believed I had retired from all forms of further employment. One day, out of the blue, I was amazed to be invited to lend a hand in the negotiation of a manufacturing agreement between a Japanese motorcycle company and an Italian combine. With an almost negative knowledge of the world of commerce this was to enter a realm of unreality, so I said I would have a go. Put it down to a weakness for the ridiculous, and a chance to return to Italy — it had possibilities.

My instructions were to go to Milan, there to meet a man called Carris who would introduce me to the Italian combine. No one seemed to be certain of Carris's nationality; he could be Italian, or English, or even Greek, for that matter, with a name like that; in any event he was reputed to be a leading engineer-negotiator, and he would start the ball rolling.

On arrival in Milan I found myself booked into a comfortable hotel; all I could then do was to hope that the hurriedly made arrangements for our meeting were understood by Mr Carris. He was to call for me at the hotel at 11.00 next morning.

Shortly before the appointed time I enlisted the help of the concierge and the telephone exchange to avoid missing my quarry, then took up position just inside the entrance to one of the public rooms from where it was possible to command a good view of the entrance hall. Eleven o'clock came and went. At 11.30 I re-visited the concierge and the hotel exchange, with no result. At noon I had almost given up hope when my attention was caught by a door opening at the other end of the room — an entrance I had not known to be there — to admit a tall grey-haired man who advanced slowly, scanning the faces of the guests as he went. For perhaps ten seconds I wasn't sure — then I was quite certain. I got up and went to meet him.

'Giuseppe. Orbitello. Remember?'

He stopped to stare in astonishment until recognition dawned; then he laughed and held out his hand.

'*Commandante*! What are you doing here?'

'I've come out on business.'

He was still floundering. 'But — how long are you staying?'

'I have no idea. I am to meet an engineer over a business deal but he hasn't turned up.'

He fixed me with an uncertain stare, and then began to laugh. 'Motorcycles?'

The coincidence was certainly strange. I had known him only as Giuseppe, the General's chief organizer, nearly twenty years earlier. With the passage of time he hadn't changed much; he was still the same suave man-of-the-world that he had been then, with white hair only a fraction thinner. Giuseppe and I did no business together — someone else got there first, so I believe — but we took the opportunity to hark back over the past for a couple of hours or more while consuming an excellent lunch. It certainly made the trip worthwhile for me — for us both, I would like to think. He, it was who gave me the sad news of the General's death.

* * *

II

In 1948 I went overseas on a three-year appointment which stretched itself, ultimately, into a stay of well over five. Thereafter, in common with many others of like age, a busy working life and a growing family left little time for looking backwards. The accent was firmly on the future.

Despite this I did manage to rough out the first draft of this book in the belief that at some far-distant date it might amuse if not interest the family. Only recently did I decide (after some really quite pointed prompting) to see what the world of publishing might think of it. That they accepted it was a pleasing surprise but their conditions for doing so — in fact, their main condition — seemed to destroy any hope of actual publication. They wanted supporting photographs. To the best of my knowledge none existed. From earliest days Captain Slocum in his official capacity as DDOD(I) had operated a strict order forbidding photographs of any personnel or ships under his command. (The same applied, more rigorously still, to pictures being taken of passengers). For obvious reasons of security it was a sensible order, and, as far as I knew was scrupulously observed. This bit of news impressed the publishers not at all; they insisted that some photographs *must* exist *somewhere*. In vain did I try to convince them that they were asking the impossible. As well talk to a brick wall for all the effect it had. Already depressed I asked how many they wanted. About 35 to forty, they said. I couldn't believe it, and all but abandoned the whole project on the spot. Airily (I thought) they brushed aside all opposition: the photographs would materialize, they said. Just try a little harder they urged (like Nanny after breakfast), with a strong hint that no photographs, no publication.

Well — such omens as there were seemed pretty low class. At the same time there was no alternative. The question was, where to start? I went to the only possible source I knew — Roderic Suddaby, a senior member of the Imperial War Museum with whom I had had some dealings in the past. He was, as always very courteous and most helpful, causing many photographs to be dredged up from his vast archives; his staff showed admirable patience, rewarded by the examples in the earlier pages. He also recommended approaches to other sources such as the Public Record Office, and the Maritime Museum, both of whom went out of their way to help. Everyone was tremendously kind, but always few, if any photographs.

The next move was a dual approach to the Naval Attachés of the United States, Captain Joseph R. McCleary, USN, who had arrived *en poste* only four days previously, and of Italy, Captain Rondonotti, Italian Navy. Both responded in the way I had almost come to expect — with courtesy and expressions of goodwill and co-operation. From Captain McCleary I received some suggested addresses I might write to in the United States, while through the efforts of Captain Rondonotti — after a pregnant silence — I received a selection of photographs of MAS boats direct from the Ufficio Storico in Rome. They regretted that they could not provide photographs of officers, and it was not difficult to understand why, even after all these years.

The real breakthrough began when my wife and I were invited to stay with an old friend in Brittany, Hervé Coatalen, and his charming wife, Anna. Hervé had been the Chief Engineer Officer of the British flotilla of 'Dog' boats (D class MTBs) in Bastia. Not only did he have some photographs of Bastia, and some of the boats (unfortunately a bit small for reproduction) but he was also able to begin what turned out to be a most successful 'tale of the horseshoe nail'. On his recommendation I got in touch with Douglas Hunt, the lynch-pin of British MTB ex-officers and men, who passed me on to Ed Garvey, his opposite number in the American Peter Tare (PT) Association, who, in turn copied my letter to him to a number of former PT captains and officers, among them being an old friend, Stanley M. Barnes (he, who it will be remembered, was so good in providing help when help was needed for our operations) now a Captain US Navy (retired), Captain

David J. Morrison, US Naval Reserve (retired), Fred Rosen, and a few more besides. Almost immediately photographs — some of them originals torn out of personal albums — started to arrive with offers of every sort of help. It was a wonderful display of generosity without which this book might never have been possible — a point I have tried to make elsewhere.

By happy chance not long after the photographs began to flow in there was a reunion in London of American PT and British MTB officers — a vast drinks party where some 180 (so I believe) turned up to make or renew friendships. It gave me the chance to thank some of the donors in person. Sadly, four of the PT Captains with whom I had worked, Lieutenants Pressly, Eldridge, Clifford and Steele had all made their last sailing in the intervening years. It was, however, a great pleasure to meet Stan Barnes once again. In the course of discussion he told me that our clandestine sorties were quite popular among his PT boat Captains, and I was glad to hear as much. We certainly enjoyed working with people who seemed to take to the unusual with such competence, cheerfulness, and ease. It was not just the confidence which they inspired, where we were concerned, but also the thoughtfulness for those of us operating in the dinghies. The return on board after each landing was a moment of regaining safe refuge, and to prove it there was always hot coffee waiting and, on occasion, the loan of dry clothes. For their part, perhaps the cloak-and-dagger aspect, and the overriding call for stealth had their attractions as a welcome change from their normal aggressive role. If they thought it was 'fun' then they certainly played their part to make it so for all of us.

From Fred Rosen came another bonus, the address of Lieutenant Peter Karlow, USNR, who so nearly lost his life when *MAS 546*, Tenente di Vascello Paolo Iappelli in command, was mined and sunk off Capraia. As it was he was wounded in the head and had to have a leg amputated a little later. Dimly, I recall meeting him in Washington not long after the war ended, but from then on all traces vanished. It was, therefore, all the more pleasant a surprise to receive a letter from him a few days ago: he now lives in California where he has almost, but definitely not quite, retired after what sounds like a very busy career devoted to international affairs in the fields of trade and investment. Now, he says he is engaged on a work-when-you-please basis as a West Coast editor. He sounds like a contented man, and I sincerely hope he is.

In his letter he mentioned that, sadly, Russell Livermore, head of the local OSS office in Bastia — he who commanded the 'capture' of Gorgona in somewhat comic circumstances — died some five years ago. Of his colourful second-in-command, Tom Stonborough, he had no news. On the other hand I did have a report that in the 1970s he was to be found in Austria but what he was doing is anyone's guess. If he is still alive — and I very much hope he is — wherever he may be, life is unlikely to be dull for the neighbours.

★ ★ ★

While a stroke of good fortune had been responsible for re-establishing contact with the Americans, no such luck seemed even remotely possible where the Italians were concerned for the distressing reason, described elsewhere, that two out of the three MAS boat Captains I had known best and worked with most, had been killed in 1944. Only the Marchese Giulio Centurione remained. Or, *did* he remain? In the light of the earlier reluctance of the Italian authorities in Rome to produce photographs of any of the officers of their flotilla in Bastia, there was no obvious channel of enquiry to pursue. A frustrating situation, but there it was. That left just the British survivors, quite a few of whom I knew to be still around and active.

One of those I got in touch with early on was Tom Maxted whom I knew to be fruit farming in Norfolk. The longest-serving of the young ops officers, and certainly the most skilled, he had finished the war with a DSO and a *Croix de Guerre*, and continuing after the war in the Royal Naval Reserve to reach the rank of Commander before retiring from the service — but not from the sea. To this day he remains a keen sailor in his own yacht which he sails down to the Mediterranean whenever he can, sometimes with Ranald Boyle, our then youngest officer who joined us almost straight from Eton.

When Tom told me that he had a few photographs (in defiance of the embargo), there was only one thing to do — go and see him. But he didn't only tell me about photographs; he gave me news of Prof. In correspondence with the Americans I had heard of a number of deaths, each one of which created its own sadness, but when Tom told me that Prof had died some ten years earlier it was very hard to take in. It was a great shock. There was a widow with whom Tom was in touch occasionally: would I like her address? As we were talking on the telephone a plan was already forming in my mind to visit Tom and Mrs Prof — perhaps in one big tour. Meanwhile I made a note of Mrs Prof's address and telephone number. Later the same day I rang her up. She was charming, and, once she knew who I was and why I was ringing her, she was both interested and anxious to help in any way she could. Yes, she too, did have some photographs of Prof, but not, she thought, of Bastia or our boats or personnel. Evidently Prof had obeyed the rules. Plans moved on another step.

216

In an effort to find any trace of any or all of the dinghymen, especially Petty Officer Bates, and the Heavenly Twins, Leading Seamen Downes and Johnstone, I had at the suggestion of Roderic Suddaby of the Imperial War Museum, put an advertisement in 'Navy News'. Soon after my conversations with Tom and Mrs Prof (Joan Sylvester-Bradley) the telephone rang one evening, and a voice said from the other end, 'This is Jim Bates speaking. I've just seen your advertisement.' It was strange hearing a voice of 43 years earlier. He was living in Gloucestershire, retired a good many years as a Lieutenant-Commander, with a DSM and a *Croix de Guerre*. We talked for quite some time. He, too, had photographs. (The publishers, and Nanny were beginning to justify themselves.) Jim Bates was added to the list of people to see on my tour.

When, a week or so later, I set out, Jim was the first person I called on. He and his wife, Susie, gave me a very warm welcome as the sun rose 'over the yard-arm' — although the phrase may have lost some of its menace in these days of strict drink-drive laws. We talked a lot. He had a good career of steady hard-earned promotion after leaving Bastia, including one short period when he was in the same ship as one of the Heavenly Twins — Downes, who by that time was a Petty Officer. But he had had no news of either of them since. After lunch we went through his album of photographs when, generously, he offered me a selection of himself to have copied. Time had been kind to him although he had altered quite a bit. Now he takes life easily but, I fancy, is seldom idle.

The following day I drove to Leicester to meet Mrs Prof. First impressions were well borne out. As a bonus one of Prof's sons, Ben, normally an accountant in Australia, was by lucky chance also present. He sounded just like Prof if, perhaps, a little shy. Mrs Prof — well, it was not difficult to see why she and Peter had had such a happy marriage. (It was the first time I had heard him called by his real name.) They were married in 1945 and had three sons, each of whom, as might be expected with such parents, is proving successful in his own field of technology. Curiously, after the war Prof remained very discreet about his work in Corsica; quite a lot of what I was able to tell her about our life in those days came as a surprise: his sense of security made him reluctant to say anything. When he reverted to his peacetime profession he seemed to have lost nothing of his expansive and cheerful enthusiasm for whatever he might be doing, researching, travelling, teaching, or listening to his favourite composer, Verdi (on whom he was something of an expert). Small wonder that he was so successful as a scientist, admired and respected by his students. His capacity for logical common sense seemed infinite (and quick, too), and this com-

217

bined with a sense of humour never far from the surface, made him not just a dependable and imaginative First Lieutenant, but a splendid companion to all who had the good fortune to know him.

Joan showed me dozens of photographs of Prof, most of them when he had reverted to his real profession, but she did have one of him in uniform. Together we selected two or three others as we pored over the albums. He was only 64 when he died very suddenly, at the height of his career. By then he had become the real thing — Professor Peter Sylvester-Bradley, F. W. Bennett Professor of Geology at Leicester, enjoying international fame in his profession, well described by *The Times* in their fulsome obituary.

It wasn't until I was on the point of departure and we were rounding off our long conversation that Joan said quite casually, 'And then after Bastia Peter went up to Leghorn — with the Marchese —' For a long second I wasn't sure I had heard alright. 'The Marchese, you said? You don't by any chance mean the Marchese Centurione?' She nodded, 'Yes, the two of them went up there together.' The next question was hard even to ask, 'You don't by any chance know where the Marchese is today, do you?' Again she nodded, smiling this time.

Joan and Prof had met the Centurione family after the war, and had maintained correspondence with Lisabetta, the wife, ever since. They had even visited them in Italy. As soon as she realized how important this discovery could be, Joan offered to write immediately to Lisabetta Salviati (as she now is since separating from her husband). It was all falling into place from a chance remark. I had no idea that Prof had left Bastia other than to return to the UK.

As good as her kindly word Joan wrote, and waiting a few days for the letter to reach its destination I then wrote to Signora Salviati explaining my hopes of finding photographs of just three officers — Cosulich, Iappelli, and her husband, Centurione. Not many days later, early one Sunday morning, Lisabetta rang me from her home near Genoa, expressing intense interest in what I was trying to do. I found her enthusiasm quite infectious after so much previous frustration, and there wasn't long to wait for results either. Not only did the Marchese, himself, write a long letter of surprised pleasure at the prospect of a book being written about those far-off days, he went much, much further. He provided three photographs, the very ones I had all but lost hope of being able to find — pictures of himself, 'Ginger' Cosulich, and Paolo Iappelli all in uniform, taken in 1943/4 in either Maddalena or Bastia. In his letter he asked that they might be returned, and small wonder. They were copied immediately and sent off back to him by registered post.

In passing I have been amazed at the generosity and trust which so many have displayed in lending photographs which must be irreplaceable; it has been a heart-warming experience. Not long afterwards Signora Salviati got in touch again to tell me that she had found the photographs she had been looking for and that they were being copied prior to prints being sent to me. They, too, were excellent photographs, packed with much care: also enclosed was a short story about one member of the Italian organization in Bastia at that time. A story of superstition, true, but one which bears repeating not just for its own sake but because it recaptures something of the spirit of those days. 'Ginger' Cosulich's unwillingness to go to sea without his green cloth helmet was of the same sort.

A certain Domenico Meleca had for some years been a retainer in the Salviati family. When war came he joined the Italian Navy, eventually becoming 'orderly' to Giulio Centurione in Bastia. At this point his services began to be shared also by 'Ginger' Cosulich, and Paolo Iappelli. These three officers, all good friends, occupied sleeping quarters in the same flat. Whenever they went to sea on operations Domenico would give each one a key so that he could let himself in on return to harbour, usually in the small hours of the morning. In 1944 Cosulich and Iappelli were both lost. From that time on Domenico refused to give a key to Centurione; instead, he would wait up for him until he returned, no matter how late the hour. The Marchese survived the war. Such superstitions were not the prerogative of the Italian Navy, alone.

* * *

Of all those who were serving in Corsica at that time the one with whom I was to be most closely associated in later life was Paddy Davies, the young RNVR Lieutenant who, as Staff Officer (Intelligence) to SOIS, provided some original briefings. This, I think, is the moment to 'round him out' a little, perhaps, indeed, to account in some measure for his unusual approach to life. Born in Brazil, of Anglo-Irish parentage to which had been infused rather more than a touch of local bonhomie, he was sent home to be educated at Stowe. When the war broke out he was back in Rio having just left school at the age of eighteen. He immediately presented himself at the British Embassy as a volunteer in any capacity which might be useful — with a preference for the Navy. In no time he found himself dressed as a Sub-Lieutenant RNVR on the staff of the Naval Attaché, knowing little more about the sea than that it was an interesting element from which the prettiest girls in Brazil could be seen to emerge with agreeable regularity on to the Copacabana (where they became fair game). He could, of course, speak fluent Portuguese. Embassy life in the 'phoney' war soon palled with the ever-increasing reports of the high toll of losses at sea due to U-boat attacks. He applied for a transfer to a more active sphere, and was told that the only way he could achieve this was to drop his commission, return to England by sea, and re-enter through the lower deck as an Ordinary Seaman, chancing his arm on getting another commission. He didn't delay. His subsequent stories of life at sea as a Leading Seaman and 'Captain of the heads' have caused as much hilarity as I can remember: he was so vastly amused by his own experiences.

At the end of the war we were both working in London offices not far separated from one another. One day he rang me up to seek my help in what he described as 'an urgent personal matter'. This could be serious or another way of suggesting a drink at lunch time. It was serious. Rather unexpectedly he had been offered a good job in civilian life; that was fine, but the snag was they wanted an immediate answer. No matter how he pleaded for time they wouldn't wait. If his priority for demobilization was low that was his bad luck — and he was pretty low down on the list, mainly due to his age.

By happy fluke — and it was a fluke — I was able to help, having had contact on a previous occasion with the authorities concerned. To them I explained that Paddy was so keen on getting the job that he was prepared to forego his repatriation money (he was entitled to a free ticket back to Brazil). The prospect of saving that much money was more than they could resist, all he had to do was to sign a waiver, and he was a free man, a civilian once more. He signed. The last place he wanted to go was Brazil. The job was in France.

About fifteen years later he more than 'repaid' any help I might have given: he gave *me* a job in *his* organization, and a very entertaining, as well as rewarding experience that turned out to be. I shall always be in his debt, on that account. He became godfather to my youngest, whilst I am godfather to his eldest. Perhaps that makes us godbrothers, a relationship I can recommend as having a limited responsibility and lots of fun.

In recalling, a few pages back, the disaster one February night in 1944 when *MAS 546* was mined off Capraia Island, I mentioned that one of those who was lost was Lieutenant Charles Buist, RN, Staff Officer (Operations) to SOIS. Recently I learned that a plaque in his memory is affixed to the wall outside where his office used to be — a fitting tribute to the considerable regard in which he was held by all those who had dealings with him.

No such memorial exists to that grizzled, sometimes dour, but thoroughly dependable small Scot, the 'Colonel' (Lieutenant Dow,

RNVR) with his wry sense of humour, but his memory remains vivid and welcome in the minds of those of us who knew and worked alongside him. In contrast to his strong doubts about the whole enterprise when he first arrived he ended by creating, in his own fashion, an aura of confidence in those on operations in which he was taking part. An enviable gift.

In further searches for photographs Andrew Croft, the local head of SOE in Bastia, showed great kindness. He *had* taken a number of pictures but only one of them could be called operational — a photograph (the only one on record, I think) of the type of dinghy we were using. The others were of some of the Conducting Officers who were responsible for handling his groups of resisters, and of more relaxing moments in the countryside. As for Andrew himself, after the war, the erstwhile explorer and soldier became Commandant of the Police Cadet College at Hendon, a post he held and enjoyed for some thirteen years when he retired — as far as he is ever likely to retire. He and his delightful wife live right on the river at Kew.

The manner in which I met that well-known hypnotist, Dick Cooper, after the war was another example of curious coincidence. Paddy and I were dining in London one night quite a few years into peacetime: at a certain hour that evening I had made arrangements to telephone to a number in a fairly remote part of France. It was a number I had called before without difficulty, although in those days it still meant going through both British and French operators; unwisely I made no allowance for delays. A quarter of an hour went by; twenty minutes; in spite of my requests for more speed nothing happened. Paddy listened to my efforts, and then said, 'Why don't you try Dick Cooper? He might be on duty.' He was — as one of the Night Supervisors. In far less time than it takes to tell, and after listening to a number of French expressions I had never heard before, I was talking to my number. It had been telephonic poetry of a very high order.

Next day Dick joined us for a drink. Nothing about him had changed. It only needed the sacrificial lamb for another terrifying seance of hypnosis. Foreign Legionary, Conducting Officer of resisters, telephone supervisor of continental calls, whatever he may be, Dick will always be what they call 'a vital man'. It fits him.

If anyone epitomized the spirit of the Allied forces in Bastia in those days, I can't think anybody would dispute that it was SOIS himself, Captain Norman Dickinson, the man with the multi-national command of — in alphabetical order — Americans, British, Canadian, French, and Italians, all of whom wanted their voices to be heard, not infrequently several of them at once.

In broad terms he relied on straightforward common sense to exer-

221

cise a firm control directed at maintaining a relentless policy of aggression against the enemy. Backing up the common sense was a gruff wit (not always understood first time by some foreigners, but they got used to it) and a deceptive knowledge and understanding of the more senior officers under him. Coupled to these qualities came the sudden, unexpected flashing charm to disarm the affronted dignity. It was a formidable combination: I never knew it to fail.

I was lucky enough to see quite a bit of him after the war. He must have got his Flag (promotion to Rear Admiral) fairly soon after hostilities ended for, when next I met him, in 1950, he came in to Piraeus, the Greek naval port, in the Indian Navy Flagship, as the C-in-C Indian Navy Afloat. Very kindly he asked my wife and me on board for, amongst other hospitality, a tour of the ship. It wasn't long after Partition, and I asked him how much of a problem was created by having so many differing religions cooped up in such limited space, all trying to work together. At times, he admitted, things could be difficult, tricky even, but, in general, he found that his own recipe of common sense and a little simple humour would usually solve the situation. For much of the smooth running of the ship he relied on the Petty Officers and Chief Petty Officers. As long as they got on together there was no fuss; it was when they fell out that matters could go awry. Walking round, watching him exchange a few words here and there it was a great pleasure to see that he had lost nothing of his old skill in getting people of disparate backgrounds and ideologies to work in harmony.

The next time I met him, well over ten years had elapsed, and he had retired from the Navy. To keep active he worked with a paint company, concentrating mostly on the marine side. It wasn't a very arduous pursuit, although he was as conscientious as ever, but he did find time now and again — round about noon, more often than not — to wander into the office where Paddy and I worked. There was a congenial bar not too far away, the haven of generations of naval officers through the ages, but now, I fear, no more.

In his civilian life he dropped all formality, to become to everyone, 'Uncle Richard' — a development, presumably, of his earlier nickname, 'Dick-o', for his real names were Norman Vincent, neither of which he cared much about. Even Rosalind, his very sweet wife, called him 'Richard'.

At about this time, or shortly after, the crippling illness which was to bow his spine so severely, was beginning to make its influence felt: as time went by the pain grew worse with the crumpling of the spine. By the time the bending had stopped, and mercifully the pain also, he was severely handicapped. He died in the mid-1970s.

Uncle Richard may have gone but he is certainly not forgotten. It is safe to say that whenever two ex-Bastians meet and the subject turns to those days, it will not be long before his name surfaces in the conversation; it is also safe to believe that such mention will be complimentary, or kindly, or both. And so it should be.

In tracing the fortunes of the principal actors in this interlude the reader may have noticed one important, indeed, sad gap. No mention of those imaginative stalwarts Leading Seamen Johnstone and Downey — The Heavenly Twins. Despite advertising and numerous enquiries, no trace could be found of their present whereabouts, the most recent news being that Johnstone was at one time to be found in Hastings while Downey was reported to be 'in the Hounslow area'. Both earned well deserved decorations. Their war effort was often unorthodox but it was certainly effective and always entertaining. Because I could not find them and for reasons readily understood I have given them pseudonyms. If either is alive I can only wish them very well indeed. I still laugh with them in their absence.

* * *

Forty-five years later, standing back a bit to survey the panorama of this Corsican interlude, the single feature which seems to stand out from the others is the extraordinary luck which blessed the African Coastal Flotilla from the start in the autumn of 1943.

On arrival in Maddalena the prospects did not look rosy. We had a single fishing-boat, the *Seadog* which, having rendered excellent service in the preceding years of relatively static warfare in Europe, was now out of date with the rapidly increasing tempo of the campaign up the spine of Italy. The resisters of Europe had to keep pace with ever more missions to and from enemy territory, and we had to carry them.

The outlook remained poor until the Italian surrender on 20 September; an event which posed problems as well as solving them. Among those created for SOIS was to find some form of employment for the large MAS boat flotilla now unexpectedly under his command. It was out of the question to expect them to fight against their recent allies, the Germans, at any rate not immediately; even less could they be used against their own compatriots. And yet they could not be left in demoralizing idleness. The ACF was the answer; it was just as much a godsend for them as it was for us. The task was non-aggressive but essential, while two birds would be killed with but a single stone.

Later, the advent of the OSS raised another problem — the risk that some of the resisters, all Italian, used by that organization, might be recognized by a member of the crews of the MAS boats. It was a long shot hazard, but it was there. Wisely OSS sought and obtained the cooperation of the PT boat squadron commander, while the ACF continued to provide the trained dinghy crews. It proved a good working arrangement and an all-important alternative, greatly strengthening our capacity to cope. Better still, as mentioned a little while back, the Americans found these ops a welcome change — a bit of light relief, perhaps — while we appreciated their cheerful company and the unaccustomed comfort of their boats. Yes, indeed, the ACF was very fortunate.

It would be doing far less than justice to the officers and men of the MAS boats to remain silent about the importance of the part they played. Nor should we forget that two of their boats were lost with only four survivors out of a total of 26 officers and men, while they were engaged on our operations. To the captains of both boats, Tenente di Vascello Guido Cosulich, and Tenente di Vascello Paolo Iappelli, must be attributed great credit and praise for the manner in which they set an example, giving their best — and their lives — in the Allied cause. To understand just how much they gave is to put oneself in their shoes at the time of the national capitulation. Who, sitting in the comfort of his peacetime armchair, can guess at his own reaction in such circumstances? Yet, in a matter of little more than hours, these young men were required to decide whether all that they had been brought up to believe was false, and that they had to change sides, or that it was still true and they had to continue as they had begun. Opinions will vary as long as the question is discussed. Side by side with the Centuriones, the Iappellis, and the Cosuliches were their counterparts who had taken the opposite course: they are unlikely to be forgotten after the horrifying defection of the MAS boat sent down to Maddalena for repairs. Fortunately, it was an isolated event which, in the long term, has served to strengthen my personal admiration and liking for those who, having thrown in their lot with us, thereafter never allowed their loyalty to waver. They did us proud.

The final, and, indeed, the highest tribute must go to our passengers, those courageous few, who by acceptance of unremitting personal risk of death, or torture, or both, at the hands of an enemy both ruthless and efficient, gave such effective account of themselves in the provision of vital secret intelligence, help to escaping prisoners-of-war, sabotage, and propaganda. Without their unswerving devotion to the Allied cause who can say by how much the war might have been prolonged, how many more lives would have been lost? It was a rare privilege to work with them and for them.

Betweentimes it was fun, too.